The Golden Horseshoe

Otto Kretschmer at U-boat Command Headquareters, Lorient.

FORTUNES OF WAR

The Golden Horseshoe

THE STORY OF OTTO KRETSCHMER
GERMANY'S TOP U-BOAT ACE

TERENCE ROBERTSON

FOREWORD BY ADMIRAL SIR GEORGE CREASY GCB CBE DSO MVO

TEMPUS

First published 2000

PUBLISHED IN THE UNITED KINGDOM BY:

Tempus Publishing Ltd
The Mill, Brimscombe Port
Stroud, Gloucestershire GL5 2QG

PUBLISHED IN THE UNITED STATES OF AMERICA BY:

Arcadia Publishing Inc.
A division of Tempus Publishing Inc.
2 Cumberland Street
Charleston, SC 29401

Tempus books are available in France, Germany and Belgium
from the following addresses:

Tempus Publishing Group	Tempus Publishing Group	Tempus Publishing Group
21 Avenue de la République	Gustav-Adolf-Straße 3	Place de L'Alma 4/5
37300 Joué-lès-Tours	99084 Erfurt	1200 Brussels
FRANCE	GERMANY	BELGIUM

British Library Cataloguing in Publication Data.
A catalogue record for this book is available from the British Library.

ISBN 0 7524 2019 4

Typesetting and origination by Tempus Publishing.

PRINTED AND BOUND IN GREAT BRITAIN.

Contents

Preface

By Admiral Sir George Creasy GCB CBE DSO MVO

This book deals primarily with the exploits of one U-boat commander, Captain Kretschmer, from the outbreak of the war until *U-99* was sunk in March 1941. I believe that he was the most efficient and the most competent U-boat Commanding Officer that Germany produced; he flourished at the time when our defences were slowly building up and were as yet woefully weak; certainly he inflicted heavier and more painful losses on Allied shipping than did any other one man, and the destruction of his U-boat and his own capture, well-nigh simultaneously with the loss of Prien and Schepke, must have been a severe blow to the U-boat Command. To us it formed one of the bright gleams of hope at a time when few such gleams lit the sombre story of the Battle of the Atlantic.

I well remember piecing together the evidence of one of his early attacks on a convoy. It was at a time when most people were thinking in terms of the orthodox submerged attack at periscope depth. I had already made up my mind that we were dealing with attacks made with the U-boat on the surface, relying on her small silhouette to give her a cloak of invisibility. And the times at which torpedoes had hit, and the position of his targets in the various columns of the convoy, convinced me that not only was Kretschmer's U-boat on the surface, but that he must have passed diagonally right through the convoy.

This was something new. But I remember, too, that I considered that the manoeuvre was so risky that he had done it by mistake. This book shows that it was a deliberate tactic, carefully thought out and brilliantly executed.

Happily, in this he had few imitators. Nevertheless the work of Kretschmer, Prien and Schepke lived on, unfortunately for us, long after their active part in the Battle of the Atlantic was over. They and a few of their contemporaries had shown the way, and their tactics led to the night surface attacks by 'wolf-packs' of U-boats in numbers which increased steadily as U-boat war production mounted. Heavy indeed were the losses in ships and the loss in life inflicted on the gallant Merchant Navies of the Allies by these attacks.

These losses began to mount at an alarming speed, far exceeding the rate at which we could build new ships, to a dangerous total. On our ability to bring material and men by sea into this country depended our ability to prosecute the war.

But there was another side to the picture. Our countermeasures were also steadily building up, The number of our escort vessels was increasing slowly at first, but later more rapidly. The numbers of aircraft available to Coastal Command were swelling. New tactics were being planned. And, perhaps most important of all, time was being found to train sailors and airmen to use this increasing strength to maximum purposes.

Moreover, the 'submersible' tactics of the enemy had their weak point, if it could be exploited. To achieve the high mobility given by surface speed, the U-boat accepted the vulnerability inherent in surface operations once the problem of location had been solved. Aircraft in sufficient numbers could cover wide areas of sea and would have a maximum chance of locating and then attacking a surfaced U-boat. Ships with efficient radar could offset the U-boat's advantage of a small silhouette, and what the human eye could not see would be visible to the radar eye in the darkness.

The Battle of the Atlantic indeed became a race. Could we turn the tables and start to inflict unbearable losses on the U-boats before the enemy had imposed unbearable losses in merchant shipping, ships and men on us?

The Allied victory is now a matter of history, but we went through times of deep anxiety before that victory was achieved. However, by the end of 1943 we had inflicted heavy losses on the U-boats, and by this time American ship production was in full stride and new merchant shipping was coming forward at a rate which put defeat out of the question.

But here I must emphasise that the victory which was won was the defeat of Dönitz's U-boat submersible tactics which had proved so dangerous to the Allied cause. The U-boat as a submarine was by no means defeated and, indeed, it was not long before the enemy had fitted their U-boats with the Snort to enable them to use their diesel engines whilst submerged, and, thus equipped, then resumed the battle. But they had lost more than half their power of mobility and they had been severely shaken by appalling losses, and never again did they cause us any real anxiety.

Nevertheless, German ingenuity had not been idle, and new forms of U-boat were under construction with high submerged speed and the ability to remain permanently under water. These new types never became fully operational before the war ended. Undoubtedly they would have set us fresh problems and, though I have no doubt we should have mastered them, we might have faced another period of losses in shipping before we had achieved this mastery.

In conclusion, I feel I should write some word of explanation of my interview with Kretschmer after his capture, which is described in this book. I did not expect to get any 'intelligence' from him. I felt sure that any officer who could handle his ship with such efficiency would guard his tongue with equal efficiency. Nor was I wrong; he gave away nothing. But I saw him because I was anxious to judge for myself what manner of man a successful U-boat captain might be; to see for myself, if I could, the state of his nerves; to measure his judgement; gauge his reactions to his seniors and to his juniors, the expected and the unexpected. In simple words, to 'size him up'.

It may be of interest to record the impression he made on me. I saw a young and obviously self-confident Naval Commander who bore himself, in the difficult conditions of recent captivity, with self-respect, modesty and courtesy. His record stamped him as brave and quick-witted; his appearance and manners were those of an officer and a gentleman. When he left me I sincerely hoped that there were not too many like him. My last word to him was that I hoped we might meet again one day in more pleasant circumstances. I shall be very happy if and when that day comes.

Author's Foreword

When Germany's assault on Allied shipping lanes began to take the shape of the most unrelenting struggle of the war, Sir Winston Churchill set the pattern for all Battle of the Atlantic communiqués. Enemy submarines, he said, were to be called U-boats, the term 'submarine' to be reserved for Allied underwater vessels. He defined the difference as: 'U-boats are those dastardly villains who sink our ships, while submarines are those gallant and noble craft which sink theirs'. This is the story of the most 'dastardly villain' of them all – Captain Otto Kretschmer, the German Navy's greatest 'ace', who caused more destruction on the High Seas than any other commander of any nation in any war.

Before his capture he had sunk nearly 350,000 tons of Allied shipping, including three armed merchant cruisers and a destroyer. He earned the highest decorations Germany could bestow. Post-cards carrying his photograph were sold throughout Germany and Occupied Europe and a special military march was composed in his honour. Yet he resisted every attempt by the master propagandist Goebbels to 'glorify' his name in books, articles and films. Since the war, this horror at the prospect of being portrayed as a 'hero' – he despises heroics – has persisted so stubbornly that he has previously refused to endorse any published material concerning his exploits. He has co-operated now only on my assurance that every available source of information would be explored to ensure that the experiences of *U-99* and her crew were portrayed as accurately and objectively as possible. This has been achieved only through the kind and generous assistance of several senior British officers intimately involved in the Kretschmer story.

Admiral Sir George Creasy, Commander-in-Chief, Ports-mouth, reconstructed the scene in his flat at Buckingham Gate when he interviewed Kretschmer alone for two hours in the hope that a private talk with the captured 'ace' might yield vital clues to the mind and personality of Dönitz. Further, Admiral Creasy has helped in every way to keep me on the tramlines of technical accuracy in those parts which deal with the Battle of the Atlantic as a whole.

Captain Donald Macintyre, who held the post of Senior Officer of the Reserve Fleet at Chatham, obtained official Admiralty consent to provide in detail the vivid story of that wild night in March 1941 when, as captain of the destroyer *Walker*, and in company with another destroyer, *Vanoc*, he brought the curtain down on Kretschmer's operational career by sinking *U-99* against a backdrop of blazing, stricken merchantmen.

Strange coincidences marked the meeting of these two opponents. Both sailed under the crest of a Horseshoe, and while Kretschmer became the top-scoring 'ace' of the U-boat Arm, Captain Macintyre became one of the Royal Navy's top scoring U-boat killers,[1] with seven U-boats confirmed and at least one damaged.

Commander R.P. Martin, former senior executive officer of the armed merchant cruiser, *Patroclus*, who described so accurately the amazing night when he and a few volunteers fought a gun duel with *U-99* while their ship sank beneath them.

Colonel James Reynolds Veitch of the Grenadier Guards, who was Commandant of the Number One PoW Camp at Grizedale Hall, near Lake Windermere, gave generously of his time to recall the long months in which he fought a battle of wits against Kretschmer, who had arrived at the camp as Senior German Officer. He filled in the gaps of the astonishing secret Court of Honour story in which Kretschmer found the First Lieutenant of a surrendered U-boat guilty of cowardice, and of the 'dummy chair' escape that just failed to succeed.

On the German side I received kind co-operation from:

Captain Otto Kretschmer, who for many long weeks worked patiently with me to ensure that every point was clear and unmistakable.

Volkmar König, the one-time midshipman, who gave so much invaluable information about their activities at Bowmanville PoW Camp in Canada, in particular about the famous 'Shackling Incident' that led to the Battle of Bowmanville.

Jupp Kassel, the former Chief Petty Officer (Wireless) of *U-99*, who assumed again the mantle of Public Relations Officer for the crew and gave me every assistance in recapturing the 'soul' of the U-boat through the experiences of various crew members.

Hans Clasen, who contributed valuable photographs, which today represent all he possesses to remind him of *U-99*.

I am grateful also to the former Colonel Hefele, of the Luftwaffe, who for many months shared the role of senior German officer at Bowmanville with Kretschmer and who looked upon the 'ace' as a 'stickler for discipline' – a factor which made Bowmanville one of the smartest PoW camps in Canada and earned for its inmates the title 'Cavaliers of Canada'.

Note

1 The late Captain F.J. Walker was the most famous U-boat killer of the war. According to Admiralty records, his escort group were credited with the destruction of twenty U-boats. But his personal successes are not known. A statement issued on August 23rd, 1944, by the Ministry of Information, announced that Captain Macintyre had sunk his eighth U-boat. However, Admiralty files allow him a personal score of seven.

One
The Ring Round Britain

In 1934, when German arms were limited by the Treaty of Versailles, the first Army cadres and Luftwaffe squadrons took shape under a variety of skilful guises. Only the Navy launched a reconstruction programme openly, and then it was impossible for anyone outside the inner sanctums of authority to determine if it was confined to the limits laid down by the Allies. Under the energetic guidance of Admiral Raeder, newly-appointed Supreme Commander of the Navy, the vast jungle of dockyards in Bremen, Hamburg, Wilhelmshaven and Kiel became the breeding grounds of a new fleet with modern battleships, cruisers and destroyers slipping from beneath canopies of cranes and scaffolding. But Raeder was not satisfied. At the last Führer's Naval Conference of that year in Berlin he told Hitler: 'The key to German power at sea lies below the surface. Give us submarines and we shall have the teeth to attack.'

Hitler gave him his reply six months later, when he summoned Raeder to the Reich Chancellery and handed him a message with the curt comment: 'There are your teeth.' It was a telegram from Ribbentrop in London bearing the news that Britain had signed the Anglo-German Naval Treaty of 1935 giving Germany the right to build a surface fleet of up to thirty-five per cent of Britain's. Then came a clause which provided Raeder with the 'biting' power he had demanded. The Germans could build a new submarine service of forty-five per cent of the Royal Navy's and up to parity if 'a situation arose which in their opinion made it necessary'. U-boats had taken a dangerously firm grip on Britain's lifelines during 1917. Now a British Government gave its blessing to a new German Navy which could legally build more submarines than any other class of warship.

The first round of the desperate struggle, to be known not so many years later as the Battle of the Atlantic, had been won on the deceptively calm seas of diplomacy. Raeder swiftly turned this paper victory into a practical programme of construction.

He rescued Germany's leading U-boat 'ace' of the First World War, Captain Karl Dönitz, from the cruiser *Emden*, and charged him with the task of building up a new U-boat Arm.

Dönitz, overjoyed at returning to submarines, contacted his former submarine colleagues who were still interested, and with their help laid the basis for a long-term training programme. The existing 'Anti-Submarine School' at Kiel became the centre not only for the teaching of the defensive tactics implied by its name, but also for offensive training. By the end of 1935 the technical hurdles had been overcome, and early the following year the first batches of officer-trainees arrived at Kiel, all little more than twenty years of age. They were welcomed with a reminder of their heritage and a hint of the intense work ahead.

'The Navy,' Dönitz told them, 'represents the cream of the Armed Forces. The U-boat Arm represents the cream of the Navy. A few of you will command your own submarines one day. But most of you will be sent back to the big ships you came from. The future of each of you depends on your individual efforts to meet the standards I require of you.'

Among the first of the young officers to feel the impact of these words were Gunter Prien, Joachim Schepke and Otto Kretschmer, three sub-lieutenants who had rebelled against the obscurity of 'big-ship' wardrooms and arrived at Kiel in search of freedom for their individualistic personalities. Apart from this common denominator, they differed widely in appearance and character.

Prien was a dapper, slim wire of a man with a mild expression that hid a stubborn, impetuous nature. His quick temper, as yet unfettered by maturity, found exit in a biting wit which kept at bay would-be friends whom he regarded as invaders of his personal life.

Schepke was the reverse. Tall and cheerful, he was the fortunate possessor of great charm and fair good looks that attracted the admiration in which he revelled. This was to be revealed as his major weakness.

Kretschmer, the twenty-four-year-old son of a teacher in Lower Silesia, was in many respects the toughest of the trio. Every sea-power produces its quota of men who prefer ships to women. They find greater contentment on the bridge than in a fireside chair. Kretschmer was of this breed; his searching mind was ruthless in its quest for knowledge of the sea and ships, and he carried himself with the confident bearing of a man who, though still young, knows instinctively not only what he is doing but also why he is doing it. Alongside these characteristics, less desirable qualities were already reaching the surface; a cruel contempt for weakness; an intolerance of anything that did not conform to his personal standards; a bigoted refusal to allow ordinary human failings to interfere with duty; and a self-sufficient pride which was saved from becoming insufferable only by a ready sense of humour and a willingness to listen to the problems of others providing they did not trespass on his privacy or lead to familiarity. During the next three years this trio became linked by reputation; their rapid rise to command and their adventures forging between them a loose friendship nourished more by rivalry than affection.

In the first few months of training, Kretschmer became a cigar chain-smoker, rarely being seen without a black cheroot or some other kind of cigar clamped firmly between his teeth.

This inevitable cigar led him into trouble before the year was out while he was serving as Second Lieutenant of *U-35*.

One day they had been taking part in diving exercises in the Baltic, and by dusk everyone except the captain was sick and tired of behaving like a porpoise. Shortly before nightfall they surfaced, and Kretschmer joined the captain on the conning-tower to relax and light a cigar. He took a first long, pleasure-filled draw and glanced speculatively at the captain, and satisfied himself that for the time being at any rate they would stay on the surface. Then he saw the captain grin widely, as though at some secret joke, and his confidence was replaced by a strong suspicion that an unexpected 'alarm dive' was about to be sounded. He tried to head off the impending dive by diverting his commander's attention to the faulty stopper in the muzzle of the gun which was letting water leak into the barrel. He suggested going down to see if he could fix it and at the captain's nod, scrambled down to the foredeck, his cigar jutting from his lips.

He took his time about draining away the water and then inspected the stopper, knowing full well it was impossible to tighten it until they returned to harbour. He had just moved the gun back to its normal sea position when suddenly he heard a frighteningly familiar sound; the loud hiss of air being blown from the ballast tanks, accompanied by the throbbing of engines increased to full speed. They were diving. Frantically, he rushed to the conning-tower, to find the hatch closed. He stamped on it furiously, hoping that someone inside would hear him. In a few seconds they reached periscope depth. He attempted to swarm up the raised periscope column, but it was kept well greased, and this, plus the weight of his now sodden clothes, dragged him back. It occurred to him that if he hugged the periscope column, the pressure of water would force him upwards to the top, and then he could peer through the 'eye' lens and let the officers inside know that he was out.

He was dragged down to about thirty-five feet in as many seconds, and the sea around him became a thick, impenetrable green wall. He could hold his breath no longer, and reluctantly he allowed himself to be shot to the surface. He came up gasping and spluttering, and at once found that the weight of his clothes made swimming an effort that would tire him dangerously. He decided to float, and the last things he saw before darkness fell were his uniform cap bobbing alongside him and near it, the soaked, mashed remnants of his cigar.

U-35 surfaced nearby and a Petty Officer rushed to the bows to throw him a lifebuoy. He had just enough strength to grab the buoy, but not enough to climb on board. He had to be lifted on to the deck and helped to the conning-tower.

Weak with cold and fatigue, he could think of nothing adequate to say to his captain, so he tottered to attention, attempted a salute, and whispered: 'Lieutenant Kretschmer reporting back on board, sir.' The astonished captain returned the salute and replied automatically: 'Thank you, Lieutenant.' Kretschmer was taken below and hot-water bottles were packed against his skin while hot rum was poured down his throat. He slept until morning, and wakened to find the bitter cold of the Baltic had been sweated from his body, leaving him fit and well except for a sore throat and a severe hangover from the amount of rum he had swallowed.

By mid-1938 the U-boat Arm was a going concern, growing rapidly from one or two ancient training boats to thirty modern ocean-going and coastal attack craft. More important, trainee crews were waiting impatiently for submarines still on the assembly lines. In Berlin, Raeder was feeling happier about the state of his under-water weapon. The 'teeth' were appearing, and the forty-five per cent permitted under the Naval Treaty had been reached. He was ready to let the baby fostered by the London Treaty flex its muscles.

On the eve of the third meeting between Hitler and Neville Chamberlain at Munich in September 1938, Dönitz, now promoted to Admiral and appointed Commander-in-Chief of the U-boat Arm, summoned his officers to a secret conference at his new headquarters on the Baltic. More than fifty officers crowded the small briefing room, sitting in rows facing a raised dais; and among them were the three one-time sub-lieutenants, each wearing now the extra stripe of a Lieutenant.

In front sat Prien, who had emerged from his training as commander of the 500-ton, ocean-going *U-47*. Behind him was the debonair Schepke, commander of a smaller boat. His tilted cap and casual manner towards superiors and sailors alike had given him a dashing air. It was an affectation encouraged by Dönitz, who guessed shrewdly that morale might soar if this fashion became the proud and distinctive stamp of a U-boat officer. In the rear of the room stood the still aloof and taciturn Kretschmer, who was the new commander of *U-23*, a small 250-ton coastal attack craft. He had earned in the last two years the reputation of being the finest torpedo shot in the Navy.

There was an air of nervous tension at the conference, which, they had guessed, would throw some light on the persistent rumours of war. Dönitz did not keep them waiting long. When they had all reported present, he stepped up on to the dais and opened the briefing.

'Gentlemen,' he began, 'you will know by now that the Führer has left Berlin to meet the British Prime Minister at Munich. I am assured by Admiral Raeder that he is determined to reach an agreement with England, but it is our duty to be prepared for the failure of any political settlement and the consequences which may result. You will therefore hold yourselves in readiness for hostilities as from now until further notice.

'Before leaving here you will be issued with sealed envelopes containing secret orders, and I must impress upon you that the seals are not to be broken until you receive signals from me indicating that hostilities have been declared. You will receive sailing orders from your flotilla leaders, and every operational submarine must be at battle stations within the next three days.

'Tomorrow a public announcement will be made that the German Navy is carrying out fleet exercises in the North Sea and the Baltic. This will serve to cover our real purpose. I hope – indeed I am confident – that the Munich Conference will succeed in reaching a settlement with England. But should it fail, then you will serve Germany in the forefront of the armed forces. Good luck.'

Within the next twelve hours, twenty-five submarines sailed into the North Sea from Kiel and Wilhelmshaven and dispersed to take up patrols ranging from the Shetlands in the north to the Atlantic coast of France in the south. In effect, Dönitz had thrown a loop of steel round the British Isles, while in Munich Chamberlain argued patiently for peace with an irascible Führer.

Two days later *U-23* patrolled below the surface some fifteen miles east of the Humber, stored and fuelled to keep her crew of twenty-five at sea for a month's cruise. Her normal complement of four torpedoes had been reduced to one to allow for the magnetic mines in the tubes. In the control-room, Warrant Officer Petersen, the lean navigator who had spent some years on the mess decks before his instinct for navigation had been rewarded by promotion, handed over the watch to the Second Lieutenant and made up the Deck Log:

> 1200. *Overcast and cloudy with light rain. Visibility fair. Short sea and swell. Windforce five (stiff breeze). Depth trimmed to thirty feet. Fishing-boats bearing 310 degrees range four miles. No warship sighted.*

Petersen signed the entry and made his way to the torpedo-room, where Kretschmer and the First Lieutenant, U. Schnee,[1] were discussing the latest news from Berlin of the Munich Conference. The First Lieutenant could not conceal his anxiety at the prospect of having to probe Britain's anti-submarine defences – still virtually unknown to the U-boat Arm. A few months before, the British submarine *M.2* had sunk in the Channel, and German Naval Intelligence had reported that the wreck had been located by destroyers using some form of listening device.[2] But no further details had been published in the Navy's secret memoranda for the U-boat Arm.

'Well, we will soon know what the Royal Navy has ready for us if we have to open those sealed orders,' Kretschmer told him. 'I don't like carrying mines. It is not too comfortable to think we might have to close the coast to lay them.'

At dusk they surfaced to charge batteries, and spent the rest of the night keeping clear of fishing-boats and coastal steamers. At dawn they returned to periscope depth and resumed their patrol across the Humber approaches. In this way, submerged by day and surfaced by night, *U-23* remained at battle stations for three days.

To the north lay Prien, in *U-47*, patrolling off Scapa Flow, main anchorage of the Home Fleet, only too unhappily aware that a declaration of war might send him into operations on the Royal Navy's personal doorstep. Having assumed that his sealed orders would reveal some such brain-wave on the part of the High Command, he reasoned that if any harbour in Britain was well defended against U-boat attack it would be Scapa Flow.

Less concerned about the efficiency of Britain's coastal defences, and not a natural worrier about future problems, was Lieutenant Schepke, in the southern North Sea. He delighted his crew with caustic comments as he carried out dummy attacks on passenger liners and large freighters ploughing to and from the Channel.

On the evening of the third day Dönitz signalled his commanders afloat: 'All units return to base with utmost dispatch. Exercises completed.' Overnight the steel noose round Britain melted away as twenty-five menacing, black-painted shapes slipped unseen into the protection of their bases. Hitler had given Chamberlain his word that Germany had no further territorial ambitions, and the Prime Minister had flown back to London to wave a slip of paper promising 'peace in our time'. The cheers of the London crowds struck a sympathetic chord in the hearts of the U-boat crews. Their relief was just as great as that of the millions who listened to Chamberlain's broadcast report of his Munich Conference. Particularly pleased was the wily 'ace' of the first war, Admiral Dönitz. His cubs had shown they could prowl. When the next crisis came, he would see if they could fight.

On their return Dönitz instructed flotilla leaders to have all captains unseal their secret orders and hold inquests on them. There was to be free discussion, and the opinions expressed were to be sent to him in a composite report. The result was a howl of protest heard in Berlin. The commanders found they had been expected to lay mines in the entrances of harbours and rivers round Britain and attack targets under the noses of shore batteries and inside what they regarded as a well-defended belt, in which they would have to cope with a variety of unknown anti-submarine devices. In their view, to undertake operations inside several miles from the British coastline might easily amount to suicide, or at least to the crippling of the U-boat Arm.

Dönitz replied: 'I shall see to it that those orders are modified should the need for them arise again. I have no intention of throwing away either you or your boats. You cost too much to be lost easily. So don't wet your pants before the shooting starts.'

Notes

1 He became a wartime 'ace' as commander of *U-66* and *U-200* with 198,000 tons to his credit. He received the Knight's Cross and Oak Leaves.

2 This was the Asdic, a listening device that enabled the Royal Navy to hunt down and 'kill' submerged U-boats. The Official History of the War at Sea says: 'The Germans do not seem to have obtained any knowledge of our Asdic.' The *M.2* incident shows this to have been only partly correct.

Two
Battle Stations

Admiral Raeder, as the Navy's Supreme Commander, was a weak influence indeed when faced with extracting production priorities from a Führer who favoured the Army, and against a Field Marshal politician who cherished the Luftwaffe. Despite all his entreaties that the U-boat Arm should have top priority in the factories, it was tanks and planes that filled the assembly lines, while submarines arrived in the Baltic at what was a mere trickle when related to the dream of a three-hundred-strong underwater offensive. But the trickle was consistent enough to make it possible in April 1939 for the Navy to recommend to Hitler that the parity clause of the Naval Treaty be invoked on the ground that 'in their opinion circumstances made it necessary'. This was followed by the scrapping of the Treaty.

In May, the Navy promulgated its Fleet Battle Instructions, which called for all operational U-boats to be at battle patrols *before* the outbreak of any major war in the West. And in August, when Dönitz had a total strength of fifty-six U-boats,[1] of which forty were operational, he decided the time had come to put the Battle Instructions into effect. He moved his headquarters from the Baltic to Wilhelmshaven, as he had done in 1938, and issued his commanders with sealed orders. This time there was no public statement to the effect that they were taking part in Fleet exercises. Instead, officers and men of the U-boat Arm were placed under strict security restrictions and banned from communicating with friends or relatives 'until the position has been clarified'.

After nightfall on the 19th, seventeen of the large 740-ton, long-range U-boats slipped their moorings and vanished into the North Sea en route to patrol points stretching from the southern tip of Ireland to Gibraltar. By the 27th, six of the 250-ton coastal attackers had taken up positions in the northern North Sea. Two days later another six of this class were deployed across the central North Sea and four more entered the Channel, ready to attack British and French ports. On the 30th six ocean-going 500-tonners were dispersed between the Orkneys and Iceland. Among the last to leave harbour was *U-23*, bound for the same patrol she had made the year before – off the Humber. Once again the unanimously disliked magnetic mines filled the tubes at the expense of her torpedo power, and, as in 1938, the prospect of having to lay them inside the Humber entrance provided little comfort for officers or crew.

Dawn on Sunday, September 3rd, revealed a dismal morning in the North Sea with intermittent showers falling heavily like the wringing of some gigantic mop. It was usual for the off-duty watch to clean up the mess-decks in the morning, a pastime that was accompanied by plenty of noise and lively chatter. But on this particular morning the whole crew stood or sat around in groups waiting stoically, in the manner of all naval crews, for their commander to relieve their uncertainty and anxiety by telling them what was happening. At 11 a.m. signals streamed out from Wilhelmshaven to the U-boat fleet.

In *U-23*'s control room, Kretschmer stood by the radio operator reading each message as it was decoded.

1105/3/9/39.

FROM NAVAL HIGH COMMAND STOP

TO COMMANDERS-IN-CHIEF AND COMMANDERS AFLOAT STOP GREAT BRITAIN AND FRANCE HAVE DECLARED WAR ON GERMANY STOP BATTLE STATIONS IMMEDIATE IN ACCORDANCE WITH BATTLE INSTRUCTIONS FOR THE NAVY ALREADY PROMULGATED

The next was from Dönitz, the expected signal ordering captains to open their sealed orders.

1116/3/9/39.

FROM COMMANDER-IN-CHIEF U-BOATS STOP

TO COMMANDING OFFICERS AFLOAT STOP

BATTLE INSTRUCTIONS FOR THE U-BOAT ARM OF THE NAVY ARE NOW IN FORCE STOP TROOP SHIPS AND MERCHANT SHIPS CARRYING MILITARY EQUIPMENT TO BE ATTACKED IN ACCORDANCE WITH PRIZE REGULATIONS OF THE HAGUE CONVENTION STOP

ENEMY CONVOYS TO BE ATTACKED WITHOUT WARNING ONLY ON CONDITION THAT ALL PASSENGER LINERS CARRYING PASSENGERS ARE ALLOWED TO PROCEED IN SAFETY STOP THESE VESSELS ARE IMMUNE FROM ATTACK EVEN IN CONVOY STOP DÖNITZ

Kretschmer opened his safe and took out the secret orders. He felt strangely unexcited as he broke the seals of Battle Orders for the first time. He opened the folded slip of paper, and in a few seconds was gazing with amazement at the terse typed sentence. He was instructed to penetrate into the Humber estuary, find the main shipping channel and blockade it with his mines. These were the same orders he had received during the 'exercises' of 1938. For some unaccountable reason, he thought, Dönitz had been unable to have them modified. The control-room crew looked at him expectantly as he ordered 'Up periscope' and issued instructions while peering round the choppy sea.

'What is the course for the Humber channel, Petersen? I want to be five miles off at dusk. First Lieutenant, we shall try to unload our mines tonight. We should be ready by 10 p.m. Down periscope.'

Under cover of darkness, Kretschmer brought *U-23* to the surface five miles from the channel buoys marking the entrance to the Humber. On the conning-tower, he was deciding upon the best method of entering the shipping channel when another signal was received from Wilhelmshaven.

FROM COMMANDER-IN-CHIEF U-BOATS STOP

TO *U-23 U-47 U-35* RETURN TO BASE IMMEDIATELY STOP PRESENT OPERATIONS CANCELLED STOP ACKNOWLEDGE STOP DÖNITZ

The following afternoon *U-23* followed the cruiser *Emden* into Wilhelmshaven. The cruiser had just tied up alongside the jetty when screaming air-raid sirens heralded the first air attack of the war. A squadron of RAF Wellington bombers swept from behind the clouds and dived on the cruiser.[2] The next few minutes were confused for *U-23*. Kretschmer took her hurriedly out into the centre of the basin and turned to look at the *Emden*. Only one bomber penetrated the flak fire, but it crashed in flames over the harbour. As suddenly as it had begun, the raid was over and the sky was clear. A few minutes later the steady throb of the 'All Clear' brought the harbour to life again. *U-23* tied up at the U-boat pier, Kretschmer and the crew thankful that in their baptism of fire another ship had been the principal target.

That night in the wardroom of the submarine depot ship the commanders of some twelve U-boats ordered back from patrols compared notes and discussed the war, then thirty-six hours old. Kretschmer, who believed privately that the German armed forces would be far better employed in the East, if they had to be employed at all, was mildly surprised that so many of his brother officers held similar views. And overshadowing all was the nagging worry of the unknown, of the defences they had yet to probe and penetrate, of defences that once before had beaten down a U-boat menace.

Their high respect for an adversary who had fought and triumphed over another German U-boat Arm was natural. They were convinced that since those days the Royal Navy had perfected modern weapons and methods in readiness for anti-submarine warfare, whereas they had started from scratch only three short years before with a training programme largely based on tactics of the first war.

Three days later, Dönitz sent for Kretschmer and asked him how long it would take to prepare *U-23* for sea.

'About twelve hours, sir.'

Dönitz smiled. 'You are the first commander who seems to recognise that we are at war. You will sail at 8 a.m. tomorrow, the 8th. I want mines laid.'

The following morning *U-23* sailed into the North Sea to make the first half of the crossing to the Scottish coast on the surface. They saw nothing to excite interest during the three days it took to cross the North Sea, and after dusk on September 18th, *U-23* nosed her way into the bay at periscope depth, expecting at any minute to run into anti-submarine defences. The tension of being so close to the enemy shore plucked at their nerves, but the minelaying went off without incident and with an ease that gave the crew new confidence.

That evening, off the Firth of Forth, *U-23* came to grips with the enemy for the first time. Under cover of darkness the U-boat was surfaced, charging her electric motor batteries, when Petersen, the officer-of-the-watch, sighted a dark shape heading towards the coast. A few minutes later, Kretschmer saw with satisfaction that the darkened ship was approaching on a course that would bring her within one mile of the U-boat; an ideal attacking position. Slowly, without a light showing, the merchant ship held its closing course.

'Torpedoes ready,' Kretschmer ordered suddenly.

'Fire one.'

The torpedo shot out from the tube, the crew silently waiting for the detonations that would perhaps signal their first success. Below, the control-room calculated that the torpedo should have reached the target, which continued on her course completely unaware that for some unexplained reason she had just escaped being blown out of existence. *U-23* nosed her way nearer, in readiness for the second attack. It was a dark, calm night, and they could see the faint fluorescent wake left by the second torpedo as it streaked towards the ship. But again there was no hit. After a third shot,

Kretschmer gave orders to break off the action and took *U-23* out to sea.

He went into conference with his officers and torpedo-men to try to work out what might have caused three such dismal failures at a perfect target. He felt sure the torpedoes had passed under the ship without detonating – an event that had never happened during exercises in the Baltic, when he had rarely been known to miss.[3] They failed to reach any verdict, and Kretschmer signalled Kiel to the effect that he was returning to harbour. Although their mines had been laid successfully, Kretschmer's anger was aggravated by having to report that his first action against an enemy ship had ended in failure.

On the way in through the Skagerrak they stopped several neutral ships to enforce contraband control. Under the international Prize Regulations, belligerent Powers could prevent the transport of vital war materials to an enemy in neutral ships. Lists of these cargoes had been published by France, Germany and Britain, and the Royal Navy had already set up a vast contraband control point off the Goodwin Sands, near Margate, where all neutral ships were stopped and searched.

The Admiralty's list of goods banned to Germany was a lengthy document designed to enforce total blockade. The German reply had been to try to set up a counter-blockade by stopping all neutral shipping plying between the Baltic and England's East Coast ports. But lacking the experience and the means of the Royal Navy, the German Naval High Command treated contraband control as more of an irksome sideline to the major war effort than a vital corner-stone of naval planning. To the disgust of the commanding officers of both U-boats and surface units, the list of banned cargoes was so vague and ill-assorted that their attempts at control became largely wasted effort.

U-23's armament consisted of a single two-centimetre machine gun, and Kretschmer could not help smiling faintly as he ordered his gun's crew to fire the time-honoured 'shot across the bows' of a small Swedish freighter heading for England, and which had already ignored his signals to stop. The gun chattered its warning and a flurry of tiny water-spouts appeared ahead of the steamer. Immediately she altered course and ran up the International Code signal for: 'I am stopped.' The Second Lieutenant boarded her, and a minute or two later appeared on the bridge to shout: 'She is bound for Newcastle with timber, sir.'

Kretschmer looked hard at the typed list of banned cargoes, as though by some magic the word 'timber' would appear before his eyes. But the magic let him down, and with a resigned shrug he called his officer back and ordered the Swede to proceed. Later he wrote a report for Dönitz, saying: 'It seems strange that Germany should allow cargoes of stout timber to be moved freely to England, thereby making the enemy a gift of pit props for mines that produce coal to make steel which, in turn, is manufactured into the weapons used to kill German troops.'

This lack of authority over neutral ships was to infuriate him even more in the weeks ahead when merchant skippers, aware that timber was a legitimate cargo as far as the Germans were concerned, would stop when challenged and then give huge grins as they shouted 'Timber' and proceeded on their way, leaving the German commander raging impotently. From a British viewpoint, this acceptance by the reputedly ruthless commanders of the German Navy of a situation caused by incompetent thinking ashore is surprising. The explanation lies in Hitler's firm belief in those early days that Britain and France could be persuaded to sign an 'honourable' peace once Poland was defeated.

Back in Kiel for the first time since August, Kretschmer sent his crew on a brief leave and reported his torpedo failures to Dönitz. To his surprise, the Commander-in-Chief said that so many other commanders had reported torpedo failures that the High Command had appointed a commission of inquiry to root out the cause.

Notes

1 The Royal Navy's submarine strength was fifty-seven.

2 This raid was intended to be an attack on the pocket battleship, *Admiral Scheer*. So early in the war air crews could not be expected to identify surface units with accuracy.

3 In those days the Germans used a magnetic firing device for torpedoes.

Three
Orkneys and Shetlands

Kretschmer received orders to put to sea on October 1st and take up a patrol on the western entrance to the Pentland Firth, the approach channel to the Orkneys and the Fleet anchorage at Scapa Flow.

During the three-day trip to the Orkneys, *U-23* was sometimes submerged, but for the greater part on the surface. The lack of British air reconnaissance over the North Sea had given submarine captains confidence in surface travel. Kretschmer and Petersen studied charts of Scapa Flow and worked out plans to penetrate the Fleet anchorage through one of the three entrances; Holm in the east, Hoxa in the south and Hoy in the west. By the time they had reached the Fair Isle Passage, Kretschmer decided that he might attack through Hoxa. He could not have known then that this was the most heavily guarded entrance of the three and the principal gateway for British warships entering and leaving the anchorage.

His plan was to approach the boom defences after dark, creep round one end of the booms and blockship, fire his torpedoes and retreat in the same way. It was a daring and simple scheme from the beginning, and dangerous, for one of the strongest cross-currents in British waters is to be found in the Pentland Firth, and a submarine approaching Hoxa at slow speed might easily be swept ashore.

That night, while they were on the surface, a lookout spotted a darkened ship, and as they drew closer, trimmed down in the water to reduce their silhouette, their quarry could be seen passing through a host of little bobbing lights. These turned out to be the lights of a fishing-fleet, and patiently Kretschmer stalked the darkened vessel until she had drawn well clear. He thought it possible that the fishermen might at any moment sprout into fast patrol-boats, so he waited until the last light had faded in the distance before closing his target for attack.

Through binoculars, it looked like a small coaster, not a particularly inspiring target, but worth attacking, if merely to find out if a magnetic torpedo would detonate in these waters.

He brought *U-23* right to the surface and came abreast of the coaster at a distance of 1,000 yards. A burst of tracers from his machine-gun cut across the target's bows, but instead of stopping, the coaster seemed to increase speed in an effort to outstrip her attacker.

The radio operator called out to the conning-tower that she was sending out distress signals on the 600-metre international waveband in plain language. 'Target calling for assistance, sir,' he shouted. 'She is saying *Glen Farg* attacked by U-boat using gunfire.' The action was taking place too near Scapa Flow and possible Fleet patrols for Kretschmer to waste much time.

'On the bridge this time,' he called out to the gun's crew. A second burst of tracers raked the coaster's bridge and superstructure, sending the crew scrambling for their lifeboats. Kretschmer gave them time to get clear and then fired his first torpedo.

For about twenty seconds only the lapping of the waves on the sides of the U-boat broke the stillness. Then a blinding sheet of flame leapt skywards from the middle of the coaster. When the smoke and spray had subsided, the little ship was already sinking fast. In less than a minute the sea had closed in over her, and Kretschmer had sunk his first ship.

A bridge lookout had kept his eyes on one of the lifeboats, and now Kretschmer took *U-23* nearly alongside the boat and called out:

'What ship and what were you carrying?'

The response was immediate.

'Glen Farg, in ballast.'

'Right. Head Southeast and you will get the advantage of the current. Are any of you hurt?'

'No.'

'Sorry you are landed in this position. I am leaving now.' There was momentary silence in the lifeboat. Then a gruff voice replied: 'Thanks for coming over.'

With a cheerful wave, Kretschmer gave quiet orders to the helmsman and U-23 slid into the night.

Meanwhile, at his headquarters in Wilhelmshaven, Dönitz; had developed a plan for the attack on Scapa. Air reconnaissance showed that the most weakly defended entrance was Holm in the east. The aerial pictures showed that the entrance, split into three channels by two small rocky islands, was only partly defended by anti-submarine booms and blockships, and it seemed to the wily tactician that in the northern channel, Kirk Channel, there was room at both ends of the defences for a U-boat to penetrate, always assuming a certain amount of luck was on the attacker's side. The U-boat would have to navigate a mile-long channel with fewer than fifty feet clearance on either side and in water no deeper than forty feet. He needed for the attack a 500-

tonner which could stay below more than twenty-four hours and had the added advantage over the smaller boats of greater fire-power with double the number of torpedoes.

Prien, who had already completed two patrols in the area, was briefed and a signal sent to Kretschmer ordering *U-23* to take up a patrol line in the North Sea, away from the Orkneys.

At 10 p.m. on October 13th the attack plan came into operation, and Prien, who had elected to stay surfaced, approached Holm Sound without incident and reached Kirk Channel just before midnight. Conditions were ideal. A dry, crisp, clear night with no moon and a light breeze. Overhead the flickering Northern Lights threw an eerie canopy over the drama being enacted below. *U-47* passed round the northern end of the anti-submarine boom, with only feet to spare, at exactly midnight. Nearly half an hour later she was through the Channel and into the Flow.

Ahead lay the vast undisturbed main anchorage of the Home Fleet. Prien's orders were to sink as many capital ships as he could with his twelve torpedoes, and here he was, intact, and at liberty to take his choice of targets from the sleeping Fleet anchored before him. But plagued by torpedo failures, his daring and gallant penetration of the Flow netted for him an unrewarding prize. The old first-war battleship, *Royal Oak*, was expendable. The greatest tragedy was the loss of 834 officers and men who died in her.

Immediately after the torpedoes hit *Royal Oak*, the Home Fleet sent every available patrol boat and destroyer into the hunt for the U-boat or boats responsible for destroying the myth of Scapa's impregnability. They searched in vain. The exploit, regarded in British as well as German naval circles as an epic in the annals of submarine warfare, was a complete success, although the toll had been limited by the failures of more than half the torpedoes fired.
The morning after the attack, a blockship ordered by the Commander-in-Chief Home Fleet some weeks before to seal off the gaps in Kirk Channel, arrived in Scapa Flow just twelve hours too late to be of use.

The effect of the operation on the U-boat Arm was immediate. When jubilation had given way to sober contemplation of lessons to be learned, the first and most important was the certainty that Britain had no secret weapon to guard her coasts against submarine attack. Since 1918, no imaginative solution had been evolved to render submarines obsolete. Yet, having arrived at this very obvious and correct conclusion, the Command failed to extend the theory to include warships at sea.

Even allowing for their respect for the, as yet, untried Asdic defence, Dönitz at no time suggested that this listening device might possess imperfections of which a submarine could take useful advantage.

The total effect of a daring operation was to send morale soaring, and crews, once just a little fearful of operations too close to the English shores, now walked with a light in their eyes and with a swagger born of new-found confidence in their boats, their officers and their Commander-in-Chief.

But the basic training remained the same – attack from periscope depth from approximately less than half a mile and fire a fan of three or four torpedoes in order to ensure at least one hit. That had been the training concept since 1936, and Dönitz saw no reason now to alter it. It is popularly believed that Dönitz trained his crews in the art of surface attack. This became true only after the way had been signposted by individualists in operational commands who laid the foundation for a new training system not to come into effect until 1941.

Despite the temporary failure to press home their practical and moral advantage the U-boat Arm had come of age; the initiative had passed from the Royal Navy.

By the end of the year the U-boat Arm had sunk 114 British and Allied merchant ships, totalling nearly half a million tons, for the loss of 9 U-boats, of which 4 were destroyed by mines; in addition, the battleship *Royal Oak* had been lost behind the defences of Scapa Flow, and the much-needed aircraft carrier, *Courageous*, had been torpedoed and sunk in the South-Western Approaches, by accident rather than design. It was the Battle Report of this last action that attracted Kretschmer's study during long hours at sea. He was not satisfied with the existing basic principles of attack. To him they reeked of caution, encouraging captains to think more of the safety of their boats than of the necessity to attack.

U-29 had been on her way to intercept a convoy reported by another U-boat when she stumbled across the path of the *Courageous*, escorted by two destroyers. It was a flimsy enough escort, and in spite of the tendency of U-boats to avoid direct encounters with Fleet squadrons at sea, her captain found himself accidentally in such an ideal attacking position that he stayed at periscope depth and fired a salvo of four torpedoes. Dusk was gathering, and Lieutenant Schuhart, commander of *U-29*, thought it likely he might escape the hunt under the cover of approaching darkness. The *Courageous* sank in fifteen minutes with the loss of more than 500 of her crew. The two destroyer escorts began their Asdic hunt over a wide arc round the stricken carrier. *U-29* dived deep, retreated at slow speed and varying depths and was at no time in any danger from the hunting escort. Instinctively, Kretschmer felt that in this search pattern lay the clue he was seeking.

During the first four months of the war he had sunk little more than 6,000 tons (three ships), but had taken part in minelaying operations off the Humber and Invergordon. These were contributing considerably to the German Navy's toll on our shipping – more Allied ships were sunk by mines off the East Coast at this period than by U-boats – but they lacked the excitement and satisfaction of sinking ships by torpedo attacks. And in this frustration lay the reason for Kretschmer's ceaseless search for a less cautious, but nevertheless sound, approach to attack methods. He had, however, earned the Iron Cross (Second Class) for his torpedo attacks and initiative in often fruitless operations off the Orkneys and Shetlands; the Submarine War Insignia for completing three operational missions; and the Iron Cross (First Class) for his minelaying sorties in enemy waters.[1]

On his last trip before Christmas he had attacked a convoy off Farne Island, near the Firth of Forth; in less than an hour he had sunk the *Deptford* (4,101 tons) and then turned on a small ship which looked to be of no more than a few hundred tons. He fired a burst of machine-gun fire across her bows, and her crew took to the lifeboats at once. Then he fired one torpedo at the deserted ship and nothing happened. He fired a second, and still there was no explosion. The third hit her amidships and the tiny vessel was blown to pieces. On questioning the survivors, he had found it was the coaster *Magnus* (1,339 tons), and had remarked angrily to his new First Lieutenant, Lt. Baron von Tiesenhausen:[2] 'Three blasted torpedoes for that little shrimp.'

This patrol marked the first of what became known to the U-boat Arm as 'Kretschmer's Shetland Sorties'. Air-reconnaissance photographs showed that the British Home Fleet had vanished from Scapa following Prien's attack, and except for a few cruisers and an old battleship, the *Iron Duke*, already beached, the heavy ships had moved to another anchorage.

U-23 was given the roving mission of finding out if the Fleet were using the Shetland Islands and, if so, where. For Kretschmer this was a series of largely fruitless but fascinating patrols in which he explored every tiny creek and inlet in the islands, sometimes creeping in on the surface by night and, more often, nosing his way round coves and bays at periscope depth by day.

By January 12th he had been on patrol for nearly a week with nothing to show for ceaseless explorations of these bleak islands. Shortly after dusk that night, he nosed *U-23* across the entrance to Inganes Bay and to his astonishment saw two patrol-boats anchored on either side of the channel, while deeper into the bay lay the great unmistakable shape of an oil tanker, richest of merchant prizes for U-boats throughout the war. For the best part of two hours, Kretschmer cruised up and down at periscope depth trying to find some way into the bay which would take him past the destroyers without alarming them. In the end, he surfaced and decided to take the only route in, between the two escorts.

It seemed apparent that the small squadron had bedded down for the night. He would have to take the chance of discovery and go in on the surface. The swish of water down *U-23*'s sides and the low hum of her engines served only to aggravate the silence, seeming to the tensed crew to be certain give-aways as they closed the enemy. It dawned suddenly on Kretschmer that in a few moments they would be 'set up' for a deadly cross-fire if the patrol-boats were playing possum. Then they were through, the patrols pitching gently but visibly in the waves of his wake.

It was a clear, bright night with the moon shining brilliantly on the peaceful scene; gleaming white foam curled up from the bows as the range closed; orders rang out above the high-pitched whine of the fast-revving engines, and the torpedo, its wake of bubbles clearly visible, cut through the water towards the unsuspecting target. *U-23* had completed a 180-degree turn and was racing for the sea when a great red ball of fire billowed skywards with a splintering roar, revealing the low-slung, grey-painted tanker for a brief, stark second before a second larger explosion sent a sheet of white flame across the bay and whole chunks of steel superstructure were tossed into the air like sticks. Kretschmer kept his glasses fixed on each of the patrol-boats in turn. Dim blue lights appeared on their decks, and he could see the vague shadows of men running along the decks. Shouts came clearly through the thin northern air, and then they were past the crucial gap between the warships and racing for the open sea.

Kretschmer and his officers studied their books giving the silhouette of merchant ships of all nations and decided correctly they had sunk the motor tanker *Denmark* (10,517 tons).

On another occasion, this time in the Shetlands, they sighted what appeared to be a cruiser at anchor in the Fell Sound. They crept into the bay to fire two torpedoes at the darkened target. One torpedo hit with a flash and a roar. Petersen, who had kept his binoculars steady on the target, gave a sudden amazed shout: 'It's not a cruiser, it's a rock.' For a moment there was a stunned silence on the conning-tower and then, suspecting a trap, they searched hurriedly round the bay. It was empty.

At first Kretschmer could not help being angry at the wastage of time, tension and the two torpedoes. But seeing the barely concealed grins on the faces of his crew, he sent a signal to U-boat Command Headquarters saying:

'Rock torpedoed but not sunk.'

They turned and headed for the Fair Isle Passage and the North Sea. On the way home they torpedoed and sank the freighter *Polzella* and the coaster *Baltanglia*, and by the time they reached Kiel, *U-23* had been at sea longer than any other boat in their flotilla.

Immediately he reported on board the depot ship, Kretschmer found himself besieged by well-wishers congratulating him on his success. As he was disappointed in the trip himself, Kretschmer was further amazed when Dönitz asked for an immediate detailed report on the action. When this had been done Dönitz sent for Kretschmer and asked: 'What about the torpedoing of the *Nelson*?'

'The *Nelson*? Kretschmer exclaimed in astonishment.

'But I have not torpedoed the Nelson. I have never even seen the *Nelson*.'

'What!' shouted Dönitz. He telephoned the Signals Officer to bring in the signal file of *U-23*'s last trip. When the officer arrived, Dönitz took the file and thumbed rapidly through the signals.

'There,' he muttered triumphantly. 'What does that say!'

Still bewildered, Kretschmer read the signal, 'Nelson torpedoed but not sunk.' For a moment Kretschmer shook his head in bemusement, and then his expression changed as he realised the mistake. The German for rock is *felson*, and in transmission this had been changed to Nelson.

Dönitz sat down. 'A rock,' he whispered as though to himself. 'So you attacked a rock.' In a moment he was shaking with laughter. 'Oh, Kretschmer, if you could know what I am thinking, I don't think either of us would be laughing. Can you see Goebbels' face when he hears this.' He picked up the telephone and said, 'Get me Berlin; the Propaganda Ministry.' He turned to Kretschmer. 'All right. I'll get tonight's announcement stopped. They were going to say: "Where is Nelson, Mr Churchill...?" I do not need much imagination to guess what reply would come from the Prime Minister.'

Notes

1 See Appendix A.

2 Tiesenhausen shared Kretschmer's views on new tactics and put them into effect, with disastrous results for Britain, on 25 November 1941, when as commander of *U-331* in the Mediterranean, he pierced the destroyer screen protecting HMS *Bahram* and torpedoed the battleship, which sank in a few minutes, 862 officers and men going down with her. *Bahram* was the first British battleship to be lost at sea. Later, when captured, Tiesenhausen was taken to the Operations Room at the Admiralty where for several hours he and senior British officers reconstructed the action.

Four
The Front Moves West

On February 12th, 1940, *U-23* sailed from Kiel on her eighth wartime trip. It was a dreary, cold, drizzling day, and the conning-tower watch huddled behind the protection of the gunwales not expecting trouble so near home. Suddenly a look out shouted: 'Torpedoes to starboard.' As he turned, Kretschmer called automatically to the control-room: 'Hard a-starboard. Full speed.' He saw three lines of bubbles racing towards them. Their turn seemed painfully slow to the rigid men on the conning-tower, who watched fascinated into immobility by the devastating speed of approaching torpedoes. *U-23* was still on the turn when two torpedoes passed her on one side and the third on the other.

'Steady as she goes. Alarm dive,' ordered Kretschmer, and the watch leapt down the conning-tower hatch as *U-23* dipped her nose in a steep dive.

At fifty feet they levelled out and, with the electric motors just turning over, listened for hydrophone bearings on the enemy. They had no need of the hydrophones. The sound of enemy propellers throbbed through the U-boat, and they could hear the clicking of electric switches altering the speed of the engines.

'That's a British sub, too damn close,' the Engineer muttered in the control-room.

The propeller noises grew louder, and Kretschmer ordered the crew to lie down and brace themselves for collision. Then *U-23* rocked gently, as though brushed by some giant hand, and the noises from outside the hull grew fainter.

Soon afterwards they surfaced and proceeded to their rendezvous without further incident.

Six days later dusk was beginning to give way to nightfall when Kretschmer went up on the conning-tower to keep Petersen company. He was smoking the inevitable black cigar as they rested their arms over the edge of the forepart of the bridge and discussed the lack of targets, when a lookout shouted: 'Ship bearing ten degrees off port bow, sir.'

More reports from other lookouts made it apparent that a convoy was passing across their bows about two miles away. Kretschmer threw his cigar overboard.

At that moment a destroyer came into sight just off the starboard bow less than a mile away, and heading outwards on a tangent from the convoy on a course that placed the U-boat almost on the destroyer's beam – an ideal attack position. Just then another destroyer appeared out of the darkness on their port side, still some distance away, and not presenting a threat. But to Kretschmer the situation was menacing. It looked to him as though, caught between the two escorts, he had accidentally landed in a trap. Had he dived then, there was every reason, from a British viewpoint, to hope that he would have been picked up on Asdic and sunk. Instead, he decided to retreat on the surface; and to do it at speed he would have to try to sink the destroyer nearing him to starboard.

They could see the brief flashes of blue light on the destroyer's deck as her crew passed through the black-out curtains covering the entrance to the mess-decks. Kretschmer pointed *U-23*'s nose at the target and fired two torpedoes. With a quick look at the other escort, he swung the U-boat round to seawards and headed for safety. The range had been short, and almost as soon as *U-23* had steadied on her new course a sudden roar and a blazing light from the attacked destroyer illuminated the scene, throwing the convoy into stark relief and making Kretschmer feel uncomfortably naked in the brilliant glare.

Darkness closed in again, and they watched the destroyer roll over on its side and sink in a rush of hissing as air and steam boiled into the water. The whole incident from the time of firing to the disappearance of the destroyer below the surface took two minutes.

Kretschmer decided to steer a parallel course to the convoy and try another attack. It was while on this course, with the convoy out of sight, that he came on a lone merchant ship steaming without lights which he assumed was either a straggler from the convoy or one trying to rendezvous with it.

He attacked with two torpedoes, and a gigantic roar came from inside the ship as it blew up and sank. This was the freighter *Tiberton* of 5,225 tons.

Three nights later, while cruising down the cast coast of the Orkneys, they torpedoed and sank a lone freighter, the *Lock Maddy*, of 4,996 tons. Then, heading northwards and with all her torpedoes expended, *U-23* returned to base in triumph. It had been their most rewarding trip since the outbreak of war. Kretschmer's exploits in the northern North Sea were drawing to an end.

At Headquarters, Dönitz told him: 'This time I want you to patrol north of the Shetlands and report the movements of the British Home Fleet. You should not attack warships unless in self-defence, but should you intercept merchant ships you are free to take any action you think fit. But most important is to keep us informed of the activities of the British heavy squadrons. When you get back, we will have another talk about a change for you. I think I shall have to ask the Führer to make you Earl of the Orkneys and Shetlands when we occupy Britain. You must know more about those islands than any other officer afloat.'

It was a fruitless nine-day patrol during which they saw neither warships nor merchantmen, only a few trawlers from the Shetlands. On the last evening Dönitz signalled them to return to Kiel with all possible speed. They arrived on March 23rd, and with the mail waiting for them was a High Command order instructing Kretschmer to hand over command of *U-23* to a relief commander and to report to U-boat Command Headquarters for further orders.

During the next day Kretschmer packed his bags and left the U-boat for the last time. As her captain, he had made nine patrols ranging from the Firth of Forth to the Shetlands; had been at sea for ninety-six days; had sunk nine ships consisting of eight merchant ships and a destroyer totalling more than 30,000 tons; and had laid mines in the entrances along the East Coast. He had achieved this without having been depth-charged by any Allied unit.

More important was the birth of an idea that tactics would have to be changed if U-boats were to play to the full their role of underwater stranglers of Britain's lifelines. This idea, born at the sinking of the *Courageous*, had been strengthened by his penetration of Inganes Bay to sink the Fleet tanker under the noses of two destroyers; by the British submarine that had passed so close to him underwater without further attack; and finally by the sinking of the *Daring*. These incidents had brought home to him one unarguable and startling fact – it was possible to get close to enemy destroyers without detection.

Near the end of April a signal arrived at Kiel from Admiral Dönitz. It said:

On the orders of the Supreme Commander of the German Navy, you are to commission and command U-99 now ready for delivery to the German Navy at Kiel. You are to undertake dockyard trials and assume command by May 1st, 1940.

U-99 was a new 500-ton, ocean-going submarine with a fire-power of twelve torpedoes in bow and stern tubes. Her crew complement was forty-four, including her captain, and compared with the old *U-23* she would be sheer luxury. Kretschmer arranged for the transfer of Warrant Officer Petersen and welcomed to Kiel his new First Lieutenant, Lt Bargsten. With the new Engineer Officer, they went down to the docks for their first look at *U-99*.

She was lying alongside the submarine pier looking more like a floating, mummified cigar than a U-boat. Thick wire cables were wrapped round her from stem to stern and loose ends jutted forlornly into the air.

On April 30th, with a skeleton crew and several dockyard experts on board, Kretschmer took *U-99* into the Baltic for trials. She lapped the measured mile at seventeen knots. They all crossed their fingers for the first dive, but she trimmed neatly at varying depths. The first salvo of torpedoes left their tubes without a hitch, and the reloading was faster than in *U-23*. The guns completed their exercises without a jam or breakdown. Kretschmer ordered the dockyard experts to stay in the control-room while he took *U-99* through a series of acrobatics that only a commander who has experienced moments of danger and crisis could call upon.

In harbour the following day, Kretschmer signed the delivery notes and formally accepted *U-99* from dockyard hands on behalf of the German Navy. The commissioning ceremony, attended by senior service chiefs, took place two days later.

U-99 looked a different ship from the one Kretschmer had seen only a few days before. Gone were the wire wrappings, and the red patches of preservative paint had given way to a dark, business-like mixture of black and grey which gleamed in the sunlight.

Through the day, Chief Petty Officer Jupp Kassel, chief radio operator and one of the finest hydrophone operators in the U-boat command, superintended the loading of stores, for in addition to his radio duties, Kassel was also the crew's *maître d'hôtel*, responsible for their daily menus. At 8 a.m. the next day they sailed for working-up trials in the Baltic. As *U-99* left the jetty, the dockyard superintendent and the staff came down to wave them good-bye.

'She's a good ship, Captain,' he cried out to Kretschmer on the conning-tower. 'Treat her well and she'll sink the whole Royal Navy for you.'

'We will,' shouted Kretschmer. 'And I'll be seeing you when you take over Portsmouth dockyard.'

The mooring wires were taken in and the long, slender U-boat slipped out of harbour with her paint gleaming and her bows slicing the water with deadly-looking efficiency.

For a week they practised diving under every conceivable condition with each officer in turn taking over as 'captain', in case Kretschmer should ever be unable to continue in command.

The following week was to be devoted to practice attacks on convoys. Two merchant ships sailed in line ahead protected by a flotilla of destroyers which had been used for the working-up of U-boats since the beginning of the war. These destroyers were experts at beating off attacks, and having the advantage of knowing at what time the dummy attack would be made were particularly alert. Few submarines managed to pierce their screen without detection, and the result of the exercises was judged more by the actions of the U-boat once it had been discovered and counter-attacked rather than its ability to sink merchant ships.

On the way out into the Baltic, Kretschmer decided to let his officers take *U-99* down the swept channel. One of them indulged in a piece of showing off by cutting the turns round buoys as fine as possible. As Kretschmer came up to the bridge he saw that the fast approach to one buoy would almost certainly result in a collision which might damage the side of his new ship.

Quickly he took over from the startled young officer, and ordered a slight alteration of course to pass the buoy some fifty yards wider than had been intended. Kretschmer had another reason for this. From experience, he knew that British submarines and aircraft laid mines regularly in the channel, usually near buoys used by the U-boats.

It was just as well he remembered this. As they passed the buoy there was a violent explosion, and a gush of water sprouted into the air just where they would have been had he not altered course. As it was, the U-boat was thrown over on its side and the blast blew in the seams of several plates below the conning-tower. It was a near miss, but the damage was slight and Kretschmer decided to return to harbour for repairs.

When these were completed they sailed again, and on the fourth night Kretschmer took over the first attack. Shortly after dusk the squadron commander signalled his course and speed for the night and Kretschmer set his 'collision' course. To the astonishment of his officers, the interception point was later than normal, making the attack time only a few hours before dawn.

It was a lusty night with a stiff breeze and choppy sea. They were lying about five miles off the convoy course at midnight when the first ships were sighted. Kretschmer closed slowly, and for the next hour ran along a parallel course checking the zigzag of the target on his stop-watch. He was lying to windward of the convoy, and noticed that a large layer of cloud was coming up which would blot out the moon at about 2 a.m. He passed this information to his officers and said he would attack just as the moon went behind the clouds. With the temerity of youth, the Second Lieutenant asked:

'When do we dive, sir?'

'We don't.'

There was a surprised silence on the bridge, and a few minutes before the moon went behind the clouds they closed the convoy at full speed. Gradually the darkened shapes of the escorts came into sight and Kretschmer pointed *U-99* at a space about a mile wide between the two bow destroyers, and while the crew waited tensely, the submarine slipped between the escorts, who continued their zigzag unconcernedly, and headed towards the rear merchant ship. Kretschmer made his attack run, and then steamed up alongside the first ship and switched on his searchlight. There was a moment of startled inactivity, before the nearest destroyer rushed inwards to see what had happened. In a few minutes the realisation that *U-99* had penetrated the escort and sunk both targets dawned on the squadron commander, who somewhat ungraciously signalled a brief acknowledgement of defeat. Kretschmer was elated. His surface attack plan had worked against a destroyer screen alerted to his movements and with all hands on the lookout for his approach. He felt he was ready to go to sea.

Back at Kiel, Kretschmer found he had made his dummy attack just in time. Dönitz ordered him to cut short the trials and report for operational duty. He asked for a few days to make minor repairs.

At last, everything was ready and they weighed anchor. They were getting under way when there was a shout from Bargsten on the foredeck. Draped round a flange of the starboard anchor was a horseshoe, which a sailor was busily retrieving. Kretschmer acknowledged their 'find' with a disinterested wave. Then came a second shout. Another horseshoe had come up on the other flange. Kretschmer called out with a grin, 'Where's the horse?'

Bargsten ran back to the conning-tower and suggested smilingly that, as they had not decided on an insignia, they might use the horseshoes so conveniently provided by fate. Kretschmer agreed, and after *U-99* returned to harbour that evening, several dockyard workers were bribed to work overtime putting a gleaming, gilt-painted horseshoe on each side of the conning-tower. When the job was finished they joined the crew in a tot of rum to christen the 'Insignia of the Golden Horseshoe'.[1]

Notes

1 All U-boats sailed with some form of insignia painted on their conning-towers. As the paint was rubbed off during each operational trip, they regularly had to be repainted. *U-99*'s horseshoes were easily repainted before she entered harbour after each trip.

Five
The Happy Time

At dawn on June 17th, loaded with twelve torpedoes, stores and fuel for six weeks, *U-99* sailed from Kiel bound for the Atlantic. She was behaving perfectly as they made their way through the Kiel Canal and down the Elbe, and the crew were in high spirits, feeling the confidence that comes with a happy and efficient ship.

Before dusk on their first day an engineer reported sick with rheumatism of the right arm. He complained that he could not do his work with only one arm. Annoyed at this disability and strongly suspecting that it was a fake complaint born of fear, Kretschmer signalled a report to Kiel and prepared to put the man aboard some ship inward bound. Instead he was ordered to proceed to Bergen, the Norwegian port then in German hands, and put the sick man ashore before continuing on his voyage.

Another signal from Dönitz warned him that the battle-cruiser *Scharnhorst* was proceeding southwards down the Norwegian coast and her aircraft would be maintaining anti-submarine patrols for an area covering 30 miles around her. *U-99*, therefore, was to keep outside that range of the battlecruiser, otherwise she might be attacked in mistake for a British submarine. The following day *U-99* was well to seawards of the prescribed patrol limit of the *Scharnhorst*'s aircraft when Bargsten on watch sighted a British submarine. Kretschmer decided to stay on the surface, in the belief that the enemy would have spotted him. But the behaviour of the British craft soon indicated it was unaware of the U-boat's presence, so Kretschmer altered course to give it a wide berth.

Just then they were sighted, and the enemy dived, presumably to make a torpedo attack. Putting on full speed, Kretschmer was soon well out of range and was about to go below leaving Bargsten on watch when Petersen broke the news that in avoiding the enemy submarine they had come closer to his estimated position of the *Scharnhorst*. Almost at the same moment a lookout spotted an aircraft approaching.

Its nose was pointed down as though in preparation for a dive attack, so Kretschmer sounded 'Alarm dive' and they began to submerge. Although he did not know it, this was one of the *Scharnhorst's* aircraft and the pilot, seeing the submarine below him crash-dive immediately, thought it to be British and trying to escape.

He attacked. *U-99's* conning-tower was still slightly above water when the first bomb, beautifully aimed, lobbed into the water alongside it and exploded on impact with the sea. There were no leaks in the U-boat, but the attack periscope jammed, its lens was broken and both compasses were put out of action. For some of the crew it was an ironic baptism of fire from one of their own aircraft. Kretschmer cursed the engineer for taking them out of their way and surfaced again to continue to Bergen. They reached the Norwegian port shortly before dark, and lay in the entrance while a motor launch came out to take off the sick man.

With so much damage to vital instruments, Kretschmer decided to return to Wilhelmshaven for repair. He was about to signal to this effect when they received an agitated signal from Dönitz which said: '*Scharnhorst* aircraft reports sinking enemy submarine in your position. Are you all right?'

Kretschmer replied that he was quite all right, but in need of repairs. He was told to return to Wilhelmshaven immediately.

Dönitz listened to Kretschmer's account of the air attack which had clearly taken place outside the prescribed limits. The Admiral became almost incoherent in his condemnation of the aircraft's pilot, leaving Kretschmer with his first hint that Dönitz felt any affection for him. In fact, Kretschmer was not the lone recipient of this fondness from the Old Man. Dönitz had trained most of these young captains himself. They were so few for the enormous task he had set them that he looked after them as a hen might mother its chicks, liable to fly into a furious temper at any outsider who might accidentally threaten to deprive him of even one of them.

In three days the repairs were completed and *U-99* sailed on a second attempt to break out into the Atlantic. For the next week they stayed mostly on the surface, making their way across the North Sea to the Fair Isle Passage, Kretschmer's old stamping ground between the Orkneys and Shetlands, and then into the northern Atlantic and down west of the Hebrides, across the North Channel, the convoy approaches off Northern Ireland, down the Irish coast to patrol in the South-West Approaches to the Channel and the Irish Sea. This was the first of Kretschmer's Atlantic adventures. At noon on July 5th he reported himself on patrol.

At 4.15 on this sunny afternoon, with a light breeze rippling over the long Atlantic swell, *U-99* lay below at periscope depth searching for targets and at the same time keeping hidden from aircraft, when Kretschmer spotted a steamer approaching on a zigzag course.

'Port five degrees…that's it, steady as you go now.'

'Engineer, prepare to fire one torpedo. Keep the bows steady at trim.'

'Stand by to fire.'

'Fire one…' A hiss of air and the submarine rocked gently as the torpedo shot from the bows and steadied on its depth and course. Kretschmer kept his periscope up, watching the track of the torpedo. Suddenly there was a quick flash and a dull roar, and the steamer broke in two, the forward part subsiding slowly into the water while the after section stood on its end. The crew were jumping into the sea from both parts and two lifeboats got clear of the rear section, which seemed to hover on its end for an interminable time. Eventually it slid backwards into the sea and vanished.

A quick spin round the horizon at the periscope, and the lack of any hydrophone effect, convinced Kretschmer to surface and find out from the survivors what ship he had sunk. As they approached the first boat at slow speed a petty officer rushed to the conning-tower holding a sub-machine gun at the ready. Kretschmer saw the survivors take a startled glance at the threatening gun and prepare to jump overboard on the far side of the lifeboat to get some protection from the spray of bullets they thought inevitable. Kretschmer shouted angrily to the petty officer: 'Put that gun away. And go below yourself. I don't want you up on deck again while we are here.'

Abashed, but stung to reply, the petty officer said, 'I was told at training-school to expect survivors in lifeboats to machine gun U-boats when they tried to help.' Kretschmer replied, 'Get below.' He shouted in English to the survivors: 'I'm sorry about that gun. We do not intend to harm you.'

Kretschmer addressed himself to a man whose uniform showed him to be a senior officer: 'What was the name of your ship?'

'Can't say,' came the reply.

'Is your captain alive?'

'I am the captain.'

'What ship?'

There was a silence. Then 'Can't say.' Kretschmer circled the lifeboat and came closer. 'We can just see the name on your lifeboat. You should have put a few more coats of paint over it. The name looks like *Magog*. Is that right?'

'Yes.'

'That's better.' Kretschmer grinned amiably at the pokerfaced skipper. He glanced at a Lloyd's Register handed to him by Kassel from the control-room. The name *Magog* was given with a tonnage of 2,053.

'All right. You are not too far from the Irish coast. But don't let the wind take you too far south, or you'll end up in France, and you know what that means.' The Canadian skipper grinned this time and put a finger across his throat.

'No, not quite as bad as that,' Kretschmer assured him.

'You are all very wet and oily. Is anyone hurt?'

When the skipper shook his head, Kretschmer shouted an order to Kassel, who appeared holding a bottle of brandy, which he waved at the boat. At an order from their skipper, the survivors pulled nearer to the U-boat and Kassel handed down the bottle. *U-99* picked up speed and headed westwards. They were still near the lifeboat when the skipper, who had been wondering how to reply to a U-boat commander who had first sunk him and then given him brandy, suddenly stood up in the stern of the lifeboat and shouted, 'Thanks'. Kretschmer waved an arm in reply, and gradually the lifeboat vanished over the horizon.

At dusk next day they spotted a freighter heading out into the Atlantic and zigzagging at long and short intervals. It carried no lights, despite approaching darkness. Kretschmer saw its stern gun, decided it was a fair target but saw a Sunderland flying-boat circling the steamer as though in escort. Instead of attacking, he discreetly withdrew and submerged.

The following afternoon another lone ship appeared in sight obviously relying on its speed to keep out of danger. It was a perfect target and would pass him at not more than 500 yards. Exultant, Kretschmer prepared for the classic submerged attack. Creeping along at periscope depth, *U-99* was as steady as a suspended carcass. Kretschmer suffered a moment of panic. The silhouette looked like a steamer of the 'Astronomer' type, a class of ship U-boat captains had been warned were being used by the British as Q-ships – heavily-armed traps to attack U-boats. He decided to fire two torpedoes, one in the wake of the other, to pierce her armour. As the range closed, he rapidly altered his plan and prepared to fire one torpedo only.

It hit amidships, and immediately Kassel was listening to the stricken ship's SOS. She gave her name as *Bissen*, and later Kretschmer identified her as a 1,514-ton Swedish ship. He had just enough time to watch her sink in the lonely sea when Kassel reported he could hear propellers approaching on the hydrophones. Kretschmer stayed at periscope depth and moved slowly from the area.

At midnight he was smoking on the conning-tower when the lookout sighted a convoy heading out from the Western Approaches. He threw his cigar overboard, and word went round the crew that the captain was heading in to attack their first convoy. For nearly two hours they steamed at full speed on the surface to reach an attacking position on the convoy's port bow before dawn, a manoeuvre that caused some anxiety to Kretschmer, who was only too well aware that they were running low on fuel. In fact, he was so worried that he promptly decided to submerge ahead of the convoy after dawn and drop back at periscope depth. There was a moment of tension when Kassel picked up strong hydrophone effect to port, and Kretschmer swung the periscope round to see a destroyer less than 100 yards away. But the escort altered course away, and they were able to let the convoy creep above them on either side.

The torpedo-firing mechanisms allowed shots to be made at ninety-degree angles, so Kretschmer prepared to fire at ships as they passed him on the same course. His plan visualised shots to right and left until all torpedoes had been expended. When the first ships came into his sights he shouted 'Fire!', but the correct settings had not been made. Eventually one of the stern torpedoes was launched late. It turned nicely to a ninety-degree angle and sped away. Then came a dull explosion and a brilliant flash from a ship lying well astern of the one in their sights. It was large, with a silhouette not unlike that of a Union Castle liner, but it was in fact the *Humber Arm*. They dived deep to head out of the convoy to safety where Kretschmer could investigate the reason why the torpedo settings had taken so long to be correctly applied.

His War Diary describes vividly the subsequent developments in that action.

> 0806: *Propeller noises heard approaching to starboard. I order depth to be trimmed at 100 feet. I believe my crew are going to get their baptism of depth charging this time. Escort approaching fast as though to attack.*
> 0809: *Propeller noises not so loud. It is possible the escort has lost us. I maintain course and speed.*
> 0810: *Escort picking up speed. This is the attack. I maintain course and speed.*

Kretschmer believed he was being attacked by a destroyer escort. In fact, the attacker was one of the first corvettes off the assembly lines to reinforce the Atlantic escort groups. The first pattern of ten depth-charges rocked the U-boat and threw everything movable on to the decks. It was too close. They submerged further to 350 feet still maintaining course and speed. But the depth-charges still came close. Kretschmer ordered all electrical equipment to be shut down except the hydrophones and gyro compass. To conserve the batteries supplying the power for the electric motors, speed was reduced so that the propellers were just turning over sufficiently to give *U-99* enough speed to maintain depth. After two hours of almost continuous depth-charging, the oxygen supply failed under the shuddering blows of the explosions. The crew donned their rubber breathing-masks, which were connected by tubes to cases of alkali which purified the stale air.

At this listening speed and maintaining the same depth, *U-99* crept away with the hunter above running over her at regular intervals to drop more of the dreaded charges which threatened to blow in her sides. Kretschmer ordered a good ration of chocolate and biscuits to be served, and each member of the crew lay down at his diving-station to conserve what little air remained. Kassel stayed at the hydrophones monotonously reporting each run-in of the hunter above. As he shouted, 'Attacker above, sir', the crew braced themselves for the blast of the charges they knew were already tumbling down through the water around them.

After the sixth hour had passed there came a lull in the attack and Kretschmer lay down himself and soon fell asleep. But forty minutes later the attack was resumed, and he wakened to feel the U-boat leaning far over on its side under the blast of the explosions. Most of the crew were now breathing in large gasps behind their masks, and it was obvious that they could not stay alive much longer. Kretschmer began to add up his chances of survival. At any moment the batteries would run dry, and without any power to provide some sort of slow speed, the boat would sink to the bottom. He tried to remember if the depth of water in this area was too great: if they would all be crushed by the pressure before touching bottom. He thought it likely that the escort up above must soon run out of depth-charges. This proved of but slight consolation, for he guessed that other destroyers were already heading to the scene. He gave no sign of his fears.

At the hydrophones nearby, Kassel looked in amazement at his commander sitting on the control-room deck reading a book. It was a detective thriller, and Kretschmer seemed thoroughly engrossed in it, showing no sign of emotion as the depth-charges blasted them with the horrible grating of a thousand chisels on steel and rolled them around the decks. But before another hour had passed, Kassel found there was something wrong in the picture of Kretschmer reading a book. A few more glances over his shoulder and he became suddenly aware that his commander was not turning the pages; in fact, he had been looking at the same page since first opening the covers. A further, lingering look and he saw that the book was being held upside down. A lasting affection for Kretschmer was born in Kassel at that moment. It is still there today, and Kassel recalls the incident as one of the finest examples any U-boat commander ever showed his crew. Certainly it must have taken enormous reserves of will-power to have sat for hours looking at the same page of an upside-down book.

After twelve hours, the charges sounded further away. No one had been able to use the lavatory, in case the discharge should rise to the surface and reveal their position to the enemy. The air inside the U-boat was thick and foetid with the dangerous tinge of carbon dioxide that all submariners fear. Since the first attack, Kretschmer had kept *U-99* on the same course. Now he decided he might throw the attacker off the scent if he made an unexpected alteration of course. Their speed had been dropping as the batteries weakened and a check at the depth-gauge showed they had sunk to nearly 700 feet – 150 feet below the safety depth for this class of U-boat. They made a turn to starboard and steadied on a course at right angles to the one they had held for twelve hours.

On the hydrophones, Kassel heard the attacker pass directly overhead, but this time there were no depth-charges. Their respite was brief. Ten minutes later the explosions came again, still farther away, and for the first time the crew began to hope they might survive. Kretschmer glanced at the instruments measuring the power left in the batteries, and decided they would have to surface inside an hour if they were not to sink into the oblivion of a crushing depth. An hour passed and still the depth-charges fell near, but not dangerously close. At 10.28 p.m. – more than fourteen hours after the attack had begun – they counted the last explosion, and Petersen marked up the 127th depth-charge in the War Diary. It was the last. For another five hours they stayed below, praying that the batteries would hold out, although they should have been run down hours before.

At a little after 3.30 a.m. the following morning, as the last power came from the batteries, they surfaced into the calm, black night of the Atlantic, after nearly twenty hours under water and under constant attack. Kretschmer could muster just enough strength to open the hatch and rush on to the conning-tower. He turned to see the dense, yellow, stinking air inside come spouting out of the boat in a thick, sickly column. It had the greenish tinge of decay. The diesel motors started up and the crew came pouring out on to the decks to lie gasping, taking in deep draughts of clean, fresh, salt air.

Nearly thirty minutes passed before they were able to gather any energy to inspect the damage. Everything breakable had been smashed, and all movable parts had been put out of action. But vital machinery and the hull plating had stood up to the severe blasting and remained intact. Kretschmer set course to the north and headed at full speed to resume his patrol. He noted in his War Diary:

We all felt like schoolchildren at Christmas time. Everything about the depth-charging had been new to us, and we didn't know what to expect next. Each noise was strange, and every toll and crack inside the U-boat seemed to herald the end. Now we have received all the presents the enemy can give us. We all have a fresh confidence in our ship and a special prayer for the horseshoes under which we sail.

Twenty-four hours later – on July 10th – they sighted a lone ship heading inwards towards the north coast of Ireland. They surfaced in the late afternoon and headed towards this target at a speed that would bring them into an attacking position after dusk. The steamer was zigzagging at long intervals, and in the last light of the day they attacked with one torpedo. It hit just below the foremast, and they were close enough to see the crew begin lowering boats immediately. Kretschmer waited for twenty minutes before nearing her to try and hurry her end with gunfire. But before they could fire the first round, the ship gave a sudden lurch to port and her stern rose high in the air. Smoothly, but with a gigantic roar of bursting girders, she nose-dived to the bottom. At that moment a starshell lit up the sky some miles away to starboard, and Kretschmer decided that with warships in the vicinity there would be no time to question or help the survivors. They left at full speed. Kassel had intercepted the target's signal for help and had noted her name as the *Petsamo* of 4,596 tons.

They saw nothing the following day until the evening, when they sighted a small freighter heading westwards, and Kretschmer decided to try and sink her by gunfire. They closed to within little more than 200 yards and fired a shot across her bows. The steamer stopped and the crew took to the boats. One of them pulled alongside *U-99* and, to her crew's astonishment, it contained seven women. Bergman counted out loud, and there were no contradictions. Almost unable to shout because of his laughter, Kretschmer asked for the ship's name and nationality. The anxious and obviously scared merchant skipper replied in broken English. '*Merisaar*...Estonia.' With a touch of whimsy, Kretschmer decided to become the first U-boat commander to take a ship as a prize of war. In slow, carefully chosen words, he announced:

> *You are now a prize of the German Navy. You will set course for Bordeaux and on arrival inform the port authorities you have been captured by U-99 and sent there to be taken as prize. Do you understand? Do not try to get away because I shall be following you below the surface. One deviation from your course and I shall torpedo you. Do you understand that?*

The Estonian captain nodded and waved vigorously. While *U-99* stayed on the surface the boats returned to the ship, which soon turned round and steamed off on a course for Bordeaux.

Four days later, while nearing the southern tip of Ireland, they sighted a darkened ship steaming in towards the English Channel. Kretschmer had four torpedoes left, and he decided to use one on this freighter. Coming in towards the target at full speed, he put his fist before him and told Bargsten: 'When my fist blots out the ship, I shall call out fire, and we shall see what happens.'

In two minutes a torpedo went speeding towards the freighter and made a direct hit amidships. There was a burst of activity on the wireless, and Kassel reported the ship's name as the *Budoxia*. They watched while the crew of the stricken ship abandoned her and pulled well clear of the firing area. Kretschmer ordered Sub-Lieutenant Elfe to sink her with gunfire. In the next half an hour they put more than fifty shells into the hull near the waterline and some twenty phosphorus shells into the superstructure. It was a dark, overcast night, and when the target did eventually catch fire, she lit up the area for miles around them. Kretschmer could see the survivors in the lifeboats shaking their fists at him.

The ship still showed no signs of sinking, and with a gesture of exasperation, he decided to give her another torpedo. This one hit astern, and the whole after-part of the ship sank immediately, the forward section following soon after.

The next morning they sighted another steamer heading towards England from the south. They attacked submerged with their last two torpedoes, and scored one hit near the stern and another in the bows. On the 600-metre band, Kassel intercepted their SOS and recorded the name *Woodbury* – only just in time. For, as the signals were repeated, the *Woodbury* leaned inwards and cracked in two. In twenty seconds she had gone. Kassel, at the wireless, heard a lookout above in the conning-tower mutter: 'They must all have gone down with her.' He thought with acute discomfort of the enemy wireless-operator who must have been trapped in his radio-room while sending out his signals for help. But it was not so bad as they thought, for among the wreckage they sighted three rafts crowded with survivors.

Kretschmer was at a loss. The rafts might drift with the wind and current and the survivors would die of exposure. He ordered all spare blankets and a keg of rum to be brought on deck and nosed *U-99* to the nearest raft. The survivors shouted frantically for mercy, thinking the U-boat was going to run them down, and jumped into the sea for safety. In seconds the raft was empty and men were swimming for dear life. He stopped *U-99* and without speaking to the men in the water, ordered the blankets and rum to be thrown over on to the raft. Then he pulled astern and headed away to the west.

After leaving the Woodbury sinking, Kretschmer signalled Wilhelmshaven that all his torpedoes were expended and requested further orders. The reply came in the late afternoon. He was to proceed at utmost speed to the French port of Lorient.

Lorient became the 'base of the aces' when *U-99* steamed through the Narrows and entered harbour as one of the first U-boats to establish residence in this Atlantic port. On the quayside to greet her were the advance guard of Dönitz's staff who had arrived to prepare the Commander-in-Chief's new headquarters in a villa overlooking the sea some two miles from the base proper. Kretschmer's most urgent problem was to find clean clothes for his crew. Their sea overalls were filthy and still carried with them the stench of the rotten air from the depth-charging. The military commander proved helpful by telling them of a warehouse full of British battledress uniforms that had been left behind by the BEF. Kassel and Petty Officer Bergman took a work-party to the warehouse and came back with a truckload of khaki uniforms, which were handed out among the crew.

When dressed, they all lined up on the quay for inspection by Kretschmer, himself decked out in a neatly fitting battledress. Fearful that his crew might be mistaken for a marauding band of English troops, he told them to sew on their ribbons and collar bands to give them a more Germanic appearance. As a precaution, the military commander was asked to warn his troops, should they see men in odd-looking uniforms running round Lorient, not to arrest them. Then came the spring-cleaning of the boat to rid it of the smell they now associated with death, for in their hearts there was still this awful memory of the hell of depth-charging.

The staff officers had made arrangements for Kretschmer and his officers to stay with them at the Hotel Beau Sejour, while the crew had been booked into the Pigeon Blanc. The officers' mess had been established at the Prefecture, which had been set up as operational headquarters of the Command. On that first night ashore, Kretschmer, feeling closer to his men now that none had panicked under the severe depth-charging, invited them all to dine with him. The anxious-to-please staff placed several tables together to form a large U to seat the forty-three guests of the Commander.

After the meal the men withdrew to explore the possibilities of Lorient. At a naval base far removed from Germany, or even Paris, there was no Gestapo. And the military had been so correct in their relations with the French population that the sailors found that a cordial tolerance had been reached on both sides. As with sailors everywhere, there was mass migration down to the dimly-lit cafés, restaurants and clubs in the red-light district. With the memory of their narrow escape still fresh in their minds, the crew of *U-99* set about painting the district a brighter shade of red than it could remember. The petty officers, Kassel, Bergman, Schnabel and Clasen sat round a table in the café with the loudest music they could find and, with the aplomb of accustomed drinkers, proceeded to call for champagne and followed this with a variety of wines, forgetting that their constitutions were unused to the rich maturity of French produce.

Well before midnight the crew staggered back to their hotel, broke, and anything but sober. And at the bewitching hour itself, four exceedingly drunk and incapable petty officers made a riotous din steering an erratic course down the main street of the town, and approached the Beau Sejour Hotel, past which they would have to go to the Pigeon Blanc. The lounge window of the Beau Sejour came down nearly to street level and they could see Kretschmer looking out into the street. At a signal from Kassel, the four carefully sank to their knees and began crawling with exaggerated caution past the window-sill. But their whispering echoed like shouts and their giggles were heard by Kretschmer. The four petty officers stiffened and then, with wide grins and still on their hands and knees, tried to salute as they continued their crawl. One by one they collapsed on their stomachs and rolled to their feet, still grinning drunkenly. Furious, Kretschmer turned his back on them and vanished from the window.

The following morning he had the crew lined up on the quayside by the submarine and lectured them on their behaviour. He told them he expected the crew to show the same discipline ashore as on board. He demanded they have pride in their ship and their uniform – an unfortunate remark in view of the British battledress they were wearing – and promised to take the strongest disciplinary action if the scenes he had witnessed were ever repeated.

For the next few days Kretschmer welcomed into Lorient other U-boats which, on completion of patrols, had been diverted to the new base or sent round direct from Germany. The hotels filled as more of the staff arrived from Wilhelmshaven. Dönitz had arrived in Paris and set up a central communications office there. And on July 24th *U-99* was ordered to sea.

0400/28/7/40

Calm sea and long swell. Light breeze. Bright moonlight and cloudy. Course due North on patrol across North Channel approaches. Surface speed eight knots. No ships sighted during watch.

Sub-Lieutenant Elfe finished the entry in the Deck Log and said goodnight to Kretschmer and First Lieutenant Bargsten. Forty-five minutes later the moon came from behind some clouds and revealed a lone ship steaming out into the Atlantic about three miles away. Kretschmer checked the time and weighed up the nearness of dawn against the likelihood of air patrols and decided to attack on the surface. At full speed *U-99* swept round towards the target in a large crescent movement that brought her into an attacking position by 5 a.m. When the range had closed to about one and a half miles, Kretschmer shouted 'Fire one!' and the phosphorescent disturbance and hiss of air in the empty tube marked the passage of the hurtling torpedo. In less than a minute there was a loud explosion at the stern of the target, and almost immediately Kassel intercepted the plain-language call for help on the 600-metre band: '*Auckland Star* torpedoed in position 52°–17′ N, 12°–32′ W, requests help immediately.'

Kretschmer glanced anxiously to the east, where the first signs of dawn were appearing over the empty horizon. Then came the sudden whine of a shell overhead. Startled, Kretschmer swung his glasses round on the stricken merchantman. The crew were taking to the boats, but astern the gun's crew were firing at *U-99*, and the shooting was good. Not liking the idea of being holed, especially after the radio signal, Kretschmer dived and decided to give her another torpedo. He looked again at the target through the periscope and saw the lifeboats pulling away from the *Auckland Star*. His orders came quickly, and a second torpedo left on its deadly mission. This time it was a direct hit between the bridge and funnels, but still she gave no sign of sinking. Angrily, Kretschmer fired a third torpedo and scored his third hit in the same place as the second. The *Auckland Star* rose in the water and turned slowly and reluctantly over on her side, finally capsizing. She vanished at 7.33 a.m. and *U-99* headed away from the scene at full speed on the surface with Kretschmer certain that aircraft would be sent in answer to the Blue Star liner's signals.

He had gone below to shave, and Able Seaman Schmidt had decided to visit the toilet, or 'heads', as they are known at sea. At the same time that he was taking down his trousers, he suddenly heard, in this, the quietest place in the ship, the rapid, deadly throb of propellers. He shot out, leaving his trousers behind and shouted desperately to the conning-tower that he had heard a torpedo approaching. On the bridge, Petersen looked around with his glasses, saw nothing and shouted in reply: 'Don't be a bloody fool, Schmidt. Go back and finish your business.'

Schmidt, crestfallen but still convinced that he had heard something, did as he was told, and had just sat down again when there was a sudden burst of activity throughout the U-boat. A lookout had spotted a periscope. Petersen altered course to put the small silhouette of their stern to the enemy, when two loud explosions came from the opposite side. These were the torpedoes fired by the British submarine which had missed and had rendered themselves harmless.

Kretschmer dashed to the bridge and took over command. They were well up to the west of Ireland, and it seemed strange that a British submarine should be in these waters. When they had made off at high speed for some time and must have outstripped the enemy with his slower under-water speed, Kretschmer discovered he had come back to the vicinity of the sinking of the *Auckland Star*. At 8 a.m. they sighted an aircraft and dived, using the respite to reload their forward tubes. At 10 a.m. they surfaced and made their way westwards at high speed, but ten minutes later dived again with another aircraft alarm.

Kretschmer's hunch that aircraft would appear in reply to the Blue Star liner's signal had been right. They turned southwards in the afternoon, and at dusk surfaced again. Just before nightfall the two best lookouts on the ship, two Viennese, known as the 'Steamer Terrors', because of their amazing gift of spotting ships at night, gave Kretschmer a merchant ship zigzagging on long legs. He joined Bargsten on the bridge, and between them they recognised the heavy-loading gear silhouette of a Clan Line ship. It was making about sixteen knots, and Kretschmer decided to proceed at full speed to get ahead of it into an attacking position. In the long swell *U-99* could not do much more than sixteen knots herself, and would never have been able to get ahead. But the zigzagging reduced the steamer's speed along her mean course to about twelve knots.

Two hours later *U-99* was lying off the starboard bow of the target. Their first torpedo fired at about two miles range missed or failed to detonate, but the second hit her amidships. She stopped and settled down in the water by the stern, but as they watched it seemed unlikely she would sink further. Kassel at the radio set intercepted what they now regarded as the inevitable distress signal. '*Clan Menzies* in position 54°–10' N, 12°– 00' W. Attacked by U-boat and torpedoed.' Kretschmer did not want to waste any more torpedoes on this ship, so he ordered a Sub-Lieutenant to stand by to take explosive charges across to the target in their dinghy. The swell had risen considerably and the dinghy was very small indeed.

'Can't we find some other way, sir?'

Kretschmer grinned.

'No. You had better get the boat ready.'

'But, sir, the sea is much too rough. We might turn over and loose the charges, and I am not a very good swimmer.'

'Get that boat ready, Sub-Lieutenant.'

'Yessir.'

He had climbed down to the foredeck reluctantly, making it obvious that he did not think this was a good idea at all, when the *Clan Menzies* gave a sudden lurch and slipped down into the water and vanished in a cloud of steam and spray.

The Sub-Lieutenant clambered excitedly back to the conning-tower and asked:

'Do you still want the boat put out, sir?'

'No, you have escaped a ducking this time.'

The following day they patrolled the approaches to the North Channel entrance to the British Isles, crossing the paths of ships leaving or entering round the north coast of Ireland. They saw nothing all day, but on the afternoon of the 30th a small warship of the 'Kingfisher' type made them dive as it sped past to enter Loch Swilly. They surfaced about two hours later, but almost immediately had to dive again when an aircraft appeared from a cloud directly overhead. There were no bombs, and they stayed down until after dusk when they surfaced. Then one of the 'Steamer Terrors' watch cried out: 'Darkened ship forty degrees to port, sir.' The War Diary report of the action reads:

0126: *Sighted steamer inward bound in the North Channel.*
0138: *Fired one torpedo at 1,000 yards (half a mile).*
0139: *Hit near stern.*
0141: *Intercepted distress signal reporting* Jamaica Progress *torpedoed. Request help urgent*

The crew of the stricken ship took to the lifeboats immediately. Kretschmer conned *U-99* alongside the nearest lifeboat and, while they were chatting to survivors, the *Jamaica Progress* slid beneath the waves at 3.35 a.m.

Almost at the same moment they heard a sound of aircraft engines and a large Sunderland swooped low over the scene, low enough for the crew of *U-99* to see the blue lights in the nose. They dived and stayed below water, heading westwards for more than seven hours. Shortly after 11 a.m. on the 31st July, Kassel picked up the sound of propellers on their hydrophones. They surfaced, and from the conning-tower they saw the smoke and masts of a convoy appearing over the horizon to the west. There were fifteen to twenty ships from Britain with an escort of one destroyer ahead and two smaller vessels patrolling on each side. By 2 p.m., *U-99* was lying in the path of the convoy and was forced to dive deep to avoid being rammed as the convoy passed overhead.

When they returned to periscope depth, Kassel reported loud hydrophone effect, and as Kretschmer looked through the periscope he saw the view blocked by a vast red curtain. It was the red-painted side of a merchant ship passing *U-99* with only a few feet to spare.

By now only the last ships of the columns were in sight, and the crew were beginning to get restless. They remembered the depth-charging they had received after their last convoy and did not like the idea of attacking another. They considered there were sufficient lone ships around.

The nearest ship was an elderly-looking freighter of about 5,000 tons, the *Jersey City*. They fired one torpedo at half a mile range and scored a hit amidships.

'Propellers approaching fast, sir.' Kretschmer swung the periscope round and, to his horror, saw a destroyer bearing down on them.

'Dive to two hundred feet,' he shouted, and the U-boat went into a steep dive.

The first depth-charges fell while they were still diving, but although the explosion clattered horribly through the boat and a few pieces of crockery on the mess deck jumped about, they were not close. During the next hour and a half about fifty depth-charges fell around them, but not one came close enough to cause any real worry. Kassel called Kretschmer over to listen at the hydrophone loudspeaker. They fell silent in the control-room as they heard the peculiar hissing and roaring noises of the sinking steamer.

At 4 p.m. the propeller noises became fainter as the destroyer called off the hunt and returned to the convoy. They could still hear the propellers of the convoy faintly in the distance, and Kretschmer, incensed at being forced down by the escort, decided to go after it again now that dusk was approaching. He returned to periscope depth and saw a corvette picking up survivors from the *Jersey City*. When he had got well past, he surfaced to proceed at full speed to catch up with the convoy. Just then a Sunderland flying-boat appeared well to the north making for the convoy, and suddenly it banked steeply and headed straight towards *U-99*. Kretschmer ordered 'Alarm dive', and they had not reached thirty feet when the first stick of bombs fell well to starboard, causing no damage.

No more bombs fell, so forty minutes later they returned to the surface. But the flying-boat reappeared and Kretschmer was forced to dive again. This time he stayed down for half an hour before surfacing again to find the convoy still in sight. Again the Sunderland returned, and *U-99* crash-dived to sixty feet just in time to be severely shaken by a second stick of bombs.

An hour passed before he could surface again, but this time the convoy had vanished in the darkness. The aircraft appeared once more and Kretschmer had to dive for the fourth time. He was cursing furiously, and Kassel was beginning to wonder if his commander's stock of cigars would last with so many being thrown away each time they dived.

At nine that evening Kretschmer brought *U-99* to the surface again, and this time there was nothing to disturb the silence of the Atlantic night. Both aircraft and convoy had disappeared. He knew at once that the aircraft had been primarily charged not so much with sinking him as keeping him submerged while the convoy escaped. He went into conference with Petersen, working out from the convoy's mean course where it would be at daybreak.

They stayed on the surface and headed at high speed for the estimated interception point. At dawn on the 1st, Kretschmer came to the conning-tower and, as he wrote later, 'What I expected to see I didn't see. There was no convoy.' After a short talk with Petersen and Bargsten, he decided to submerge, in the hope of obtaining hydrophone bearings. Once submerged, Kassel picked up the faint sound of propellers fairly far away, and after surfacing they headed on the bearings he gave.

From the conning-tower they spotted smoke on the horizon dead ahead. Congratulating Kassel, Kretschmer ordered full speed, and by late afternoon they were in sight of the convoy. There was no aircraft around this time, and they were able to manoeuvre ahead of them on the surface. The sea was rough and a mounting wind was whipping the water into a flurry of spray, so it took till 8 p.m. to get ahead.

This was against all the principles laid down by Dönitz in attack training. U-boat commanders were taught never to wait but to attack as soon as they could get a target in their sights at periscope depth outside the escort ring and fire a 'fan' of torpedoes. Kretschmer could have carried out this formula by attacking during the day. Instead, he had worked out his own procedure, by taking most of the day to get ahead of the convoy, so that by dusk he was in a perfect position for a surface attack. Now he wanted to prove he could attack by night on the surface and carry out his personal principle of 'one torpedo, one ship'. Fans of torpedoes were, in his opinion, a waste of equipment and effort and allowed a U-boat commander to attack from a position of comparative safety in the hope of hitting something, instead of taking carefully calculated risks and by precision firing making every torpedo count. It was from this time that he became the first commander to attack convoys only by night and always on the surface. This attack was to set the pattern. At this stage of the war no other commanders followed Kretschmer's technique, considering it too dangerous, yet it was this method that led him to outstrip his colleagues in sinkings.

As he maintained the course and zigzag of the convoy ahead and on the starboard bow, he mentally checked the points he had always believed would make night surface attacks possible. Intelligence reports had indicated that escorts were leaving outward-bound convoys from Britain before they reached the longitude of twenty degrees West. They had reached the 15th meridian, so Kretschmer thought it likely that the escort would leave either that night or the next. It was a guess, and a remarkably accurate one, for at that time our escorts did leave outward-bound convoys on the 15th meridian to join inward-bound convoys. He checked the weather and the amount of cloud which might hide the moon and altered course to take him to the darker side of the convoy. At fifteen minutes past midnight the escort began signalling to each other with blue lights. They sped past the columns of the convoy and vanished at high speed to the northwards.

Kretschmer smiled excitedly. Twenty merchant ships were now at his mercy. His attacks would be limited only by the number of torpedoes that remained, and he had only four left. He had time to choose his target, and in accordance with Dönitz's orders looked for the priority target-oil tankers. The third ship in the second column was the biggest tanker in the convoy. Elfe, glancing through their book of tanker silhouettes, reported it to be of the 'Baron Recht' Dutch-type tanker of about 9,000 tons. Unaware of approaching danger, the convoy continued on its mean course, without zigzagging.

Kretschmer took *U-99* right into the convoy. The crew were astonished. On the bridge Bargsten and Elfe held their tongues, not daring to call their commander mad, but thinking that he must be. As they crossed the bows of a merchant ship in the outer column safely and with no alarm, they began to see what Kretschmer was doing. They were now less than 600 yards from the tanker, ready to fire at point-blank range.

The torpedo hit the tanker near the stern in the engine-room. She listed heavily and began sinking by the stern. As *U-99* swept past her along the convoy lane to attack the second tanker, a lookout reported that the leading ship in the centre column – the commodore – was showing a red light.

At this signal every ship began zigzagging independently. To Kretschmer's astonishment, the whole convoy began twisting and turning in all directions. 'It was an awful muddle,' he wrote in his War Diary. 'I was in the middle of twenty, no, nineteen now, ships freewheeling around to try and avoid attack.' He kept his eye fixed on the second tanker, and from a range of less than 500 yards fired the next torpedo. This hit the target near the bows, and at once Kassel was able to read her distress signal. She was the *Lucerna* (6,556 tons). With this sinking the convoy dispersed, each ship steaming as hard as she could away from the site of the two attacks.

This was *U-99*'s first experience of getting inside a convoy at night and having each merchant ship career about all around the submarine. It was alarming, disconcerting and not conducive to the best attacks. Kretschmer was convinced by this time that at any moment some ship was going to ram him without knowing it. But a large freighter loaded well down in the water was in a perfect attacking position. Beyond it Kretschmer saw a third tanker, but he had to sink the freighter to get at it.

'Fire when ready, Bargsten,' he called out and pointed the nose at the freighter.

To their anger, the torpedo, an extremely precious one, headed straight for the bottom of the sea. Kretschmer ordered his First Lieutenant to fire the last torpedo. But, as Bargsten fired, the freighter blew a long blast on her whistle and altered course towards *U-99*. The torpedo flashed past her and scored a hit amidships on the tanker Kretschmer had been trying to reach. There was a great sheet of fire, and the wounded ship burst into flames, sagging dangerously in the middle. Kassel intercepted her signal for help and reported that she was the *Alexia* of 8,016 tons. Kretschmer regained his good temper. By missing the freighter and hitting the tanker, he had sunk three tankers with four torpedoes. His conviction that it should be possible to sink one ship with one torpedo inside or near a convoy was proved. Momentarily, he forgot he had only gained undisputed access to the convoy because the escort had been ordered away.

Suddenly a frightening crash and splintering roar brought his eyes round to his starboard beam, where he saw two ships that had been heading towards him – possibly intending to ram him – had collided half a mile away. They were locked together and one seemed to be settling down by her bows. Within thirty minutes, only the stricken wrecks and the two collided ships remained with him on the battlefield. The rest of the one-time orderly convoy had vanished in a dozen different directions.

Kretschmer steered towards the last tanker (the *Alexia*), which, although burning, was still afloat. He decided to assist its end by shelling from a range of just under a mile. Sub-Lieutenant Elfe and his gun's crew put thirty well-placed shells into the dying hulk and Kassel intercepted a further signal from her saying she was damaged and being shelled by a U-boat. Bravely the crew of the *Alexia* returned *U-99*'s fire and Kretschmer was astonished that a ship with smoke pouring from its funnel, its deck alight, its middle sagging and the stern sinking slowly, could even consider fighting back. By now the *Alexia*'s gun had straddled *U-99*, one shot falling little more than fifty yards over her, and the next twenty yards short. It was too close for comfort, so he altered course away while continuing the action.

A searchlight beamed over the horizon, and while still pumping shells into the *Alexia* and twisting rapidly to avoid being hit in return, Kretschmer saw a destroyer approaching at high speed. He broke off the action and withdrew discreetly into the darkness, still on the surface. They watched the destroyer race up to the *Alexia*, and then returned to the scene of the first sinking. Only wreckage wallowed bleakly in the water – a grim reminder of the tragic end to a ship's life. While looking around for survivors, always with one eye ready to sight the approach of the destroyer, they heard depth-charging in the distance. That decided Kretschmer. Thankful that the destroyer was hunting in another district, he ordered Petersen to set course for Lorient. With all torpedoes expended, it was time for home.

On August 7th Kretschmer anchored in the Narrows approach to Lorient harbour and waited for the minesweeper to escort him into harbour. The crew were ordered to clean up the ship, to wear their British battledress uniforms and shave. On the 8th, *U-99* sailed into harbour to be welcomed by the military band and members of the Staff. From her raised periscope flew seven victory pennants each bearing the Horseshoe Insignia in recognition of seven ships sunk.

Six
Convoy HX72

Kassel, Clasen and Bergman sat drinking round a table in the café they had found after their first trip. They had dined with the rest of the crew at the officers' hotel as guests of their commander. Now they were getting down to the real business of a night ashore.

Most of the crew were there, dancing and enjoying themselves generally. Eventually the petty officers joined in the fun, and by the early hours of the morning it had developed into a wild party with the crew of *U-99* still in their light summerweight British uniforms. They were all sweating profusely when suddenly Clasen let out a startled yell and pointed at his tunic. It was falling apart; first the sleeves disintegrated, then the bodice fell apart, and after a while the trouser legs began to shred. There was a yell of laughter from the rest of the crew and their girl friends. But this soon stopped as each one glanced down at his own battledress and found it coming to pieces as well. In a desperate attempt to remain decent they rushed in a shouting mass from the café and ran back to the Pigeon Blanc. They discovered later that before quitting Lorient, the British troops had poured acid over the uniforms and, with the heat of their bodies, it had eaten away the cloth. They had escaped from the café just in time.

Before going ashore, Kretschmer covered his action in not attacking the convoy during the day while submerged and waiting until nightfall. He noted in his report that the rough weather made it necessary to stay on the surface to maintain contact. Dönitz could hardly blame him for not carrying out the standard procedure for attack in such weather.

The following day he was summoned to the telephone ashore. It was Dönitz calling from his headquarters in Paris.

'I've just been reading your report, Kretschmer. Congratulations on an excellent attack. Come up and see me this afternoon.'

That evening in Paris, Kretschmer learned he had been awarded the Knight's Cross to the Iron Cross for the greatest number of ships and total tonnage sunk by a commander in one voyage and for 'continuous determination and skill' in handling his ship in face of the enemy. He was informed that he could not be spared to receive it from the Führer in Berlin, but that Admiral Raeder would visit Lorient the next day to make the award in person.

All naval crews in harbour were lined up in Lorient Harbour on parade for inspection by the Commander-in-Chief. The other officers and crews were immaculate in their dress uniforms and daggers. But in the place of honour, in the centre of the parade, was *U-99*'s crew in hastily adorned new battledress tunics to replace those destroyed by the acid. Kretschmer, as senior officer, called the parade to attention as Admiral Raeder appeared through the gates.

The German Navy's Commander-in-Chief looked a little startled to see, that the crew he had come to congratulate and the commander he was to decorate were wearing British uniform, but he recovered and paid Kretschmer the compliment of saying that his crew looked the smartest on parade – 'no doubt due to their extremely smart and efficient uniforms'. The rest of the parade was dismissed, while *U-99*'s crew was told to remain for a special address. Raeder congratulated them on their success and handed Kretschmer a flat box containing the Knight's Cross and sash. It was an austere, yet moving ceremony. When Raeder had gone, Kretschmer and his crew celebrated together on the deck of *U-99* with bottles of beer for all hands.

Kretschmer took some of the crew with him to Kiel in a special plane ordered by Dönitz. They collected their uniforms and personal belongings and returned to Lorient by train. Kretschmer reported to Staff Headquarters, now occupied by Dönitz, who had taken over his villa. There he was told that a minesweeper had picked up survivors from a merchant ship that had been bombed by a Focke-Wulff in the Bay of Biscay. Dönitz had heard their story and had remembered Kretschmer's report of his first trip. They were the survivors of his prize, the Estonian *Merisaar*. So, through no fault of his own, Kretschmer could now claim another 2,136 tons. This did not temper his anger against the Luftwaffe for sinking, as far as he knew, the only prize ever taken by a submarine on the high seas. At the same time he learned he had been the only U-boat on operational patrols in the North Atlantic for the last week of his second trip.

On August 26th, 1940, Admiral Dönitz arrived at the Hotel Terminus in Lorient and went to bed with a heavy cold. He called all his commanders in harbour to his room for an urgent conference. As they walked in, some six of them, he leaned against his pillow and chuckled at the concern on their faces. 'Don't worry,' he said. 'I'm only having a child.' He was really suffering from severe stomach trouble and his Flag Lieutenant was at his side. 'Gentlemen,' he began, 'you are here to receive your orders for Operation *Sea-Lion*.'

There was a sigh of excitement round the room.

'The day for invasion has been set…September 15th. Those of you on patrol in the Atlantic will receive orders telling you to proceed to Cherbourg to refuel and reload with torpedoes. Your task will be to bar entry to the Channel through the western entrance. No warship of the Royal Navy is to get through to interfere with our cross-Channel supply lines. I must stress this point. No British ship must enter the Channel.'

This was all the Lorient commanders were allowed to know of the overall operation.[1]

A few days later Kretschmer was called to the Hotel Terminus to be introduced by Dönitz to an Italian submarine officer, Commander Longobardo, who commanded a submarine based at Bordeaux.[2] The Italian Navy had sent him to Dönitz with the request that he be allowed to make at least one trip in a German U-boat to study attack methods. After the introductions, Dönitz said: 'Kretschmer, I want you to take Commander Longobardo with you on your next trip. You should be ready to sail within twenty-four hours. I think you had better see that his gear gets aboard *U-99* today.'

Kretschmer greeted this with a sour look. It was customary for U-boats to have a 'guest' on every trip but, so far, these had been U-boat officers making a study of operational methods before assuming their own commands. This was going to be different. Outside Dönitz's room Kretschmer tried to speak to the Italian in German. Longobardo replied in Italian. This was just dandy, thought Kretschmer. A 'guest' for perhaps three weeks who could not speak German. Then, with sudden inspiration, he said in English: 'We will make you as comfortable as we can, Commander. I hope you think the trip worthwhile.'

In equally good English, the Italian replied: 'Thank you, Commander. I expect to be under your orders, and I will do my best not to get in the way.' Kretschmer breathed his relief. They could talk to each other in the language of their common enemy. Never had he been so grateful that he had studied English as a boy.

At the local school near his home in Lower Silesia he had shared his father's love for languages and natural science. This tendency to absorbing study moulded his character into one of quiet, unassuming reserve and gave him a gentle modesty foreign to his more exuberant classmates. While others romped in the snow or played their pranks in the rich countryside, he learned the meaning of prehistory and archaeology. Yet he could ski with the best, and in time became the friend of none, but popular with all. From this serious and intensive study came the tremendous power of concentration that was about to reflect brilliantly in the practical application of his theories on U-boat warfare.

While still a boy of little more than seventeen, his father had sent him to Britain, France, Italy and Austria to perfect his knowledge of languages and science. In England he had studied privately under Professor Schopp, then teaching at Exeter College. He stayed in Exeter eight months before leaving for Paris, but it was sufficient to enable him two years later to take and pass the Naval Interpreter's examination in English. In 1930 he had thrown aside his studies to join the Navy as a cadet. This was not surprising, as it had been a consistent boyhood desire and the switch was made with such characteristic courtesy that it left not a ripple on the surface of family dignity. It was a move that Great Britain was to regret more than his father.

On September 1st there was a loud knocking on Kretschmer's bedroom door and Prien burst in with the news that Schepke was due in harbour in the early evening. He suggested a party, and that evening the three 'aces', together for the first time since Kiel, drove to a tiny village near Lorient and drank wine until the early hours of the next day. When they returned to the Beau Sejour, Kretschmer received orders to sail that afternoon.

U-99 slipped from Lorient and ran out into the Atlantic across the Bay of Biscay along the route known to the escort groups of the Royal Navy as 'U-boat Alley'. Sub-Lieutenant Elfe gave up his bunk to the 'guest' who, three days later, joined Kretschmer and Petersen on the conning-tower. They were about to go below for lunch – Kassel had instructed the cook to produce plenty of spaghetti for their ally – when a lookout shouted: 'Aircraft on starboard beam, sir. Height about forty degrees.' They all swivelled round to see the flyingboat coming in their direction. 'Alarm dive,' Kretschmer ordered, and they scrambled hurriedly through the hatchway as the boat tilted her nose downwards and the engines throbbed to full speed.

'Take her to thirty feet, Schröder,' Kretschmer told the Leading Engineer.

He stood by the periscope well ready to take a look at the aircraft's intentions. Instead, the submarine continued her downward plunge past periscope depth. In fact, they had crash-dived too steeply, and the boat refused to answer to the trimming vanes. Kretschmer ordered compressed air to be blown into the forward ballast tanks. This righted the submarine, and eventually she settled back on trim at the correct depth, the air being let out again. Kretschmer glanced sourly at his First Lieutenant and the Engineer. The Italian commander was having his first experience of working with the German Navy, and this would hardly help to create a good impression. He turned to Longobardo.

'Sorry about that. These things happen at times.'

'That's all right. I was sure you would right her easily.'

That afternoon was bright and sunny when they sighted a small, curiously-built steamer zigzagging a mean course heading inwards to Britain. Kretschmer approached cautiously and identified it as a Canadian Great Lakes steamer. It was small enough to attempt an attack with gunfire. The first shot went across the bows, and Kassel at once picked up the inevitable signal for help. It was the *Luimneach* (1,074 tons). They saw her crew abandon ship, one man leaping from the bridge into the water and three more jumping over the stern.

Kretschmer closed the range to 100 yards and about twenty ordinary armour-piercing shells and six phosphorous shells were enough to send her down, a blazing hulk. From the conning-tower he could see that two men in a lifeboat were wounded. He had rolls of bandages and packets of cigarettes tossed into the boat before *U-99* drew away into the dusk.

At 6 p.m. on September 8th they sighted an outward-bound convoy and spent all that night and the following day shadowing and getting ahead into an attacking position on the bows. In the evening they surfaced, only to be sighted by a destroyer which spotted their wake on the fluorescent sea. Kretschmer tried to get away at full speed on the surface, but the destroyer, with its greater speed, kept up the hunt until he was forced to dive. Depth-charges fell around them at once and they submerged to more than 300 feet, counting thirty charges on the way down before the propeller noises became fainter as the destroyer lost their echo on her Asdic. Half an hour later they surfaced and were spotted by another destroyer coming up fast from the stern of the convoy. Kretschmer dived again, and another pattern of depth-charges, better aimed than the first, heeled them over on their side and sent most of the control-room crew rolling on the deck. But the destroyer broke off the attack and steamed off.

For fifteen minutes Kretschmer steamed towards the convoy on hydrophone bearings, and at 10.20 p.m. surfaced inside the escort and alongside the port outside column of the convoy. He was little more than 500 yards from a large freighter, well down in the water with her cargo. The torpedo hurtled from the tube and, to Kretschmer's astonishment, leapt from the water and careened off like a porpoise on an erratic course. It missed the target. The second torpedo was fired at once and behaved exactly as the first, leaping around in the water and heading off at a tangent from the course on which it had been fired. Another miss. Kretschmer closed to within 200 yards of the freighter to fire the third torpedo. This one repeated the performance of the first two. The Italian officer watched with a wicked-looking smile playing at the corners of his mouth. Kretschmer was too angry to offer any excuses. Then came two explosions from inside the convoy. By checking the times, it was obvious that the first and third torpedoes had scored hits on other ships in the convoy.

While dropping back behind the convoy, Kretschmer again met the stern destroyer escort and was chased off in the direction of the North Channel. This was the last straw. With the Italian officer on board everything had gone wrong. He was supposed to be learning something from a German 'ace'. All he was learning was how not to handle a submarine. In his War Diary, Kretschmer wrote: 'I was supposed to show him how we sank ships. I had missed with three torpedoes, and missing ships was something Italians knew about already.'

Worse was to come. For five days they prowled around the Western Approaches without sighting anything. Just before dawn on the sixth day, September 15th, they sighted a darkened ship sailing alone on a zigzag course westwards off Rockall. It was a black, gusty night, and Kretschmer decided to attack from close range. But the sea was so heavy he could not make enough speed to get close before daylight. So he fired one torpedo from 3,000 yards. It hit, and the inevitable call for help followed. It was the Norwegian steamer *Hird* (4,950 tons). Kretschmer waited to see if another shot would be necessary, but as the first signs of dawn appeared the *Hird* vanished.

Shortly before dusk on the 17th they sighted their fourth target – the *Crown Arum* (2,392 tons) – zigzagging in short, wild spurts heading inwards towards the North Channel. Kretschmer fired one torpedo and scored a hit near the stern. They watched the crew take to their boats while the ship settled slowly in the water. Kretschmer ordered Elfe to set her on fire with phosphorous shells and the ship burned like matchwood for nearly half an hour before subsiding in a sizzling mass into the water.

Meanwhile, Prien in *U-47* had expended his torpedoes and had been sent out into the middle of the North Atlantic on a weather patrol for the Luftwaffe. This was a mission every U-boat tried to avoid. When they had no more torpedoes left, Dönitz sometimes ordered them to this weather patrol, which meant days of inactivity, signalling weather reports from which the Luftwaffe meteorologists could work out conditions over Europe and Britain. Then, on September 20th, the spell of bad luck for *U-47* broke when an inward-bound convoy crossed Prien's weather patrol, and gave him the excuse he needed to leave the tedious weather-reporting 'beat'. He signalled the convoy's position, course and speed and announced he was taking over as shadower. His reports were so infrequent that, at Lorient, Dönitz believed he had lost contact. So, basing his calculations on the last known course and speed of the convoy, the Admiral ordered five U-boats, including *U-99*, to form a stationary 'stripe' across the probable path of the convoy. These boats stayed on the surface at the limit of visibility from each other, approximately five miles, and covered a frontage of some thirty miles.

At dusk Prien signalled another position, course and speed, and with this evidence that he was still in contact, the 'stripe' was dissolved automatically without any further signals breaking radio silence. Each U-boat proceeded independently to attack in her own way. But, to Kretschmer's fury, one U-boat commanded by a new captain, kept up a stream of signals to Lorient. First he informed Lorient that he had taken up his position on the 'stripe', then he signalled that he intended leaving the 'stripe', and followed this with a report that he was half-way to the convoy. Kretschmer was certain that at least one of these transmissions would be picked up by the enemy, and was tempted to signal them to shut up. He decided not to risk giving away his own position by adding to the welter of words filling the air. Instead, he headed at full speed on the surface on a 'collision' course to the convoy.

After nightfall they arrived at the interception point, but there was no convoy. It had altered course after dark, and Kretschmer was certain that the signals had been picked up by the escort, who had ordered a new course to avoid attack.

He was probably wrong, for it was common practice for convoys to make a drastic alteration of course after dark to try and shake off possible shadowing U-boats. He submerged to try to get hydrophone effect, and Kassel managed to pick up faint propeller noises to the south. On this bearing they surfaced and steamed at full speed. At nearly 2.30 a.m. the following morning they sighted the convoy and headed round its stern to get into an attacking position on the dark side. On the way Kretschmer spotted a U-boat almost stopped on the surface. Carefully, he slowed down and stealthily crept up behind it until he was close enough to ram. There was panic on the stranger's conning-tower. Their propellers churned the water as they made off at high speed, quite certain they were being attacked. But before becoming lost in the night, they turned round in a broad sweep and a tiny blue light blinked out a recognition signal. They replied, and the other boat came alongside in the rough swell. Kretschmer and his conning-tower crew were grinning hugely, and broke into outright laughter when they saw they had 'bumped' Prien in *U-47*.

Prien called across: 'You wouldn't have got away with that if I had been on the bridge, Otto. You scared my watch stiff.'

'You need some lookouts,' Kretschmer replied tartly. He felt a little annoyed that Prien's crew had been so slack as not to see him approach. A precious U-boat could be lost like that. He was still on the wrong side of the convoy and the moon was playing hide-and-seek behind the clouds. It was quiet and lonely as they closed to attack.

He decided to fire at a target on this side first; a tanker he had seen before the incident with *U-47*. He watched the zigzag of the stern destroyer escort, and when it launched out on a wide leg, he crammed on speed and passed the escort to get near the convoy, planning to get to within 500 yards before firing. But when he was still more than a mile away, the moon came out from behind a cloud to shine brilliantly on the scene.

Kretschmer was still uncomfortably close to the destroyer, so he fired one torpedo before turning away. From this distance they could see their target – the largest ship in the convoy – and for a moment it seemed that the torpedo had missed. But suddenly there was a tremendous flash from the bows of the tanker. Kassel intercepted the radio signal giving the ship's name as *Invershannon* (9,154 tons). They stayed long enough to see the crew take to the boats, and then the *Invershannon* settled down by the nose.

As soon as the torpedo exploded, the destroyer nearest to *U-99* turned at right angles to the convoy course and began firing starshells astern of the convoy, lighting up the area behind. Prien was back there somewhere, and Kretschmer felt he would not like the illuminations. He headed *U-99* to the starboard and dark side of the convoy and sighted a deeply-laden freighter. He fired one torpedo at 800 yards, and it hit amidships. There was a huge sheet of flame and a splintering crack as the freighter broke in two and sank in forty seconds.

The crew of *U-99* were startled. No ship in their experience had sunk that fast after being torpedoed. This sinking left open a gap through which Kretschmer could see another large freighter. The range was just over half a mile. He fired another torpedo and scored a direct hit amidships and the freighter stopped. It sent out a distress signal picked up by Kassel which read: '*Elmbank* torpedoed. Am stopped in position 55°–20' N. 22°–30' W.' Kretschmer halted *U-99* and let the convoy draw away from him, not attempting to retreat himself. They stayed like that for an hour, watching the escort fire starshell and illuminating rockets out to sea on either side of the convoy.

Kretschmer wondered vaguely why no other U-boat from the 'stripe' had attacked. The only explosions of the night were from his own torpedoes. Suddenly he realised that they would be carrying out orthodox attacks from outside the escort screen and would have had to retire hurriedly when the starshell started coming their way from escorts hunting outwards from the convoy. To him, it spelled the final evidence supporting his theory that U-boats should penetrate escort screens and attack alongside or in the convoy itself. When the convoy had drawn far enough away, he turned his attention to the stopped *Elmbank*, which had failed to sink. Sub-Lieutenant Elfe pumped shells into her on the water-line at point-blank range without result. The *Elmbank*'s crew had taken to their boats and stood off at a safe distance, watching.

They saw the cargo drifting from the holes torn in her side. It was timber, and it struck Kretschmer immediately that she was floating on her timber cargo. He decided to use another precious torpedo, but this one hit some of the floating cargo before reaching the ship and exploded uselessly. He was worried about the time it was taking to send this ship to the bottom. It was a bright night, and he expected to see at least one of the convoy escorts come racing back to hunt him or to pick up the survivors of the *Elmbank*. He decided to take a chance and reloaded his tubes with deck torpedoes – a long and difficult operation on the surface – and have another try. It meant sacrificing any hope of diving in the event of a counter-attack. All this time the *Elmbank*'s crew made no effort to pull away into the night, but stayed where they were, watching the proceedings with detached interest quite close to *U-99*.

The gun's crew expended eighty-eight rounds of ammunition on the *Elmbank* without success before Kretschmer decided to return to the *Invershannon*, which still floated with a list of port. He tried to sink her by riddling her water-line with bursts from the machine gun, but the bullets bounced off. Meanwhile, Longobardo had stayed silent on the bridge, standing out of the way behind his host. Kretschmer did not want to waste more torpedoes on ships already half-way to the bottom, so he decided to send Bargsten over in a dinghy with a petty officer and some charges to blow more holes in her side below the water-line. They put out the tiny dinghy and were half-way to the *Invershannon* when a wave caught them broadside on, capsizing the frail boat. Kretschmer could scarcely conceal his chagrin from the Italian 'guest'. The two men swam back to *U-99* and were hauled on board.

Kretschmer was annoyed that his First Lieutenant could not do a simple thing like taking a dinghy across a few yards of water without capsizing. He decided to rescue the dinghy and make them try again. Taking *U-99* over to the waterlogged boat, he told Bargsten, still standing on the foredeck, to have it pulled aboard. *U-99* was pitching considerably, and Bargsten had reached the prow and was leaning over to grab the dinghy, when he suddenly slipped and teetered for an agonising second before plunging head first into the Atlantic from which he had been rescued only minutes before. This was too much for Longobardo, who burst into loud laughter. It was also too much for Kretschmer, and when his First Lieutenant had been hauled aboard, dripping and gasping for the second time, his own laughter was added to the Italian's.

Dawn was approaching, and with it the danger of aircraft patrols. From 500 yards he fired another torpedo at the *Invershannon*, which suddenly broke in half, and for a few minutes the crew of *U-99* were the sole witnesses of a sight reserved only for sailors in wartime. The two separate parts of the oiltanker sank gently inwards and the two masts locked together at their tops, forming a great Gothic archway, under which black smoke and flames were thrust upwards from the bowels of a ship in its death-throes – a magnificent and terrifying scene bathed in pale moonlight. Around them the flurrying sea heaved and subsided, while over in the west a huge bank of black cloud gathered to emphasise the loneliness and vastness of the watery desert around them. Five minutes later the *Invershannon* gave its last, almost human, gasp of pain and was swallowed up by the waves.

Kretschmer returned to the *Elmbank*. On the way he saw an astonishing sight. 'It was like a Punch cartoon,' he wrote in his Diary later. 'A tiny raft was wallowing in the swell with an oar erected as a mast with a white shirt flying from it stiffly in the wind. Balancing himself by holding on to the makeshift mast was a lone man in his underwear.' They passed him and approached the *Elmbank*, now lower in the water. Kretschmer was about to order Elfe to fire a few more shots into her, when a lookout saw a submarine approaching. Kretschmer recognised it as German, and a few minutes later was welcoming Prien to the scene.

Prien shouted across: 'You seem to have caused quite a lot of damage tonight, Otto. I feel like an old man without any teeth. Mind if I take a shot at this one with you? I'd like to give the crew some target practice.'

Kretschmer shouted his consent and together the two U-boats poured shells in the *Elmbank* without any noticeable effect. Eventually, Prien gave up.

'No more ammunition left. Am going home now. See you at the Beau Sejour.' And with a wave, he took *U-47* away into the darkness to the south.

Kretschmer told Elfe to fire some phosphorous shells, and the first few shots set alight the deck-cargo of timber. Within some minutes she was a blazing hulk. They stayed long enough to see her go down with the water boiling over her, and then Kretschmer decided to find the man on the raft. He steamed slowly back in the direction of the *Invershannon* lifeboats and soon sighted the stiff white shirt. They went alongside the raft and carried the half-unconscious survivor aboard. When he was helped up to the conning-tower, Kretschmer greeted him in English and told him to go below and get his clothes dried and something warm to drink. Still speaking in English, he called down to Kassel to do everything he could for the survivor. Kassel replied in English and put the man in the captain's bunk. Describing the incident later, Kassel said:

> I stripped off his clothes, wrapped him in blankets and put him to bed. Then I gave him a tumbler full of brandy, which he swallowed in a gulp, and some colour came back to his face. He kept complaining about his head, and when the captain came down and we both talked to him in English it was obvious he had some sort of concussion. He swallowed some coffee, and the captain tried to get him to tell us the name of his ship. He could remember the cargo, which was iron ore, but no matter how hard he tried he could not recall the name of the ship. At first we were inclined to think he was being difficult, but in fact he could not remember. He kept moaning with the pain in his head and eventually dropped off to sleep.
>
> About an hour later he wakened and saw me sitting at my radio set a few feet away and called across. He was hungry. I remembered we had some tinned pineapples on board, part of the stores of the British Army which had been left behind at Dunkirk and on the Führer's orders distributed to U-boat crews. I gave him a tin of these and called the captain down from the conning-tower. We questioned him again about his ship, and he muttered something like Baronisewood. The captain glanced through Lloyd's Register and found a merchant ship called the Baron Blythwood. He asked the sailor if he was trying to say Baron Blythwood, and he nodded. The captain said that explains why,

with a cargo of iron ore, she had gone down in forty seconds. He asked for more coffee, and through the conning-tower hatch he could hear the captain and the Italian officer talking in English. When I brought the coffee to him, he gave me a shock by saying: 'Thanks, mate. A bloody U-boat torpedoed the ship, but those blasted Nazi swine didn't get me.' Then he gave me a wink and grinned as he said: 'I foxed the buggers and got myself rescued by a British submarine, eh? That fixed the bastards.'

I didn't know what to say. I heard the English conversation on the bridge and looked at the can of pineapples lying by his bunk. It was stamped 'California'. I realised that the survivor had not heard a word of German spoken on the boat. In his concussed state he had not assimilated his surroundings properly, and only the superficial things such as the pineapple and the English language had registered with him. Besides, in our sea-going overalls there was nothing to identify us as Germans. To clinch matters, the Italian commander came down to see him and exchanged a few words, and asked me in English if I had received any signals from Lorient.

Meanwhile, on the conning-tower, Kretschmer had decided he could not take a survivor with concussion back to Lorient with him – there was no room and there were no facilities on board for looking after him – and determined to find the *Invershannon* lifeboats and hand him over to them. It was daylight now, and they saw the sails of the lifeboats to the eastwards. It took Kretschmer thirty minutes to reach them, and he called down to Kassel: 'Have that man dressed, bandage his head and bring him up here. I am transferring him to a lifeboat.'

When he heard this, the British sailor grew panicky. 'Why can't I stay here?' he asked Kassel belligerently. 'I don't want to get into no lifeboat. This is comfortable enough for me.'

Kassel explained that they were out on patrol and would not be returning to harbour for some days, possibly weeks, and he would get home sooner by going in the lifeboat. He was careful not to say to which harbour they were going back. He was afraid that by letting the man know he was on board a German U-boat he might suffer a relapse. He wracked his brains trying to think of some way to break the news gently.

'Listen, chum,' he said. 'When you go up to the bridge you will see our captain. He is dressed like me, but he has the stripes of his rank on his shoulder-straps. Take a good look at them. You will find that on his forage cap is a naval badge with a swastika. We are a German U-boat.'

He did not have the heart to say it was the one that had sunk his ship. But the survivor just laughed and thought it a good joke. Kassel heaved him up through the hatch on to the conning-tower, and the captive was about to plead with Kretschmer to let him stay aboard when he saw the cap badge. He went pale and stared fixedly at the swastika. Kretschmer held out his hand and said: 'I'm sorry you have been hurt and I hope you feel better. We will see you have enough water, food and bandages to last until you get home.'

Alongside, the lifeboat from the *Invershannon* bumped against the U-boat while its crew, two white men and nearly a dozen Lascar seamen, looked up in astonishment. The survivor clambered down into the boat without saying a word, probably speechless with shock. He had spent two hours being nursed on board a German U-boat and he had called them 'swine' and 'bastards'. And he was still alive to remember it.

The man at the tiller of the lifeboat – a young blond giant who said he had been the boatswain of the *Invershannon* – took the bread and water handed down to him and stored the rolls of bandages under his seat. Then he made a note of the course Kretschmer gave him to steer for the coast of Ireland, and pushed his boat away from *U-99*. Kretschmer waved and shouted, 'Good luck'; before he could move away, the shipwrecked boatswain reached down into the lifeboat and stood up to throw a carton of 200 cigarettes on to the foredeck of *U-99*. It was his way of expressing his thanks at being spared death from machine-gun fire. To Kretschmer, it was always odd that survivors should live in terror of being mowed down by U-boats.[3]

It had taken all of one night and most of a morning to sink these ships, and now, with no attacking power left, Kretschmer headed for home. The following day they tuned their radio into a news broadcast from Berlin and were astounded to hear the announcer say:

Another of our brave U-boats has struck a mighty blow against the enemy's supply lines. U-boat Command Headquarters state that on the night of September 21st, U-48 torpedoed and sank two British merchant ships steaming in convoy. They were the Elmbank and Invershannon.

Kretschmer refused to break radio silence to correct U-boat Headquarters. Three days later, on the 25th, cleaned, shaved and in their best uniforms, *U-99*'s crew lined the decks and she slid into her berth alongside the mole in Lorient with seven white pennants carrying the insignia of the Golden Horseshoe flying from the raised periscope.

Notes

1 All U-boat captains received sealed orders to be opened when the code word putting *Sea-Lion* into operation was sent out. The German High Command made the defeat of the RAF and Luftwaffe control of the air a necessary prelude to *Sea-Lion*. When this failed, the operation was cancelled and the U-boats captains were ordered to destroy their orders.

2 He became one of the few Italians to achieve glory in the Battle of the Atlantic and received the Iron Cross from Hitler.

3 According to the Admiralty there was only one proved case of Allied survivors being machine-gunned by a German U-boat in the North Atlantic. There may have been other cases in such areas as the South Atlantic, Mediterranean or Indian Ocean. In many instances U-boats tried to sink ships by gunfire at night. If their shots were 'short' or 'over' and fell among lifeboats the survivors tended to believe that they were being gunned.

Seven
One Torpedo, One Ship

On their first night ashore the crew dined as usual with Kretschmer at the Beau Sejour, and after the toasts – a few more than usual, to celebrate their success – they were told that a rest camp had been provided for them near Lorient at Quiberon, where all facilities were available for sports and entertainment. They were to be taken there for a week the next day.

After dinner Kretschmer shook hands with Longobardo, and the Italian left to catch a late-night train for Paris. The military commander and Prien then joined him to discuss the last trip. Kretschmer was indignant about the German radio claim that *U-48* had sunk ships rightly belonging to *U-99*. 'Don't worry about that,' said Prien. 'It was a staff mistake. When I left you and got well clear of the area, I sent a signal saying those ships had been sunk without giving a source for the signal. The Chief thought it must have come from *U-48*.'

Their discussion was closed by a loud clatter in the hotel foyer as the familiar tall, handsome figure of Schepke burst into the lounge. He had returned to Lorient fresh from triumphs on land in the nightclubs of Paris, where he had spent two days, and wide grins came to the faces of his listeners as he described tactics not to be found in the Submarine Manual.

Kretschmer sat in his room writing his Standing Orders for the efficient running of *U-99*. They covered points ranging from the cleanliness of the ship and crew to the tactics he had decided to use in convoy attacks.

1. Of primary importance in all submarine operations is an efficient lookout system. During sea operations the finest possible organisation is the first precept of success. A weak link in the system can mean the destruction of the ship and the death of her crew.

2. It is not enough that lookouts should sight every object that appears on the surface: they must sight in good time every object that appears in the sky. Aircraft are playing an increasingly important role in the enemy convoy organisation.

They are a deadly menace to submarines on the surface. We rely on lookouts to give us the time we need to dive and hide from detection or bombing at depths below sixty feet.

3. Lone ships, not wearing neutral flags or carrying a red-cross sign, and in every other way giving the appearance of behaving as a belligerent, should be sunk by gunfire if possible to conserve torpedoes for more difficult escorted targets. They may be torpedoed if gunfire is obviously impracticable.

4. Survivors are to be assisted if there is time and by doing so the submarine is not exposed to undue danger. The crew should be made to realise that should U-99 be sinking and there is time to abandon ship they would expect to be rescued by the enemy. That is precisely what the enemy have a right to expect from us.

5. Only attack convoys by day if it is not convenient to wait for darkness. Day attacks on escorted convoys presuppose the necessity for taking a calculated risk, and should be made only after the most careful consideration of all the factors involved, particularly those concerning the question of whether the results to be achieved make the risk worth while.

6. In normal circumstances U-99 will use daylight hours for shadowing a convoy and working up to a favourable attacking position by nightfall. A favourable attacking position is on the dark side of a convoy when there is moonlight, so that the convoy will be silhouetted to us, while our small bows-on silhouette will be almost impossible to detect.

7. When there is little or no moon, U-99 will always attack from the windward side of the convoy. Enemy lookouts peering into a wind and sometimes rain and spray are less efficient than those with their backs to the wind.

8. U-99 will abide by my principle that fans of torpedoes fired from long range are not guaranteed to succeed and must prove wasteful. It should not be necessary to fire in the first instance more than one torpedo for one ship.

9. The principle stated above makes it necessary that we should fire at close range, and this can be done only by penetrating the escort's anti-submarine screen and at times getting inside the convoy lanes. This should be the objective of all our attacks.

10. Once an attack has been opened under these conditions, at night, we must not under any but the most desperate of circumstances submerge. As a general rule I alone must decide when to dive. This instruction is based on my belief that a submarine on the surface can manoeuvre at high speed to avoid danger, and if necessary can fight back with her speed and fire-power in torpedoes. If we are being chased, it is a general principle that once a submarine submerges and loses the use of speed she is at the mercy of the hunter.

11. Remember that at night on the surface it is almost certain that you will see a surface vessel far sooner than she will see you. This applies to enemy destroyers and other anti-submarine vessels which might detect you with their Asdics the moment you dive, but would be unaware of your presence if you ran away on the surface.

12. U-99 *will dive for two hours just before dawn each day at sea. This will serve twofold purposes: first, it will avoid the risk of running into ships and planes we have not seen during the night and which might see us first; and secondly, it gives us a chance to use the hydrophones to sweep for unsighted ships. In addition, it gives the crew an opportunity to relax, clean up and have breakfast in peace.*

At the same time as Dönitz received his copy of these Standing Orders for *U-99* with those of other U-boats, Britain had taken the first step in replying to the U-boat menace by appointing a new Director of Anti-Submarine Warfare.[1] This was a former destroyer commander, Captain George Creasy.[2] But with the confusion that often reigns in high circles, once the decision had been made to create a centralised office for the direction of the Atlantic battle, Creasy was left alone to overhaul this office, to make it possible for him to advise the Chiefs of the Naval Staff on what action should be taken to stem the tide of losses and to beat the U-boats. It seemed to Creasy that to carry out this broad briefing effectively he should consider himself the direct opponent of the German Navy's Commander-in-Chief, U-boats.

From this moment dates the official opening of the Battle of the Atlantic, which was to ebb and flow with the relentless duel of wits between George Creasy and Karl Dönitz. Creasy's most immediate task was to co-ordinate intelligence; the various convoy headquarters; air and sea operations in convoy protection and U-boat hunts; and lastly, the reports of U-boat attacks on convoys. In a short space of time he reached certain conclusions concerning the tactics being employed by U-boats that they preferred attacking at night;[3] that they used the daylight hours for shadowing; that their favourite attacking position was broad on the bow of the convoy; that the next operation would be to fall back on a firing position on the convoy's beam and then, increasing speed, they would fire a salvo of four torpedoes and, turning away at full speed, would fire their stern torpedoes and withdraw to a safe distance to reload their tubes.

Creasy was largely right on all these points, but he did not realise at the beginning that these were tactics employed by such 'aces' as Prien and Schepke, and not by all the boats, most of which still clung to the methods they had been taught in the Baltic. He did not guess at that time that one commander alone had carried the 'ace' formula even further by discarding the salvo, and laying it down as a firm instruction to his officers that the escort screens must be pierced to carry out the basic principle of 'one torpedo, one ship'.

To counter these methods, the British Naval Staff recommended to all escort groups a standard counter-attack procedure to be put into operation the moment an attack had developed. The moment a convoy was attacked at night, the escort would turn outwards and fire starshell and other illuminants, such as the 'Snowflake' rocket, to illuminate the area seawards of the convoy and reveal the whereabouts of the U-boats, or at least to force them to submerge, where they could be picked up on Asdic – a useless device if U-boats remained on the surface. Radar, still in its infancy at sea, was not yet a factor to be reckoned with by either side. Escort-group commanders took over from there, working out by their individual experiences a form of developing counter-attack once the attackers had been located.

By coincidence it was this very standard procedure that made Kretschmer's more daring method of attack successful, while in itself proving of some effect against other commanders. And his next trip was to illustrate this with results as disastrous for Britain as they were cause for satisfaction to the Germans.

On Friday, October 13th, 1940, *U-99* sailed on her fourth Atlantic voyage. The crew grumbled, and eventually one, more superstitious than the rest, actually requested Kretschmer to anchor somewhere and start the Log Book for the trip on the 14th. Kretschmer was surprised when Petersen added his weight to the request. They had been together since 1937, when they took over *U-23*. Kretschmer had seen the flashes of superstition that affected Petersen in various predicaments, but this was the first time he had tried to intervene in sailing instructions. Kretschmer reminded him curtly that he was a responsible non-commissioned officer, but, as it happened, an engine-room defect delayed their sailing, and they cleared harbour at 1.30 a.m. on the 14th.

When entering the Narrows exit between the islands, they received a signal timed 2.20 a.m. from the Commander-in-Chief stating that Lorient harbour was closed because of mines. Kretschmer showed the signal to Bargsten, who looked startled. For the last hour they had been steaming out of a harbour blocked by enemy mines and probably still patrolled by British submarines. Just then a lookout sighted a periscope and they dived, staying down until dark, and then surfaced again to head out due west along 'U-boat Alley'. The next two days were uneventful except for two alarm dives for aircraft sightings, but at 4 p.m. on the 16th they received a general signal from *U-93* giving the course, speed and position of a large convoy outward bound from England. They altered course and headed to intercept this convoy by the 18th.

On the 17th it began to look as though *U-93*, the shadower, had lost contact with the convoy, and late in the afternoon *U-48* made contact and took over. Kretschmer adjusted his course to intercept, and by noon next day seven U-boats were converging independently on the convoy.

Lorient was uneasy at *U-48*'s silence, and ordered an interception 'stripe' across what they considered was the path the convoy. The signal sent to *U-*

93, *U-100, U-28, U-123, U-101, U-99* and *U-46* ordered stations on the 'stripe' to be taken up by 8 p.m. Kretschmer noticed that Schepke in *U-100* would be with him on this attack, checked his own position and signalled to the Commander-in-Chief: 'Cannot comply with orders as I am too far away.' In fact, by hard steaming, he arrived an hour later, and sighted *U-46* already in station. To the northwards he exchanged recognition signals with *U-101*, and found, incidentally, that it was heading by mistake in the opposite direction to the 'stripe' patrol. At midnight a ninth submarine, *U-38*, reported the last known position, course and speed of the convoy as seen some hours previously. No one knew what had happened to *U-93* and *U-48*, who seemed to have lost contact. This latest information made it likely that the convoy would pass well to the north of the 'stripe', and the U-boats proceeded to act independently. Kretschmer heard a rushing of water beside him as he prepared to head off on what he considered an interception course and turned to see Schepke waving cheerfully from the conning-tower of *U-100*. He shouted that he thought the shadowers had made a mess of things and that he intended heading southwards for a while and sweeping to the west. Kretschmer was sure the convoy lay in the opposite direction, and they parted company.

Meanwhile, in London, it was known by signals from the escorts that this convoy, S.C.7, was being shadowed. A violent alteration of course was ordered to shake off a possible mass attack by a 'wolf-pack'. There was little anyone could do after that but wait for the first blow to fall. In the operations room, Captain Creasy and his staff watched the pattern of disaster unfold as signals flowed in from the escort.

Heading northwards, Kretschmer was only five miles away from *U-101* when she reported a sighting of the convoy. By now dawn had broken, and he contented himself by closing to visibility distance and exploring the strength of the escort. He counted three destroyers and several smaller warships – a strong escort for those days.

He was happy now to stay in sight of the convoy and wait for darkness to fall. At dusk he was edging in to have a crack at a wing ship when suddenly she disintegrated before him, torpedoed by another U-boat. The attack had begun. In London and Lorient an anxious Creasy and an excited Dönitz watched the development of the attack.

After dark, a slim, dark shape appeared across Kretschmer's bows and he exchanged signals with *U-123*. Just then a destroyer appeared heading fast in their direction. *U-123* dived, but Kretschmer turned away and raced off at right angles on the surface. It took him nearly two hours to regain the convoy, and at 10 p.m. began the classic attack which was to set the stamp of the 'ace'. While seven other U-boats, including Schepke, attacked from outside the screen, firing salvoes, *U-99* headed for the starboard side, covered by three destroyers – one ahead of the convoy, one on the beam and another on the bow.

Trimmed up, not down, to get maximum speed and manoeuvrability, he headed between the bow and beam destroyers, passing between them with about a mile to spare on either side, but they gave no sign of spotting him. Within three minutes he was through and approaching the outer column of the convoy. He aimed at the first ship and fired one torpedo from 700 yards range. It missed. It was a clear night with a bleak yellow moon bathing the vast calm sea in a brilliant glow; the 'Hunter's Moon' silhouetting each target. The second torpedo hit amidships and the ship sank in twenty seconds. Two more explosions came from the other side of the convoy, and suddenly the long lines of ships made a complete alteration of course. Kretschmer swept down the outer column only 100 yards away, and stumbled on a large gap in the column. With a curt order, U-99 heeled over and steamed right into the convoy itself. At 10.30 she was heading down the first lane towards the rear and fired at a large freighter. The torpedo missed. Bargsten, who was setting the range, courses and speed of the targets on the aiming director, remembered it was a new instrument that had not been tested before they sailed. Kretschmer decided to aim by guesswork.

Just then a large cargo ship sighted U-99 and turned to ram, firing starshell at the same time. They tried to dodge round it, but the freighter altered course rapidly and still came directly at them. They retreated out towards the escort screen, and the freighter turned and fired a few rounds with her stern gun. By this time Kretschmer was near the stern of the convoy. He turned back towards it and fired a torpedo at the end ship of the outer column. As the torpedo left the tube, the target altered course on a zigzag and the torpedo missed, but hit another ship in the next column. This ship broke in two, and both halves sank in little more than a minute. Her radio signal for help gave two words once: 'Empire Brigade.'

With this ship gone, the way was open to return into the convoy again, and Kretschmer, standing at the front of the conning-tower, turned to Bargsten and Elfe and said: 'Well, here goes. We are going in to tear down this convoy.' U-99 throbbed at full speed towards the next column, and at midnight fired another torpedo at a large freighter. The torpedo hit forward, and a second later there came a huge spout of yellow-and-red flame from amidships and the ship ripped apart before their eyes. The smoke-cloud mushroomed up in a large billowing column to about 500 feet and the ship vanished in the calm, almost undisturbed sea in less than fifty seconds.

Ten minutes later three destroyers raced up to the wreckage in line abreast and stopped to search the area. Kretschmer, still running at full speed, was astern of the third column now creeping up to the beam of the last ship. He allowed himself to relax for a few minutes and watch the illuminations around him. The escorts were firing starshell on either side and in front of the convoy out to seawards. The explosions of torpedoes from other U-boats were becoming infrequent. 'Kassel,' he shouted, 'note the times of detonations for which we are responsible.'

Down below in the control-room, Kassel drew another line down the sheet of paper on which he was already recording the number of their own torpedoes fired, the number of hits and the sinkings. It was nearly 1 a.m. when they fired at the biggest freighter in the convoy, recorded by Bargsten and Elfe as 'about 10,000 tons'. The torpedo missed, and Elfe wrote in the Log Book that 'it could have been a fault in the torpedo's steering device'. The range was about 500 yards. They tore into the convoy and hit the next ship ahead in the fourth column. This leaned over on her side and capsized completely, taking several minutes to hiss and boil her way to the bottom. In the second column a smaller ship altered course to cross their bows. Kretschmer took a snap shot, and the detonation broke her in two near the stern. She had time to send one signal saying, 'SS *Fiscus* torpedoed' as the larger section keeled over and vanished, the second section following suit a little later.

There was a curious silence over the convoy at this point. The 'wolf-pack' had broken off the action and the escort had ceased firing starshell. It sounded peaceful...and ominous. Kassel recorded the last detonation from the other side of the convoy at 1.33 a.m. Well up inside the lane between the third and fourth columns of the convoy, Kretschmer fired at 600 yards at a large freighter in the fourth column, hitting it near the stern. She sank in forty seconds, but not before a weak signal had been made giving her name as *Thalia*. Suddenly the starshell firing began again on the port side of the convoy, followed by depth-charging. More depth-charges fell on the starboard side. Up in front a bright light shone on the water. Elfe muttered to Bargsten:

'They are driving off the others. Thank God it's not us.'

'No, our turn is to come,' Bargsten replied grimly.

Kretschmer was shouting orders down to the helmsman, conning *U-99* to the big freighter they had missed once already. Suddenly he turned hard to starboard and ordered: 'Stern tube, fire.' The torpedo hurtled out and scored a direct hit amidships at a range of 300 yards. The cargo ship reared up in the air and began to settle by the stern. Kassel intercepted the distress signal: 'SOS...*Shekaticka* torpedoed in convoy.' A few minutes later they saw the crew jumping over the side into the water.

The next target was a large cargo ship up ahead in the third column, and while getting into position, the peace of the night was wrecked by a rapid burst of machine-gun fire out in front of the convoy. With a brief prayer that whatever U-boat was being attacked would get away, Kretschmer ran into the target to about 700 yards and fired a bow torpedo while still turning towards its stern. The torpedo ran wild and hit the tip of the target's bows; and they watched in amazement as the ship continued ploughing ahead, sinking more and more by the bows. This ship gave her name as the *Sedgepool*, and before their startled eyes she executed a perfect crash-dive, as though she was a gigantic submarine, with propellers churning the water as she drove herself down into the sea with a deafening roar of grating, twisted girders as the water flooded the boiler-rooms and cargo-holds. She vanished, and the turbulent battle around the rear of the convoy caused by one deadly U-boat died away.

U-99 had cut a swathe through the convoy, leaving a trail of wreckage in her wake. Kretschmer decided it was just a question of time before the escort guessed where he was and came rushing to bar his escape route from inside the convoy. He slowed down and allowed the remnants of the convoy to pull ahead of him. But fifteen minutes later he discovered he had forgotten one of the stern ships, a small straggler that now came tossing innocently towards him. His first torpedo missed but the second hit under the bridge, blowing the superstructure into the air in a shower of sparks and flame. The ship settled only slightly in the water and the convoy was drawing ahead at maximum speed, leaving behind the stricken straggler and battle-weary U-boat.

Starshell was still being fired on either beam of the convoy in spasmodic bursts, having a curious ineffective result in the pale glow of the moon. The nearest flares were falling ten miles away, and looked to the U-boat crew to be about as effective as a small child playing with matches in the middle of the Sahara desert. Kassel intercepted the small ship's message giving her name as the *Clintonia*. Suddenly, to *U-99*'s astonishment, the sound of gunfire came from the other side of their target and shells whistled over to land alongside them. Rapidly, *U-99* retreated to a safe distance and made her way warily round the bows of the victim to see who had been firing. It was *U-123*, who thought to hurry the demise of what her commander considered an abandoned ship. *U-123* had dropped well astern of the convoy to take over as shadower in the event of anything going wrong with the attack. Now she had caught up with the *Clintonia* while the convoy itself forged ahead in the distance. Kretschmer let him continue, but to take credit for the sinking, he had to stay there until the shellfire put the target down. This took some twenty minutes, and Kretschmer acted as an invisible fall-of-shot referee, noting grimly that *U-123* was wasting her ammunition, with most shots falling over the target, while those that hit landed on the deck, making no difference to her eventual sinking from the hole in her side. By now Kretschmer had expended all torpedoes and decided they had achieved enough. He had proved his tactical methods with disastrous effect to the Allies.

In London, Admiralty operations recorded the loss of seventeen ships in two nights from S.C.7. In Lorient, Dönitz watched the brief radioed reports of the night operations from eight U-boats and drew the attention of his staff to the astonishing fact that *U-99* had sunk more than half the total.

On October 22nd, *U-99* arrived at her usual 'cleaning-up anchorage in the island bay off the approach to Lorient. They had been at sea only nine days – Kretschmer's shortest Atlantic trip – and had spent four days getting to the convoy, one day at it and four days returning to base. In a total of three hours on one night he had sent nine important ships to the bottom. On the chart table in the control-room lay a signal from Dönitz: 'You have won two battles this night. Prepare for formal welcome into harbour.' Kretschmer would have preferred the clean white sheets of a shore bed and undisturbed sleep for several days and nights. He had not slept for forty-eight hours during the attack. Instead he ordered Bargsten to see that the crew wore their clean overalls and tidied up the boat before entering harbour.

After lunch, they weighed anchor and made their way into the approaches. As they closed the entrance, a large 740-ton U-boat returning from a South Atlantic patrol raced from the southwards and cut in front of them, her crew lounging on deck with their faces covered in several weeks growth of beard and their sea overalls grimy and stained as though with the dirt of battle. On the conning-tower, also bearded, stood the commanding officer in a white roll-necked sweater, and on his head, set at an angle, was the white-covered cap of a U-boat captain. Kretschmer winced at this lack of discipline. He and his crew wore their best overalls and he himself wore his cap without a cap cover, the correct winter dress for a naval officer. He never forgot that the U-boat Arm was just a branch of the Service. Still, he had to admit that the crew of the other ship looked like any young man's – or young girl's – dream of what a warrior of the sea should look like. Bargsten put it succinctly. Fixing his glasses on the conning-tower, he said: 'They look rather picturesque, sir.'

They followed the oil-streaked South Atlantic veteran through the boom defences and steamed slowly into the harbour basin to give the other boat time to go alongside. While they were stopped, a pinnace came out from the main mole and raced towards the ship ahead, and an officer in the stern waved for the U-boat to follow him. While Kretschmer and his crew watched, the 740-tonner made a wide turn to dock at the main berth, where crowds of officers and women carrying flowers waited expectantly. The faint sounds of a military march reached them as Kretschmer pointed their nose at the only vacant berth, a little-used jetty unpopular with crews because it was a long walk from the town. The sailors on the foredeck looked up at the conning-tower with angry faces.

Behind Kretschmer, young Elfe murmured to Bargsten the thoughts that were in all their minds.

'That's our reception over there, and we have earned it. He's not going to let them get away with it, surely.'

Bargsten grinned good-humouredly. 'You ought to know the commander as well as anyone by now. He is about the most relieved man in Lorient today. He can't stand this sort of thing, and I can see him relishing the idea of slipping ashore leaving all the brass hats running around in small circles wondering what happened. Tell you what, if I know Dönitz, the captain won't get away with it. I'll bet you a bottle of champagne the Admiral finds out in time and orders the other boat away.'

Elfe looked at the distance separating them from the jetty and said: 'Done.'

They had just tied up, and Kretschmer was preparing to go ashore and report at flotilla headquarters, when the pinnace came speeding up on the outboard side and an officer waved agitatedly to Kretschmer.

'Commander Kretschmer, there has been a mistake. Admiral Dönitz and the military command have turned out to greet you. You are to take your ship over to the main berth now. The Commander-in-Chief says you are not to waste any time and keep him waiting any longer.'

Kretschmer laughed and waved in reply, while Bargsten called the watch on deck to move ship. They left the jetty and Kretschmer decided to give the watchers a bit of a show. He made a wide turn at speed and came up alongside the main berth as though he were driving a speed-boat. *U-99* shuddered as he put both engines astern and brought 500 tons of submarine to a stop only a few feet from the amazed crowd on the quay. It was a blatant bit of playing to the crowd, but for once Kretschmer felt a secret satisfaction at being able to do it. A slight smile played on his lips as he passed Bargsten on his way from the conning-tower and the widely-grinning First Lieutenant reminded Elfe of their bet.

Kretschmer crossed the gangway ashore, and Dönitz stepped forward to greet him. Cameras flashed as the crew followed their captain and lined up to be addressed by the Commander-in-Chief.

War correspondents and photographers clustered around, demanding pictures and 'first-person' accounts of what was already being described in Lorient as 'The Night of the Long Knives'. In a hoarse voice, Kretschmer called for Kassel and, after introducing him to the journalists, told him to take over and speak for *U-99*. Three days later Kretschmer called at his flotilla leader's office and was shown a copy of his Battle Report with a footnote written by Dönitz. It said:

Excellent led attack on a convoy which has been rewarded with corresponding success. Signed. Dönitz. Commander-in-Chief, U-boat Command.

These few sober words written in judgement on his tactics were more satisfying to Kretschmer than the reception on the quay. The legend was born of the lone seawolf, soon to be heard throughout Germany and described by Goebbels in a broadcast to the nation as 'the greatest adventure story of the war.

Notes

1 The Anti-Submarine Division of the Naval Staff was first established in the First World War, but as a post-war economy measure it was abolished and incorporated in the tactical Division. It was re-established in the autumn of 1939.

2 Now Admiral Sir George Creasy.

3 Dönitz himself was familiar with the principle of night attack. In the First World War the concept of night surface attack outside an escort screen had been used with success by a few U-boat commanders. But without the number of submarines he needed, he 'based his training programme on the safer submerged-attack technique'. Now his commanders worked out for themselves a technique of attack which in reality continued where the tactics of the first war left off. He was impressed by reports from his commanders, and allowed them to develop their own ideas freely from practical experience.

Eight
Hunter's Moon

On November 3rd, 1940, *U-99* was on patrol off Bloody Foreland. It was a magic night. Overhead the stars shone brilliantly from a navy-blue sky brushed at intervals with thin wisps of low-lying clouds which did not dim the 'Hunter's Moon' to the south. A large, long swell lifted them high before dumping them into deep valleys of water, but the wind was light and the sea only slightly ruffled by its gentle touch. All around in the far distance, huge banks of black, menacing clouds reared into the heavens like a great circular range of mountains. It was the sort of night on which the largest ship afloat would look frighteningly small; to the crew of *U-99*, their slim shell of a submarine made them feel like a match tossed into a pond.

From the dark, mysterious shadow cast by the cloudbanks in a vast crescent to the south-west, appeared a lone steamer zigzagging its slow passage across the Atlantic. On the conning-tower, Kretschmer gave orders that would take them into an attacking position. He wondered what the deck watch on the steamer were thinking at that moment. Did they ever think they would be torpedoed? Did the officer-of-the-watch dream for one moment that this was to be his last night on the bridge?

Kretschmer had never really thought seriously of the people who manned the ships he sank. They were the enemy, and if they were human beings as well, it had not bothered his conscience. But now he felt unaccountably weary of the stealthy approach and the fast racing attack, ending in the blinding flash of the explosion and the flame and smoke which spelled the death and destruction of which he was the architect. On this night he felt he would be glad when peace once again sent him back to train others in the Baltic. For a moment he was tempted to let this steamer go, but the mood passed quickly as the nervous tension of the attack welled up, cleansing him of thoughts forbidden in a U-boat commander. Yet he had weakened; the strain of command was increasing with every trip.

As he prepared for the run-in to attack, Able Seaman Wald the port half of the 'Steamer Terrors', sighted a large ship heading fast in *U-99*'s direction. A quick calculation of distance, and Kretschmer decided he had time to sink the steamer before the arrival of the larger ship. At 10.13 p.m. the attack developed. The target steamed towards him, and, as she turned broadside on to take up her mean course, he shouted: 'Fire one.' The range was less than a mile and they watched fascinated as the torpedo wake, gleaming, in the fluorescence of the sea, sped straight and true. There was a dull, almost expressionless, detonation just aft of the steamer's bridge and a splutter of flame that quickly died as the ship began to settle hesitantly in the water. Now *U-99* swung round and found the second ship was still a good distance off, but, surprisingly, a third ship had appeared as if from nowhere and was little more than a mile away.

Kassel at the radio was busily intercepting plain-language messages from all three ships. The first, he found, was the *Casanare*. The second ship was reporting a submarine in the vicinity and gave her name as the *Laurentic*, while the third identified herself as the *Patroclus*. Both were in Lloyd's Register, but more interesting to Kretschmer was that they also appeared in the Navy List as armed merchant cruisers. He decided to attack the first warship to appear, *Laurentic*.

He turned towards her, calculated the range of 1,500 yards and fired on the turn – now a favourite Kretschmer method – and the torpedo streaked towards the massive target, striking her amidships in the boiler-room. Clouds of smoke billowed from inside and spread over the ship, but she gave no sign of sinking or of being affected in the least by the hole torn in her side. They watched boats being lowered and some pull away. After half an hour of waiting for some evidence of sinking, they fired another torpedo which hit near the stern. Once again there were no visible signs of sinking. Kretschmer decided to fire a third torpedo at the hole torn by the first in an effort to make the hole bigger, and thereby break the back of the ship. He closed to within 250 yards and the third torpedo hit again in the boiler-room. The *Laurentic* sent out more signals, intercepted by Kassel, and fired starshell over the scene. Then she opened fire with a heavy gun, sending salvo after salvo at the submarine. These soon gave way to well-placed shots of anti-personnel shrapnel shells.

Kretschmer did not like this, so he withdrew rapidly at speed. While carrying out this manoeuvre, he found that the second ship had reached the scene to pick up a boatload of survivors from the *Laurentic*. Taking time to check that this was HMS *Patroclus*, he closed to 300 yards and fired without being sighted. The torpedo struck near the stern, and *U-99*'s crew gaped as dozens of empty barrels shot from the hole like corks from a champagne bottle to bob happily on the sea. Kretschmer fired his second shot at the stern, but the torpedo went off on an erratic course and hit below the foremast. Once again there came the deluge of empty barrels. Now it was the turn of the *Patroclus* to open fire at him. The first two high-explosive shells fell dangerously close, and Kretschmer, worried at the prospect of the single hit that could immobilise him, retired again and contemplated the appearance of so many barrels spreading now over the battlefield. He concluded, rightly, that these cruisers must be filled with barrels to give them extra buoyancy in the event of torpedo attack. He sheered away towards the first steamer he had hit, the *Casanare*. There was no sign of her, only two boatloads of survivors. Then came a sudden roar of aircraft, and they looked up to see a Sunderland flying-boat swooping so low the lights in the cabin outlined the heads and shoulders of the pilot and crew. Kretschmer sounded 'Alarm dive', and they plunged down, waiting tensely for the bombs they felt sure were already falling. But nothing happened, and Kretschmer ordered the torpedo crews to reload the tubes.

By now it was 3 a.m., and half an hour later they surfaced again to make their way back to the *Laurentic* and *Patroclus*. The cruisers, one more than 18,000 tons and the other nearly 12,000, sat like great wounded bears, hardly moving in the swell while the tiny U-boat tossed and pitched like an agitated puppy. There were about six lifeboats in the water, all of which had pulled away from the danger area and were sitting there watching the scene play itself to a finale. A conning-tower lookout sighted a destroyer coming up fast over the horizon. They had been at action stations all night, but Kretschmer was now thoroughly angry at his un-obliging targets and announced loudly: 'We have got to sink those ships before the destroyer gets here.' With sudden decision he turned and, increasing to full speed, headed straight for the *Laurentic*. They closed to 250 yards and Kretschmer shouted:

'Hard a starboard. Fire one.' They heeled over on the turn and the torpedo shot towards the Laurentic.

It hit the stern, and a whole section of the ship fell away to sink in a matter of seconds. The depth-charges on it, set to not more than a few feet, exploded, and the blast rocked *U-99* over on her side, throwing the conning-tower into confusion. As they picked themselves up they were in time to see the rest of the great ship rise high in the air and slither stern first to the bottom.

They had about fifteen minutes left to sink the *Patroclus* and, closing her at high speed, fired at 300 yards. This shot hit amidships again, and there was another eruption of barrels. They turned rapidly at speed and raced in for the fourth shot. This one hit forward, and again there came the astonishing barrage of barrels. A fifth torpedo hit amidships. This time there were no barrels and the *Patroclus* seemed at last to be sinking. Kretschmer looked in the direction of the destroyer now in gunfire range. He ran in for the sixth torpedo shot and hit amidships again. Almost simultaneously the cruiser seemed to convulse and leap into the air. As she subsided, she broke in half and both sections dropped straight out of sight, as though the sea had opened and they had fallen into the holes.

Trimmed down for escape, *U-99* retreated southwards, leaving hundreds of barrels and ten lifeboats for the destroyer to pick up. But the destroyer by-passed the wreckage and chased after the vanishing U-boat. Kretschmer dived, and they braced themselves for a depth-charge attack. It came in a deluge, and the submarine rocked and nearly turned over as patterns of depth-charges fell around her. For some inexplicable reason, the explosions then stopped and Kassel at the hydrophones reported the propeller noises growing fainter. After an hour Kretschmer risked surfacing. They were about twelve miles from the scene of destruction, and in the first light of dawn could see the destroyer picking up survivors. They headed discreetly to the south into the protection of the vast cloudbanks on the horizon.

While returning to his patrol area, Kretschmer noted in his War Diary: 'It seems strange that the second cruiser, *Patroclus*, should have gone out of her way to approach the scene and deliver herself into my hands.' It was not so strange to Commander R.P. Martin, at present working in the City, who was then the senior executive officer of the *Patroclus*, and a personal friend of his captain, 'Bill' Wynter. During the morning of November 3rd, *Patroclus* had sighted the steamer *Casanare* and had stayed in company with her as an ocean escort against surface raiders. Before lunch, Captain Wynter, Commander Martin and the navigator, Commander Harrison, RNR, had discussed what action they should take if the *Casanare* were torpedoed. Both Martin and Harrison stood by Admiralty instructions concerning the role of armed merchant cruisers which, in effect, banned any action which might expose this type of ship to undue danger from U-boats. The menace of German surface raiders was beginning to be felt, and with warships scattered across the oceans of the world, armed merchant cruisers played a vital and important part in the escort system by patrolling the convoy routes as protection against attack from German surface units. To these two officers it seemed that to stop and pick up survivors from the *Casanare* would merely provide the attacking U-boat with a perfect target. Captain Wynter dismissed their arguments by saying: 'The Admiralty don't run my ship. If we didn't stop I could never show my face in Liverpool again.'

That evening *U-99* attacked the *Casanare*, and Captain Wynter altered course towards her to pick up survivors. As he did so, the *Laurentic* appeared on the scene, and they saw the flashes of the torpedoes striking home into her hull. On the bridge of *Patroclus*, Commander Martin told his commanding officer: 'If we go over there and stop we shall be sunk within half an hour, sir.' The two officers were old friends who had served together at Jutland in the first war. Wynter[1] was a stubborn man, possessed of great courage and dash, but at this moment it seemed to Martin that he was being downright reckless. Irritated, Captain Wynter replied obstinately: 'I am going to help those poor chaps.' Commander Martin left the upper bridge and began supervising the preparations to bring survivors of both the *Casanare* and *Laurentic* on board. The result of Captain Wynter's decision is described vividly in the following Battle Report submitted to the Admiralty through the Port Naval Offices at Largs by Commander Martin after his rescue.

SECRET
LOSS OF HMS *PATROCLUS*
Naval Offices
Largs
6th November, 1940

Sir,

I have the honour to forward the following report of the circumstances attending the loss of HMS Patroclus *on 3rd November, 1940.*

At 2100 on Sunday, 3rd November, 1940, I received a message from the Bridge that the SS Casanare *had been torpedoed some miles off on our starboard bow and the Captain was going to endeavour to pick up survivors.*

We had, during the day, discussed such an eventuality, even going so far as to name this particular ship, and the opinion had been freely expressed by myself, the Navigating Commander, and Lieutenant-Commander Hoggan, that such a proceeding would gravely imperil the ship and expose her to needless risk. The Captain, however, had decided on his course of action, and nothing we could do would dissuade him.

We circled round the position for some time until it was judged to be sufficiently dark for us to close, and then came in to pick up survivors. In doing so, just before reaching the position, we dropped two depth-charges set to 150 feet, with the object of scaring away any submarine which might be in the vicinity.

Boats were observed in the water, and we stopped and hailed the nearest alongside. It was just coming alongside the starboard side of the forward well-deck, in fact, it was to all intents and purposes alongside, when the ship was struck by a torpedo. The time was approximately 2255.

The torpedo appeared to strike underneath the boat, which I am convinced was blown to pieces.

Some of our men were killed instantaneously by the explosion. Some were blown overboard, and the forward well-deck was reduced to a shambles. This explosion, amongst other things, broke both Lieutenant Piddocks's legs.

Lieutenant Atkinson, at this stage of the proceedings, dived overboard to rescue some of the men who were swimming about, and eventually he clambered on board and took charge of one of the cutters after it had been lowered.

It was quite obvious that the ship had been torpedoed, and the crew immediately went to their 'mine-and-torpedo' stations, which consisted of falling in abreast their respective boats with lifebelts and warm clothing on.

Mr Maddox, the gunner, about this time appeared on the Bridge and reported that both depth-charges had had their primers removed and had thus been made safe.

I then took up a megaphone and spoke to the ship's company, told them that the ship had been hit by one torpedo, that there was no need to abandon ship yet, but I wanted them to remain fallen in abreast their boats until further orders.

Illustrating the spirit of that ship's company, they responded by clapping. I had, every patrol, been in the habit of giving the crew a lecture on the war in general, and they always, at the end of my lecture, used to give me a clap, and I was rather surprised that when I gave them this bald announcement, they again responded by clapping and somebody yelled out, 'You're telling us, sir.'

CPO Brooks of the Fore TS then reported to me that the action TS crew were closed up and that the organisation for fighting a submarine was in order, though I think No. 1 gun had had some casualties.

Shortly after this another torpedo struck us in No. 4 hold and the Captain ordered 'Abandon ship' – and magazines were flooded.

I ordered Lieutenant-Commander Hoggan to supervise the lowering of the boats and I personally said good-bye to the Captain, whom I never saw again, and then made my way down to the boatdeck generally to supervise and see what was going on.

I remember speaking to Sub-Lieutenant Harmsworth, the signal officer, who told me he had thrown the confidential books overboard and was then going to lower the starboard cutter, which he did very efficiently. I went to the wireless-room and told Mr Johnson to report to the Commander-in-Chief Western Approaches that we had been struck by another torpedo.

It struck me forcibly that it was an unpleasant task having to launch boats in the dark when the ship had been hit by two torpedoes. She had a big list on her. I was also struck by the way in which the organisation worked. Boats seemed to go out smoothly without any panic, and the men managed to get away from the ship, though there seemed to be a few swimming about in the water. I think a good number had been blown overboard, and numbers one and five lifeboats had been smashed by explosions and people in them killed. Boats were ordered to lie off the port side, well clear of the ship, and await events.

Immediately after this the ship was struck by two more torpedoes simultaneously, one in the cross-bunker and the other in No. 6 hold, the latter taking No. S3 gun overboard.

Shortly after this I found myself on the boat-deck with Lieutenant-Commander Hoggan, Lieutenant Murchie, Lieutenant Kirkpatrick, Sub-

Lieutenant Davie, Mr Johnson, Mr Barron, CPO Creasey, P/O Kemp, P/O Naylor and two or three other ratings. There wasn't anything we could do; the wireless was out of action. All the boats and carley floats had left the ship. Sub-Lieutenant Davie reported the engine-room was dry and not making any water, which showed the bulkheads were holding, and he was particularly good in going below and starting all the pumps, but we did not know for how long this would be the case. The sea was calm with a slight swell.

We discussed thoroughly the question of saving the ship, but we came to the conclusion it was only a matter of time.

About 1 o'clock the submarine started to shell the ship. We had often debated beforehand what we would do under such circumstances, and so on a pre-arranged plan we at once manned the starboard 3' HA and opened fire. CPO Creasey, the chief-gunner's mate, was gunlayer. AB Ellis, the trainer. I was loader, with Lieutenant-Commander Hoggan ammunition supply. We opened fire, and both Creasey and Ellis reported they were dead on the target. Creasey is a first-class chief-gunner's mate. We think we hit with the fourth round because we were firing fuse setting 022, which is extreme fuse setting, but bursts on impact. This shell was seen to burst and the submarine was not more than 1,000 yards off.

After our fourth round the shelling ceased and our target disappeared, so ending the action.

We had been hit twice, once amidships and once aft, but the enemy shells had apparently done no damage beyond starting a small fire in the after-well-deck over the after-magazine. I watched this very closely with some apprehension, but the ship was almost awash there and it very soon went out.

About ten minutes after the action ended, the ship was hit by another torpedo in No. 3 hold. This was now about 1.15 a.m., and we saw nothing more.

We walked about the boat-deck, had some rum and whisky, just enough to keep us warm, laid down together and covered ourselves with blankets etc., and we were really very comfortable. We took it in turns to keep watch for the submarine coming back, but it was just a question of waiting until it was time for the ship to sink, and ourselves to get off.

About 4 o'clock the ship was hit by another torpedo, right forward underneath the Bridge. This collapsed the Bridge completely, and we all laughed because we realised the enemy had put four torpedoes in nearly the same place. The total effect was practically to break her back forward of the Bridge. Five minutes afterwards she was hit by another torpedo amidships, which appeared to strike her in the engine-room, and this time we realised the end had come. She started to list very rapidly. I gave the order, 'Come on, over the side.' We had previously swung in life-lines, and had got all kinds of movable gear ready. We slid down into the water. I yelled to everybody, 'Push away from the ship. Don't get caught by the suction.' We swam away, and when we were about twenty yards off we could feel all kinds of disturbance going on in our rear, and could feel the suction and the ripples of the ship going down and a terrific noise as all the girders twisted and bent, and the drums rolled about and crunched together. I turned and looked over my shoulder. She was half-way down. She rolled over on her starboard side and slid into the water, and when I looked at her practically only the bows were sticking up. I swam away, and when about 150 yards off got everybody I could around me in a cluster.

We supported ourselves on the wreckage and held on to each other as far as we could. The ship's bows were still in sight, and they did not seem to go down for a long time. I don't think they disappeared for two hours. We did not try and swim much, as there was no point in it. We just stayed together, moved our legs up and down and paddled. At one moment we started a song, but came to the conclusion that we'd better reserve our energy, but we wise-cracked the whole time and joked each other and jollied about. In my little party there was Lieutenant Murchie, Creasey, Kemp, Kirkpatrick, Davie and two ratings, AB's Ellis and Rondean.

The time we got into the water was about 4.30 and I estimated we had to wait until 8.30 for daylight, with no chance of being picked up in the dark.

From time to time I could hear Lieutenant-Commander Hoggan's voice in the distance, yelling out, 'Boat ahoy', and we kept shouting 'Boat ahoy', back.

After we had been in the water an hour and a half I produced my brandy-flask out of my Gieve waistcoat, and we all had a tot. That revived us a lot.

About 7 o'clock we each had some whisky from a bottle which Lieutenant Murchie had brought.

About 7.30 Lieutenant Murchie died, quite peaceably. There wasn't anything I could do. His voice had been getting weaker and weaker, and I realised he was dying from exposure, but he went out quite peaceably.

P/O Kemp was also getting very weak at this time. It was a pity, because star-shells were being fired all round us, and we knew destroyers were on the scene looking for us and would find us as soon as daylight came.

Daylight started to break about 8 o'clock. At 8.30 HMS Achates stopped close to us and we made our way alongside. They got them all on board with the exception of P/O Kemp, who had, I think, by this time gone, and myself. I, unfortunately, was the last man to come out of the water. The Sub-Lieutenant of the Achates had come down to give me a hand, and I was about half-way up the side when I think HMS Achates got a 'ping' and went ahead with both engines. I think she went full ahead because I dropped back into the water, and I remember being hit on the head by what seemed to me to be every bit of wreckage in the sea. I bobbed up astern and remembered somebody firing a depth-charge.

About what seemed half an hour afterwards, another destroyer[2] came along *and I shouted to them and they saw me. They lowered a whaler and hauled me into it. I told them there was another officer further on, and we picked up Lieutenant-Commander Hoggan, but there was no sign of Murchie and Kemp.*

Looking back on that night's proceedings, I can't help remembering how much strength I gained from the conduct of the men I had with me. Time after time they came to me and said, 'You know, sir, we wouldn't have missed this for anything.'

If I could, I'd like specially to recommend Chief Petty Officer Creasey, Lieutenant-Commander Hoggan and Sub-Lieutenant Davie. These three men were, to me, a tower of strength.

I am also grateful to Mr Johnson, the Senior Wireless Officer, who stuck to his wireless-room until everything had gone dead.

I have the honour to be, Sir,

Your obedient servant,

COMMANDER

THE REAR-ADMIRAL

COMMANDING NORTHERN PATROL[3]

Captain Wynter did not survive to explain his decision to the Court of Inquiry. When the last boat had left and he thought the ship was clear of men, he dived overboard and was drowned despite the fact that he was a strong swimmer. He was thought to have been physically weakened by heart trouble, bronchitis and exposure, which, when coupled with the shock of having lost his ship through a stubborn and brave determination to save other sailors, despite orders, drained him of the resistance necessary to live in the cold of the Atlantic in winter. According to Commander Martin, it is quite certain that had Wynter realised that volunteers were remaining on board, he would never have considered leaving them. But it was disturbing to the small group of officers and ratings gathered around Commander Martin to learn their Captain was no longer aboard. When they found they could do no more and were forced to abandon the heavily-listing ship, two stokers who could not swim appeared from the engine-room and asked Martin if they could get themselves a bottle of whisky and some blankets and use the ship's motor-boat, which was jammed by wreckage in its chocks.

Martin was certain they would drown if they jumped overboard and equally certain they would drown in the motorboat, so he gave his permission, believing that they would face death more comfortably in the boat than in the water. Then he had to abandon ship himself, and as he slid down a rope into the water he heard one of his gun's crew call out: 'Oh, God, save us.' They had swum away for what seemed a long time when the stricken *Patroclus* heaved her last sigh and subsided into the sea. They turned to look back, and Martin was amazed to see the motor-boat float clear of the wreckage and drift away into the darkness. The two non-swimming stokers were found by a destroyer later the next day curled up inside their blankets sound asleep with an empty bottle of whisky between them.

Curiously, the destroyer *Hesperus*, which picked up Martin and his volunteer gun's crew, was commanded at that time by Commander Donald Macintyre, who was to play such a large role in the Kretschmer career at a later stage in the Atlantic struggle.

When the survivors of *Patroclus* – 230 of them – were landed at Greenock and taken to the station to be sent to their bases, they were joined by Commander Martin. Most of them had believed he had gone down with the ship, and they cheered and carried him shoulder-high round the station hall. Newspaper reports, based on the assumption that as a Commander he must have been the commanding officer, described this scene and gave his name as Captain Wynter. The *Daily Telegraph* story of November 7th said: 'The men hoisted their commander shoulder-high, and after repeating their cheers sang: "For he's a jolly good fellow." Captain Wynter had survived the ordeal of four and a half hours in the sea.'

This and other Press reports emphasised the alleged cruelty of the U-boat commander in this action. The same report in the Telegraph was headlined: 'Torpedoed whilst on Mercy Mission: Germans shell lifeboat from *Laurentic*.' Then came a paragraph saying: 'The U-boat, not content with having torpedoed the two great liners, tried to get at the lifeboats with shell-fire.' Another newspaper ran the story under a bold headline: 'U-boat Ferocity.' In fact, as the Admiralty War Diary, the War Diary of *U-99* and the stories of Commander Martin and Captain Kretschmer all show, *U-99* was returning the fire of the *Patroclus* and *Laurentic* and at the same time trying to set the *Patroclus* on fire with phosphorous shells because of a shortage of torpedoes.

Commander Martin has given this verdict: 'Kretschmer was perfectly entitled to attack us. We were a warship on patrol, and while we went to the scene with the intention of picking up survivors, we were not actually a rescue ship. In fact, we had no right to be there at all. Bill Wynter was an old and dear friend. It just happened that on this occasion he made the wrong decision and paid for it with his own life – an eventuality that is always present when you command a ship at sea in wartime.'

Kretschmer wrote another verdict in his Diary. He found that by firing successive torpedoes into the hole caused by the first, the target was likely to break its back. Torpedoes hitting at intervals along a ship's side were inclined to let the water into the various compartments evenly, and the ship would tend to sink slowly by a gradual settling down. Kretschmer had sent six torpedoes into *Patroclus*, of which four had hit in the same place, and she had broken her back. He was convinced that if there had been no barrels, she would have sunk much sooner.

When *U-99* steamed away from the battlefield that night, the crew were not to rest for long. They sighted the smoke-trails of a convoy heading inwards towards the North Channel. On Dönitz's instructions, a U-boat which sighted a convoy had to report its position, course and speed and act as shadower for other submarines to converge on it. Kretschmer was in no mood to shadow for long. He sent his sighting signal and began moving up to an attacking position. By ten o'clock he was on the port bow keeping station on a destroyer escort. At 3 a.m. another U-boat, *U-123*, attacked from the starboard quarter, and at once the escort turned outwards, firing starshell to seawards. The port bow destroyer maintained its course, so Kretschmer held up a clenched fist at the convoy and said to Bargsten and Petersen: 'We will fire when my fist covers the width of three ships. I am prepared to waste this torpedo to see if our guesswork is as good as the director.' They checked their stop-watches and suddenly Kretschmer called out: 'Fire.'

The tanker *Scottish Maiden*, carrying crude oil to Britain, had been given a privileged and protected position near the centre of the convoy. Able Seaman Samuel Dougherty, of London, was coming off the morning watch and making his way aft to the galley for his customary morning cup of tea before turning in, but that Guy Fawkes morning, he decided to forego his tea and stay on deck a few minutes to admire the dawn. It had been a quiet, clear night, and after a few deep breaths of clean, crisp Atlantic air, he made his way to the fo'c'sle and lay down on his bunk. Suddenly a tremendous roar slit the night and the stern of the ship, including the galley in which Dougherty would have been normally drinking tea, was blown to pieces.[4] This was *U-99*'s 'guesswork' torpedo which had missed all the ships in the outer lanes and struck the more safely placed tanker. On the conning-tower, Kretschmer sighed with relief. It had taken the torpedo so long to hit something he had nearly written it off. In the control-room, the wireless operator intercepted the tanker's distress signal and recorded her name.

With all torpedoes expended, Kretschmer should have stayed with the convoy and acted as shadower, but after the previous night's battle he had no wish to stay at sea longer than was necessary. He knew that *U-123* was under attack by destroyers well astern and no other submarines were sufficiently close to the convoy to reach it before it sailed into the protection of coastal waters. He altered course away and called the engineer to the bridge.

'Chief,' he said, 'we have used up all our torpedoes. I'm not sure, but I thought that during the last attack the engines were running a bit rough. Is there a defect anywhere?'

The Chief caught his captain's meaning at once. He vanished below and a few minutes later reappeared on the conning-tower to report.

'There is a defect now, sir. And I'm afraid I can't do a running repair job at sea. We shall have to return to base to get it fixed.' He grinned agreeably, and Kretschmer smiled back.

'Very well, Chief; I shall return to base immediately.'

In the Deck and Engine-room Logs the defect was duly noted as the reason for their returning home. Meanwhile in London, Admiralty Operations had received signals from H.X.90 saying the convoy had been attacked. Further signals indicated that a destroyer had put down a U-boat astern of the convoy. It was known that Kretschmer was in the vicinity, and there was an inevitable temptation for Creasy's staff to hope that the boat under attack was *U-99*. But hope told a flattering tale, for Kretschmer had already dropped astern of the convoy and was steaming slowly to the boatload of survivors from the *Scottish Maiden* to check their position and their course home. He made off southwards, wincing slightly at the dull, distant roar of depth-charges falling on *U-123*. Four days later he arrived in Lorient to hear the news that *U-123* was overdue. She limped into Lorient two days afterwards. He also learned that on November 4th the Führer had awarded him the Oak Leaves to the Knight's Cross.

Notes

1 Captain Wynter won the DSO in the First World War when as a destroyer commander he sank a German cruiser at Jutland.

2 This was HMS *Hesperus*.

3 When Kretschmer read this report in MS form, he said: 'Martin nearly caught me in a trap. There was no reply to my gunfire, and I closed *Patroclus* confidently. Then they opened fire, sending spray over the conning-tower with their first shot. It seems obvious that, having got my range, Martin and his crew mistook the flash of my gun for the explosion of their shell – a natural mistake in a pitch black night…'

4 This story was told by Mr Dougherty in a letter to the *Evening Standard* published in September 1954.

Nine
Hitler's Guest

Coming into harbour after this fifth trip, Kassel took down a signal from Dönitz saying:

TO COMMANDING OFFICER *U-99*
WELL DONE STOP COMMANDING OFFICER KRETSCHMER AWARDED OAK LEAVES TO KNIGHTS CROSS STOP WARRANT OFFICER PETERSEN AWARDED KNIGHTS CROSS STOP COMMANDER KRETSCHMER WILL RECEIVE DECORATION FROM FÜHRER STOP COMMANDER-IN-CHIEF U-BOATS

When they had docked, Kretschmer learned that Dönitz was at his Paris headquarters in the Avenue Souchet and an aircraft was waiting to fly him there first before continuing on to Berlin. The following day he was in the Admiral's office answering the usual inquest questions put to every commander after a trip. Dönitz was punctilious about claims of sinkings and demanded the names of ships, tonnages and descriptions of silhouettes where possible. Even then, claims were not announced until confirmed either by intelligence agencies, BBC announcements or both. Dönitz congratulated him on his Oak Leaves, the highest decoration Germany could award for valour in face of the enemy – the equivalent to Britain's Victoria Cross.

'Now,' he said, 'I have authority to allocate five other decorations to *U-99*. Who will get them?' Kretschmer shrugged.

'That's an unfair question. All my crew deserve medals, I suppose. You have read my reports; you know the names I have mentioned in them. I think you should decide.'

'All right, but there must be someone whose behaviour in action is consistently good. Who is it?'

'Well, I think I should like my chief radio operator Kassel to get something. He earns it ashore as well by keeping the war correspondents off my neck.'

Dönitz smiled. 'An Iron Cross, First Class?'

'Yes.'

'All right, I'll send you the list of five I intend to decorate. You can make any alterations you like. Now I should get some sleep and go on to Berlin tomorrow.'

That night Kretschmer sat at the corner table in the Club Chez Elle, which hummed with gaiety. He drank his wine thirstily and swayed to the rhythm of a nostalgic chanson. He returned to his hotel in the early hours of the morning purged of tension by the champagne and the soft voice of a lovely singer.

At Quiberon, Kassell Bergman, Thorens and Clasen stood near the sports-ground when a sergeant of a cavalry unit stationed nearby approached them.

'Do you chaps know anyone that wants to ride a horse?'

'Why?' Clasen looked sourly at the Army uniform.

'Well, we have twenty-five horses here and only six of us to exercise them. We thought some of you would like a ride and at the same time help us out.'

Kassel looked at Bergman. 'Can you ride?'

'Certainly I can,' Bergman replied blandly, refusing to admit he had never been nearer to a horse than a bookmaker.

'So can I,' Kassel said. 'Let's take them up on this offer. In fact,' he said – somewhat rashly, 'we'll have a race. Navy versus Army.'

Bergman thought his friend crazy to challenge cavalrymen, so to even it up a bit, he chimed in.

'Yes, and just for the hell of it, we'll make it bareback.'

The sergeant guffawed.

'You submarine jockeys don't know what you are saying. We will take you on, and it's a night out on the losers.'

They shook hands and the sergeant walked away. Kassel turned on Bergman. 'You damn fool, you've never ridden a horse in your life.' Bergman looked indignant. 'You wait and see. Come to that, I'm not so sure that you have either.'

The following morning all the submarine crews resting at the Quiberon camp turned out to line the one-mile route for the race. The Army arrived with four horses, two for each team, and a Petty Officer brought a revolver and acted as starter. Bergman, who had prepared for the ordeal by consuming a considerable quantity of cognac, swayed alarmingly by his horse and eventually had to be hoisted on its back, where he steadied himself by firmly gripping the ropes acting as reins. Kassel sat more steadily, but nonetheless apprehensively, beside him, while the two Army riders made their horses prance expertly.

Suddenly the revolver cracked, too close apparently to the naval horses, for Bergman's steed bolted with its now thoroughly sober and alarmed rider hanging on by hugging the horse's neck with one hand and grabbing the mane in a tight grip with the other. Luckily, it galloped in the right direction, and scampered across the finishing line lengths ahead of Kassel's horse, which had been so thoroughly frightened by its companion's behaviour that it had bolted in pursuit. The cavalrymen, keeping their mounts under superb control, could not compete with the naval novelty-riders, who could dismount only when the horse stopped through sheer weariness. That night they wined and dined, with the cavalry footing the bill.

On the 12th the Siebel five-seater aircraft in which Kretschmer was the solitary passenger touched down at Dresden for fuel before continuing the journey to Berlin. He was taken by car to the luxurious Kaiserhof Hotel, where only the most celebrated guests of the Reich Chancellery were housed, and after a bath he reported to Admiral Raeder at the Naval Department. The Naval Commander-in-Chief looked tired as he greeted him.

'Of course we know each other, Kretschmer. I had the privilege of awarding you the Knight's Cross not so long ago at Lorient. *U-99* stayed in my mind because you all wore British uniforms. Very smart, too. Now tell me something about Lorient. Is there anything you need to help efficiency there?'

Kretschmer repeated a demand made several times by Dönitz for air co-operation in locating convoys and providing cover over the Biscay harbour approaches against enemy submarine and air reconnaissance and attack. At eleven o'clock he returned to the Kaiserhof, naïvely confident that he had told Raeder something new and had achieved what Dönitz had failed to do; 'stinging some action out of those armchair sailors in Berlin'. In the excitement he forgot that Raeder's weariness was probably caused by knowing only too well what was wanted and not having the political pull to get it. In Berlin, politics governed the actions of the powerful, and any strategic success was gained only by adroit usage of friends in high places.

At 11.30 a.m. his car called to take him to the Reich Chancellery, and he thought it ridiculous to use a car for a 200-yard trip, when the fighting services could never get enough petrol and oil. He wondered about Hitler. Like most naval officers, he knew only what he had read about the Führer and the Party high-ups, and he approached this meeting with the same sense of thrill that a Royal Navy commander would feel when going to Buckingham Palace to receive the Victoria Cross. When the car drew up outside the Chancellery, he jumped out and adjusted his uniform cap before mounting the steps leading to the vast imposing entrance dominated by a great German eagle. Accompanying him was Hitler's naval adjutant, Captain von Puttkamer, who had been sent to rehearse him in the drill of an investiture. They went through the entrance lobby into the towering reception-room in which the Führer held his audiences. Kretschmer was the last visitor on the Chancellery engagement list for the morning and learned that the first for the afternoon session was M. Molotov, Foreign Minister of their new ally, Russia. He told von Puttkamer of the delight it would give him to tell the story in Lorient that he had been placed ahead of a Cabinet Minister of a foreign Power.

At noon punctually, von Puttkamer left him for a few minutes; huge swing doors opened and Hitler walked in, accompanied by the adjutant. Von Puttkamer presented Kretschmer to the Führer and the formal investiture took place immediately. With a few words of praise, Hitler handed his leading 'ace' the gold-edged box opened to reveal the glittering Oak Leaves. They sat down on a settee and after a moment of silence Hitler began talking. 'It is good that the enemy started this war so early,' he said, as it would have been a much harder task if they had waited to build up their strength. So, for our naval warfare, we have secured the ports of the Bay of Biscay. I am most happy about that. At the beginning of the campaign I was determined to get the French Channel ports for our submarine warfare.'

He asked how the U-boat war was progressing. Kretschmer wondered how frank he should be, and then took the plunge.

'Sir, the arrival of new submarines is making things better, but it must be realised by the factory workers that the more they build and the quicker they build them, the more possible it will be to press home night surface attacks and produce wolfpacks large enough to wipe out convoys, or at least to so cripple them that the convoy system would prove too costly to maintain. At present, the British obligingly gather their ships together in large numbers for us to attack. It saves us searching the high seas for lone ships. But we need to increase our means of locating these convoys. This can be achieved only by large-scale air reconnaissance over the Atlantic. With large numbers of submarines at sea, a 'homing' signal from an aircraft could bring devastating destructive power to bear on the enemy supply routes. Air 'homing' would speed up attacks and cut out delays in patrolling for convoys which we sometimes never find.'

Hitler nodded, and having listened attentively, rose from his seat and said: 'Thank you, Commander. You have been admirably frank, and I shall do what I can for you and your colleagues. You will be lunching here with me.'

He left the room, and von Puttkamer escorted Kretschmer into the dining-hall. There, about a dozen adjutants and civilian staff administrators were standing behind their chairs waiting for Hitler to come in and take his seat first. Kretschmer was shown to the place of honour on the Führer's right.

Hitler came in and took his seat. It was a round table, so that Hitler was not at the head and no one could be relegated to the foot. It was Kretschmer's first experience of a Chancellery meal, which did not include meat. But later it became more painful for him. No alcohol was allowed at the table, and, worse still, no smoking.

All the servants were huge SS men who seemed to be doing Kretschmer a favour by bothering to serve him at all. Talk centred on the arrival that morning of Molotov from Moscow. One adjutant reported that after the Russian delegation had changed trains at the border – because of different rail gauges – they had refused to eat the food supplied on the German train, and had brought their own breakfast baskets. 'Wise, if a little theatrical,' commented Hitler.

The adjutant remarked on the number of women the Russians had brought with them. It was rumoured, he said, that the delegation feared that German women might stab them in bed, and as the Russians considered it uncivilised to sleep alone, they had brought bed companions they could trust.

'Are they pretty? ' Hitler asked.

The adjutant, warming up to his gossip, did not hear the question.

'Are they pretty? ' asked Hitler again, his voice louder and sharper.

'I have not seen them myself, Mein Führer,' the adjutant replied nervously, 'but I shall find out this afternoon.'

'Do that before Molotov comes to see me. I should like to taunt him with some of our beauties.'

When the meal was finished, Hitler stood up, shook Kretschmer's hand and wished him good hunting at sea. He left the room and von Puttkamer and another adjutant, whom Kretschmer had known before the war, joined their guest for coffee, brandy and cigars in another room. While they were smoking and chatting, Hitler, who detested smoking and drinking but tolerated them in his intimate circle, entered the room. The two staff officers jumped up immediately, but Kretschmer, not sure of himself, remained seated. Hitler nodded and crossed the room to go out by another door. It was not till then that Kretschmer realised he had not called Hitler 'Mein Führer'. It was not that he had any real political objection, but rather that he had overlooked the proper form of address.

That night the car called again at the Kaiserhof to take Kretschmer to the State opera at which 'Tannhauser' was being played. He was shown to the State box used only by Hitler and representatives of foreign governments being entertained by the Reich Chancellery. He was alone in the flower-filled box.

For his return to Lorient, Kretschmer was given the use of a bomber of the 'Führer Squadron', one of Hitler's personal aircraft. He went to Kiel, first to see some old friends and pick up some personal belongings, and then flew direct to Lorient. In all he had been away four days. It was time to prepare for sea again.

A week later Prien and Schepke joined Kretschmer for a trip to a tiny village some miles from Lorient where German officers were welcomed to a restaurant and given the best food on the Atlantic coast. It was a celebration dinner for Kretschmer's decoration.

In the interval since they had been rivals in the Baltic exercises each had matured under constant danger. Prien was liked by few of his fellow officers and by none of his crew. He was fanatical in his love of war and the Nazi cause, and sneered openly at less experienced officers who did not dare to press home attacks with the sort of determination he demanded of himself and his crew. After days of action, he would return to harbour and, instead of giving his crew a chance to rest and let the fresh, clean air of the countryside burn the greyness from their faces, he made them carry out long and irritating minor harbour exercises, while he did not appear from the day he went ashore to the moment they sailed.

Schepke was still boisterous, but there was a nervous note in the gaiety. His laughter came too loud and too often, and although his success ranked with Kretschmer's and Prien's, he was given to reporting actions in which every ship sunk was more than 10,000 tons. He was curiously unable to identify his claims by name. The Headquarters staff were saying that in his efforts to keep up with his fellow 'aces' he was 'cooking the books a bit', which, in turn, bolstered his own pride. Each of the three had reached the 200,000 tons region of sinkings. Over coffee and brandy, Schepke put on a show of bravado.

'Let us wager on which of us reaches 250,000 tons first. I offer to provide champagne for the three of us if either of you beats me to it. If I win, then you will see to it that I am wined and dined with suitable trimmings. Is it a bet?'

Prien and Kretschmer assented readily. Kretschmer had long ago decided that Schepke was a likeable and brave officer who could be forgiven his weaknesses providing only half of what he claimed were true; for even that would be formidable enough. Kretschmer himself was liked and respected throughout the U-boat Arm. He was steeped in naval tradition and his every action was designed to place himself into a proper relationship between superiors and subordinates. Throughout his training years, and now in his hour of triumph, his personal courtesy to fellow-officers and sailors alike made him one of the most popular commanders in the U-boat Arm.

His characteristic reserve had earned for him the affectionate nickname 'Silent Otto'. He was respected and admired; and Dönitz proudly described him as 'the best of my pupils'. Yet with this success he affected none of the arrogant swaggering of Prien and other commanders. Instead, his earlier contempt of weakness and inefficiency had become tempered into a more tolerant understanding of the defects of humanity and willingness to help his men overcome their handicaps. From the ruthless young Lieutenant who had commanded *U-23* had emerged Commander Kretschmer, the tough martinet, who nonetheless was a captain in whom any of his crew could safely confide their troubles.

These 'aces' were as vastly different in character as they had been in 1936. And still it was more the spirit of rivalry than friendship that bound them together to share a common destiny.

The three commanders left the restaurant late and returned to the Beau Sejour. Over coffee in the lounge, Kretschmer tried again to persuade them to carry the night-attack methods a stage further by trying his tactics of penetrating convoy screens and getting into the convoy lanes.

The hall porter came in to ask them if they wanted anything else before the kitchen closed. 'No, thanks,' said Schepke. 'By the way, I've noticed that you people at the hotel seem to know more about our comings and goings than we do. You might tell me now when I am going to sea again. I might get a good night's sleep.'

'I'm sorry, sir,' replied the old man mildly in French. 'I do not know about your orders, but I have heard it said that Commander Kretschmer will be leaving us for a spell on the 27th.' Kretschmer jerked upright. 'You mean to say you know that I am sailing on the 27th. Don't be silly, man. How could you know what my movements are going to be when I don't know myself yet?'

The old man shrugged. 'That's what the staff are saying, sir.' And he walked away.

Prien laughed. 'I'll bet you 100 francs he is right, Otto.'

'No, thanks. These people are too often right. Our security here is shocking. I only hope none of them is so foolish as to try and pass their information to the enemy.'

Soft dance-music and heavy wine were having their effect on the petty officers who were dining out in style. It was a smart restaurant, and at the end of the meal they received the bill and discovered that all the money they had pooled was still short of the total. Kassel called over the manager and in passable French said: 'We are short of funds at the moment, Monsieur, and have to meet friends at a club. Perhaps we could pay you half the bill now and I will sign a note for the remainder, which we shall pay after our next trip.' The manager beamed his approval and wished them bon voyage.

At the hotel that night they learned that in the taverns of the dock area their sailing date was being tipped as the 27th.

Clasen turned to his friends murmuring: 'Here we go again. I've never known these people ashore to be wrong yet.'

'That means,' remarked Kassel, 'that tomorrow I shall get stores aboard, whether we receive sailing orders or not.' The next morning Kassel visited the stores department and handed in his list of requirements for the voyage. He noticed a pile of cases in a corner, and was told they contained tinned duck. His demand for some was refused on the grounds that the whole consignment had been booked by Prien. Kassel threatened to tell his captain and this was enough to get him two cases. That afternoon, while the stores were going aboard, Kretschmer arrived and asked Kassel why he was storing ship.

'We have no sailing orders yet.'

'I heard last night that we would be sailing tomorrow, sir, so I thought I would be ready, in case the orders were rushed at the last minute.'

'Who told you?'

'Oh, it's known all over town, sir.'

'All right, but if we don't sail tomorrow, you will have to unload again.'

'Aye, aye, sir,' Kassel replied amiably, and went on with the loading.

At 9 a.m. the next day, November 27th, they sailed for the North Atlantic and four days later *U-99* was struggling in a heavy sea and swell and against a strong easterly wind to intercept a convoy reported by *U-101*. They expected to reach the 'collision' point at 4 a.m. the following morning. The weather was becoming increasingly worse and the conning-tower watch were chained to the steel sides to avoid being washed overboard, as they pitched and rolled in mountainous seas. At times the heavy, rain-laden sky was blacked out by great waves that hung over their heads threatening to crash down on them, but always they rushed up the sides of the hills of water and their propellers thrashed air before they sank back into another valley.

At 3.15 a.m. Petersen wrote in the log: 'Impossible to maintain speed. Reduced to half speed, making about five knots over the ground. Boat being pushed under water by the force of waves.'

A lookout, standing near Kretschmer, let out a cry as his chain snapped. He was being carried off by the rush of water when Kretschmer unhooked his own chain and barged heavily against the struggling sailor, knocking him across the conning-tower, where he fell behind the machine-gun mounting. This quick action probably saved his life.

It was doubtful now if they would make sufficient speed to intercept the convoy. It was even more doubtful if they would be able to attack even if they found a target. Kretschmer took comfort in the thought that, while this weather made efficient attacks difficult, it also caused confusion among escorts and convoys, who lost touch with each other; and enemy lookouts would be screwing up their eyes against the wind, the rain and the spray too tightly to keep a thorough watch.

At 5.40 a.m. Bargsten shouted into Kretschmer's ear and pointed dead ahead. A large, ominous shadow had appeared in the darkness less than half a mile away. Kretschmer's reaction was to attack, and they had increased to full speed in readiness to fire when a lookout sighted a destroyer ploughing towards them. It was impossible to run away on the surface, so they dived and fired a snap shot at the same time. When just under water, they heard the dull explosion of the torpedo striking its target. They were plunging downwards expecting the destroyer to drop its depth-charges before they could reach any real depth, when Kassel, on the hydrophones, reported the destroyer had passed overhead. He could not hear the target, which by that time had been forced to stop.

A little later he picked up faint propeller noises of a convoy. Kretschmer surfaced and saw, to his surprise, the target ship wallowing helplessly in the turbulent seas. Someone on its bridge was firing red and yellow Very lights towards them. Kretschmer brought *U-99* into an attacking position, slowly because of the weather, and fired a second torpedo. This hit under her bridge, and immediately Kassel picked up her distress signal on the 600-metre wavelength. It was the armed merchant cruiser HMS *Forfar*, which, it is now known, was the ocean escort for Convoy HX90. At the same time her gun's crew fired round after round of starshell in Kretschmer's direction, the lights of the flares glowing palely over the black, writhing sea. Kretschmer fired his third torpedo quickly to deliver a death blow before the cruiser's guns found his range. It hit forward with no visible effect. Her crew were making no apparent attempt to take to the boats, and Kretschmer interpreted this as meaning they were confident of their ability to survive the attack and stay afloat. Bitterly, he recalled the barrels that had poured from the holes in *Patroclus*. The fourth torpedo fired from 800 yards hit the stern and, thankfully, he saw her settle down in the water. It was nearly 7 a.m., and dawn would be breaking soon to expose him to the destroyer that must be racing to *Forfar*'s rescue from the convoy. He fired the fifth torpedo at the stern deliberately. It was a direct hit in the hole made by the fourth, and the stern broke off, to be gulped down by the hungry sea. There were several explosions as its depth-charges went off.[1] Ten minutes later *Forfar* gave up the unwilling struggle in such a gale and subsided beneath the sea.

Kretschmer was shocked. Although his torpedoes had been spaced out over nearly an hour and a half, he had not seen any lifeboats lowered. The flush of success was still-born when he thought of the hundreds of men who must have foundered with their ship. Only minutes later they sighted a destroyer driving hard into the sea as she fought to get to *Forfar*. *U-99* retreated on the surface and dived to reload tubes. They surfaced again and made their way to the convoy. Shortly after daybreak an aircraft dropped flares over the wreckage of the cruiser. The destroyer was still there, and Kretschmer scouted around him well to the south. At noon Petersen wrote in the Log: 'We have caught up with the convoy and the Captain has indicated he wishes to attack after dark at 1800.'

This was the plan, but at 1.15 p.m. they sighted a lone straggler from the convoy sailing in ballast with a gun's crew swinging the gun-barrel from side to side as though at drill. Kretschmer shadowed it, and since nothing had been heard from *U-101*, he sent out the convoy's position, course and speed, in case any other U-boats were in the vicinity favourably placed to intercept and attack. At 8.30 p.m. he attacked the lone ship and scored a hit amidships. She listed badly, but did not sink and, unwilling to waste more torpedoes, he decided to set her alight with his gun. The gun's crew scored more than fifty hits with alternate high-explosive and phosphorous shells to make her burn, and by 9.30 the ship was a blazing wreck – an awesome sight in the howling wind and tormented sea. The U-boat steamed alongside the stricken vessel and shone a signal lamp over her. She was deserted, so it was likely the crew had taken to the boats. This was the Norwegian *Samananger*. At 2 a.m. the ship heeled over and sank. By this time the convoy was so far ahead that Kretschmer could not catch up before it reached the protection of the mine barrier stretching across the entrance to the North Channel. This barrier consisted of tens of thousands of mines laid sufficiently deep to allow convoys to pass over them, but still shallow enough to trap a submerged U-boat.

Kretschmer turned southwards to take up another patrol, but an hour later a lookout sighted a darkened shape seemingly steaming northwards. It was a tanker, obviously a straggler from the convoy, which had been forced to lag more than fifty miles behind or had become lost in the storm. They closed the target and, to their astonishment, found it had stopped. Cautiously they circled and looked for signs of a trap, but the tanker wallowed up and down with her propellers idle. Kretschmer was content to lay off and wait. They stayed like that until dawn, and in the light were amazed further to see that the lifeboats had disappeared and the ship was deserted. Closing in again, they raked the decks and hull through their glasses. There was no sign of damage anywhere and the ship was on an even keel, riding well. It was a 'ghost ship' without a soul on board, and painted on the side of the bridge was the name *Conch*. They were nearly stopped when two sailors on the foredeck fished a lifebelt out of the sea also bearing the name *Conch*. At 200 yards range they fired a torpedo, which struck her amidships. She keeled over and sank in seconds.

Cruising southwards to their patrol area, the weather grew worse, the seas developing into raging torrents reaching out with claw-like fingers. They had passed through one side of what had now developed into a cyclone, ridden out the comparative, calm of the centre, and were now experiencing the other side, which struck them with increasing ferocity. It was now difficult to stay afloat and hope to carry out an attack. Kretschmer could have sought peace below the surface, but he insisted on staying 'upstairs' to report any sighting to Lorient.

At 11.35 a.m. on December 7th, when the storm was beginning to abate, they sighted another lone steamer. It was daylight, so Kretschmer decided to make a submerged attack, but when he dived and tried to use the periscope, he found it had jammed in its sheath. The smaller secondary periscope was useless because of the high swell. He surfaced and shadowed the ship, intending to attack after dark.

At dusk Kassel intercepted a signal on the 600-metre band in plain language saying: '*Aghia Eirini* wants immediate assistance. Position 32°–38' N. 22°–52' W. stop Twenty-nine on board stop Damaged by storm and all holds full of water stop.' Kretschmer decided to attack his target immediately and then head for the *Aghia Eirini* to sink her before she could receive help. But it took four hours to get into attacking position, and it was not until 10.29 p.m. that he fired one torpedo at a range of 500 yards. It jumped through the waves and hit the target in the stern above the water-line, which meant she took water only with every wave that rushed past her side. She signalled for help, and the relief radio operator reported her as the Dutch steamer *Farmsum*. The effect of the torpedo jumping from the water and hitting so high, was that the stern superstructure bearing the after-gun mounting was lifted high in the air by the explosion and thrown overboard. But it stopped the ship, and as she no longer had a gun with which to counter-attack, Kretschmer crept nearer and fired his second shot at the bows. But the torpedo veered off course and hit the stern again – this time below the water-line. There was still no sign of the ship sinking, and the third torpedo was fired at a setting of nine feet. It hit well down on the hull, and the *Farmsum* capsized at once, to sink in three minutes. On this occasion Kretschmer was much more concerned with getting away to attack the *Aghia Eirini*, and, without waiting to find out what had happened to the survivors, he headed off towards the position signalled by the damaged ship.

They arrived there at dawn, but there was no sign of her, and Kretschmer thought she might have struggled towards the North Channel. He took up the trail on what he considered her course might be, and at 9.33 a.m. Kassel intercepted another signal from their quarry saying, 'Making every attempt to come near shore in spite of ship's holds full of water stop Helm out of action.' This was followed by a position, and a few minutes later a shore radio station, which had taken a radio director bearing on the damaged ship's signals, reported her bearings from the Irish coast on the same wavelength. Petersen worked out these on his chart and placed the ship at least sixty miles from where her own dead reckoning had put her.

Shortly before noon the *Aghia Eirini* came on the air again: 'To the Admiralty Urgent stop No hope of coming near shore stop We are asking for your help stop Helm out of action and steering gear damaged by weather stop Ship filled with water three days ago stop No ships have come to our rescue in those three days stop'. It gave a correct position signed by the Master. Kretschmer grinned at his officers.

'There is a very angry captain,' he said. An hour later, while heading on their new search course, a large liner appeared heading roughly in the same direction, but converging slowly. It was travelling at high speed, and Kretschmer guessed it was on its way to help the *Aghia Eirini*. He held his course while there was still a considerable distance between them, but at 4 p.m. he sighted a destroyer also heading in the same general direction at high speed. Then the engineer rushed to the conning-tower to report that the weather had damaged one of the electric motors which powered them under water. He wanted time on the surface to carry out repairs. Kretschmer was about to agree when the destroyer altered course towards them and another two destroyers appeared on the horizon astern of them. Without waiting to argue with the engineer, he shouted, 'Alarm dive', and they began sinking, but, with only one electric motor, took longer than usual in getting down.

Kretschmer checked the silhouette book and decided the liner he had seen was a merchant cruiser. Kassel could get no hydrophone effect, so, twenty minutes later, Kretschmer decided the enemy could not have seen him and came up for a look round. As his periscope was jammed, he had to surface completely, and sixty seconds later was plunging downwards again. The cruiser had stopped only a mile or so away, and one of the destroyers was even closer, also stopped. Almost immediately, Kassel heard the sound of the destroyers approaching and they felt Asdic impulses on the hull. At the same time the slower revs of the cruiser could be heard dying away in the distance. By staying stopped, the enemy had caused him to come to the surface and had got his position.

Five minutes passed, and one destroyer moved directly overhead. Seventeen minutes clicked on while *U-99*, with propellers just ticking over and everything silent inside, lurked at 300 feet. As the depth-charges came, the U-boat jumped around like a wounded whale. Inside, the crew were thrown to the floor and the lights went out. When the auxiliary lighting came on, they picked themselves up – all except a Leading Seaman, who knelt before his locker praying to a picture of his wife. The second pattern was not so close, but near enough to scare them horribly. They counted fifty explosions before Kassel reported the propeller noises dying away. They stayed below, steaming northwards at four knots, most of the crew still tensed and nervous after the depth-charging. Suddenly a loud crack reverberated through the U-boat, bringing Kretschmer leaping from his bunk to the control-room.

'What was that? ' he shouted at the astonished Elfe, who was on watch.

'I don't know, sir.'

'Anything reported on the hydrophones?

'No, sir.'

Kretschmer paced the control-room for a while and then went back to continue his rest. A few minutes later he jumped up again, as three more cracks came in quick succession. Elfe was already ordering an inspection of the hull in case some of the plates were giving way after the depth-charging. Kassel had been sitting in the Petty Officers' mess looking thoughtful, and when two more explosions made the crew crowd round the control-room anxiously, his face went red. Kretschmer was worried. 'What the hell can it be?' he asked of no one in particular. Kassel could stand it no longer. He rushed to the storeroom and threw open the door to reveal a ghastly sight and an evil smell. Sticky brown legs and wings of duck were plastered over the walls, with the juice running in sickly rivulets down to the deck. The mystery was explained. The tins of duck were exploding in rapid succession. He called out guiltily to Kretschmer, who came storming over to gaze unbelievingly at the mess. All bent hurriedly by the open door as four more tins blew up almost together. Kretschmer's language only added to the thickness of the stale air, and Kassel felt he could safely assume that *U-99* was not to have duck again.

Two hours later they surfaced. Darkness had fallen and there was nothing in sight. With one engine out of order, his attack periscope damaged and most of his torpedoes expended, Kretschmer gave up the chase for the crippled *Aghia Eirini*, and sent a short signal to Dönitz saying he was returning to base with engine trouble, and headed for home. They arrived tired, depressed by the depth-charging and by too many trips with too many risks. Two days later Dönitz signed his official report with the words: 'Very successful, well-handled operation.'

In London, the Anti-Submarine Division had reached some fairly definite conclusions on enemy tactics in the Atlantic. In their view these tactics called for a complete re-organisation of ideas on the functions of a U-boat. Dönitz was not using them as submarines but as 'submersibles'. This in fact meant that the U-boats in the main attacked on the surface by night in the manner of torpedo boats. The Royal Navy's defensive and offensive tactics should therefore be adapted to fight them as surface craft which would submerge only in the interest of safety, generally during daylight.

At this time Creasy was setting a very high standard for the 'Enemy Strategy and Tactics' Section of the Division. The target at which they must aim, they were told, was to guess Dönitz's next move at least a week before he thought of it himself.

Notes

1 These depth-charges would explode, due to an Admiralty regulation that all depth-charges were to be set to explode at a depth of five feet while steaming at sea in normal circumstances.

July 1939: The crew of U-23 relax during training.

Commander (later Captain) Prien (right), who sank the Royal Oak *in Scapa Flow, watches preparations before sailing from a base in occupied France.*

Officers and crew of U-99 after the boat was commissioned at Kiel in May, 1940. Commander Kretschmer is second from right, lower row.

U-99 flies seven victory pennants each representing an Allied ship sunk. The pennants bear the horshoe insignia, and the gilt horseshoe hangs upside down on the conning tower.

'Hunter's Moon' *over an Atlantic convoy, easy prey for the U-boat wolves in 1940.*

Above: *At Lorient, Admiral Raeder presents the Knight's Cross to Kretschmer, who, with his crew, wears salvaged British battle-dress.* Below: *Kretschmer (second right) responds in lager to deck party toasts on his Knight's Cross.*

Kretschmer receiving the Oak Leaves of the Knight's Cross (the German VC) from Hitler at the Berlin Chancellery, November, 1940.

Kretschmer presents a lifebuoy from the 'ghost' tanker Conch *to the German Army. He refused to broadcast, but a sailor behind him recorded his speech on a wrist-microphone. Admiral Dönitz*

Left: *Grand Admiral Raeder.* Right: *Admiral Dönitz.*

A scene that became familiar, but always distasteful to Kretschmer during the Atlantic battle. Survivors leave their torpedoed ship by lifeboat.

The destroyer HMS Walker *under Commander Macintyre, put a final end to* U-99's *run of victories.*

Above left: *Admiral Sir George Creasy directed the Anti-Submarine Warfare.* Above right: *Commander R.P. Martin of the* Patroclus. Left: *Commander Donald Macintyre of the* Walker.

Kretschmer goes ashore at Liverpool as a prisoner.

The crew of U-99 *line up on the deck of HMS* Walker.

The end of a dream. A wounded German rating is carried ashore en route to a POW camp.

Monteith Camp, near Lake Ontario, where U-99's 'other ranks' staged many escape attempts.

Military honours were accorded the First Lieutenant of U-570 who was shot while attempting to escape. Chief Petty Officer Kassel is on the extreme left.

Kretschmer and fellow officers at Bowmanville Camp in Canada.

At a reunion in Hamburg, Kretschmer meets old shipmates König (left) and Kassel (right).

Ten
On Leave

The next day Kretschmer addressed his crew: 'We are having a refit, and I expect we shall be in harbour for a month. That means three weeks leave.' There was a rustle of excitement.

'You can go home or spend some of it at the rest camp at Quiberon, but those of you who want a rest in the mountains can join me for some skiing at Crumble, in Silesia. You can bring your wives, and I shall arrange a specially cheap rate for you at the hotel. Those who want to come can give their names to Chief Petty Officer Kassel, and travelling arrangements will be made so that you can leave tomorrow.'

Dönitz invited Kretschmer to dinner on his second night ashore, and after the meal the Commander of *U-99*, a man who enjoyed good food and wine, resolved never to eat at Headquarters again. The Admiral had made it a rule that the shore staff of the U-boat Command should live on the same rations as those allowed German civilians. To a U-boat officer, used to almost any sort of food he wanted, this was meagre fare indeed.

Over coffee, Dönitz said: 'I promised that if you let Bargsten and Elfe go to take over commands, you could have any First Lieutenant you want. Who is it to be? Here is a list of the officers available.'

His Flag Lieutenant passed across a short list to Kretschmer, who gave it a quick glance.

'Lieutenant von Knebel-Döberitz, sir.'

Dönitz turned to the Flag Lieutenant. 'What did I tell you?' He smiled at Kretschmer. 'I knew you would have him, so I have already sent a signal for him to take over here while you go on leave. I remembered you had served together in Kiel, and I think you got on well.'

Kretschmer knew the officer he had chosen was reliable, but he was more concerned about leave. 'How long will I get for leave, sir?'

'A good spell, I think. I should say you could take the same as your men – three weeks. Incidentally, I am going by car to Cologne tomorrow. Why not come with me, and travel back home from there? I have only one other officer coming, so there will be plenty of room.'

'Thank you, sir.'

Next morning the green-painted staff car left Lorient for Paris with Admiral Dönitz sitting in front with the driver while Kretschmer shared the back seat with Lieutenant-Commander Lüth,[1] another U-boat captain. During the drive, Dönitz made another of his periodic attempts to persuade Kretschmer to give up operational command and either join his staff or be assigned as chief instructor at the Submarine Training School. As usual, Kretschmer declined the offer, which meant in effect that he would be removed from danger and allowed to rest on his laurels.

The possibility that one day this might happen was a constant worry to him. Although little more than a year separated the 'ace' captain of *U-99* from the intolerant, aloof young officer who had commanded *U-23*, too much action and responsibility on young shoulders in too short a time had left their effect. His face had become hardened and lined; his hair was thinning and receding from the forehead.

Blatant, cocksure self-confidence had given way to the quiet serenity that comes with knowledge and experience. Yet beneath this, nerves were taut, and he never relaxed in his determination to keep his command and resist every effort to rest him ashore.

His philosophy of war was uncomplicated. At sea, he was at peace with himself, content that danger lurked behind every squall, and each patch of mist or fog. Ashore he would never fit in among the dandies of a headquarters staff. He was neither an intriguer nor a politician, and officers with desk jobs had too much time to become both. In battle it is doubtful if he ever gave much thought to the horror of the destruction he caused and faced. He helped survivors because it complied with his personal code of honour and duty. In return he expected – and never questioned – that in his own moment of peril the enemy would help him. If he had committed himself to deeper thought, he might have cracked under the strain of command. As he cut through the dark Atlantic waters to attack, there was little time to worry about the fate of the enemy or his own crew, and in the aftermath, sheer physical exhaustion cast a protective screen round his mind in an insistent call to sleep. That was his life; his chosen rôle in war. Now the warning that a shore posting was imminent rang aloud as Dönitz pressed the argument.

'You have been at sea since the beginning of the war, and you are the only U-boat captain on active service who has not had a spell at a shore job. I think you should consider taking this leave and reporting to Kiel for instruction duty.'

'Is that an order, sir?'

'You know it's not. But if you stay as stubborn it will have to become an order. No man can take what you are doing without a rest – if only for the safety of his crew. A tired captain is a menace at sea, don't forget.'

Kretschmer gazed moodily out of the window. Somehow this continuous harping on shore duty made him depressed at a time when he wanted to feel cheerful. And then he remembered. 'Incidentally, sir, Prien has not taken a shore job since the war.'

Dönitz snorted irritably. 'I know that. So there are two of you, and he is just as stubborn.'

Kretschmer knew that would not be the end of it. As his leave neared its end, Dönitz would try again to make him stay ashore and hand over *U-99* to another commander. Cold and ruthless in action as he was, Kretschmer could not think without panic of the day when he might have to give up his ship and crew.

In Paris, Dönitz left the two captains to find their own amusement. He warned them to be at his headquarters early in the morning to continue the drive by car to Cologne, where Kretschmer would leave to make his own way to Silesia. The two officers spent most of the night visiting clubs and bars aimlessly at first, until the cognac and wine began to make themselves felt, and in a mood of exhilaration Kretschmer took his friend to Chez Elle. There was little sleep for either of them, and as soon as the car got under way at dawn for the long drive to Cologne, Kretschmer ventured rather timidly to request of the well-rested and chatty Dönitz: 'Would you mind very much, sir, if Lüth and I dozed for a while?'

Without waiting for an answer they both dropped their heads on their arms and let their eyelids close thankfully. When they woke up they were nearing Cologne, and Dönitz, amused that his two junior officers should have such obvious hangovers, bade Kretschmer a cheerful good-bye at the railway station.

Crumble was a paradise to the crew of *U-99*, most of whom joined Kretschmer at the hotel. With the help of Dönitz, he had arranged that the German Navy would foot the bill for the sailors, who would be presented with only nominal charges for those wives and sweethearts invited to spend the Christmas with them. After the thick, yellow air and the stench of chloride gas, the cold, crisp air of the snow-covered mountains was the difference between grey, sallow faces weathered to unhealthy parchment and bright red, virile cheeks with the light of good health in their eyes. After a week of skiing every morning and afternoon, Kretschmer received a visitor. He was a publisher from Berlin, who lost no time in telling Kretschmer he was a very big publisher with the ear of high circles. He wanted Kretschmer to prepare a book on his exploits under his own name. *U-99*'s captain listened obligingly and gave his answer at once. No. The publisher smiled superciliously.

'But of course, I know how you people in the front line feel about publicity,' he said, with what he thought was disarming frankness, 'but it will do you good in your career, Commander. I have powerful friends who know of this request and expect you to agree. They won't like it if you refuse.'

'The answer is no. I am sorry you have made this long journey in vain, but I am about to join some of my crew. We are going to climb a mountain. You look as though something like that wouldn't do you any harm. Why don't you come along?'

Irate at this reference to his portliness, the publisher turned nasty. 'Commander, I advise you that you are expected to write this book to assist the recruiting campaign for the U-boat Arm and to boost civilian morale. I should not like to return to Berlin and report that you are not willing to help your country in this respect.'

Kretschmer exploded. 'Help my country, by God!' He controlled himself with difficulty, but his face had paled with anger. 'The answer is still no.'

The publisher sneered. 'What makes you think you are so much better than Prien, who has written one, and Richthofen of the first war?'

'I don't, but if it means so much to you, you will have to do better than you are doing now. I can assure you that I would only consent to such a proposition if I was ordered to do so by my Commander-in-Chief, Admiral Dönitz.'

The publisher took the hint, and left promising this was not the last that had been heard of the matter. Two days later Kretschmer received a telegram from Lorient, signed by Dönitz, telling him to write his story for the publisher. Puzzled, but resigned, at this order, which was so unlike Dönitz, Kretschmer telephoned the publisher and gave his consent. Two days later a special writer arrived to interview him. While this was going on, Kassel, as the unofficial publicity officer of *U-99*, was in another room writing articles on their trips for German newspapers and preparing scripts for broadcasts.

Kretschmer made the writer's job difficult, giving him as little time as possible and only essential facts. He hoped that when he returned to Lorient he could persuade Dönitz to change his mind and cancel the work. He was certain it would be nothing more than a propaganda book. He could imagine the feelings of his brother officers and commanders who had suffered as much and sailed on as many operations without having what he regarded simply as the luck provided by his horseshoes.

When the leave was over and he returned to Lorient towards the end of January 1941, he hurried direct to Headquarters and saw Dönitz. The Admiral let him finish talking and then said quietly: 'I haven't the slightest idea of what you are talking about. What publisher? What book?'

Kretschmer was speechless. 'But I received a telegram from you,' he protested.

Dönitz called in his Duty Officer and asked for the files. They found a letter from the publisher to Dönitz. There was a 'Yes' written in the margin, and the Admiral remembered he had written 'Yes' in the margin only because he agreed with Kretschmer's refusal to be used for propaganda purposes. When the Duty Officer had cleared the desk, he had picked up the letter and taken the 'Yes' to mean Kretschmer should do as the publisher wished, and had sent a telegram accordingly, signing it in Dönitz's name. The order was cancelled immediately and another one placed on record telling Kretschmer that on no account was he to lend his name to a book or assist in the production of one. The commander was satisfied.[2]

Meanwhile, one of the Headquarters staff who had been a sculptor before the war was told by Dönitz to do a bust of Kretschmer for the Officers' Mess. Patiently, Kretschmer sat each day for more than a week. It was a small bust, which took only two weeks to finish. Dönitz presided over the unveiling, also attended by Prien and Schepke. When the Admiral took his first look, he turned to an orderly and said: 'Take this away. It is no one I know.' Kretschmer agreed with some disappointment that it was pretty bad, and submitted amiably to the bantering he received from his rivals and friends who had only recently returned from their last trip. Prien referred to 'Otto the Silent' who had become 'Otto the Immortal', while Schepke reminded the other two that they had a bet to settle.

Kretschmer had reached a total of 250,000 tons sunk and become the first submarine commander to do so in the war. Now it was time to claim his champagne.

The following day he called Knebel-Döberitz to his room and asked him to arrange details of a presentation to the Army. The Military Commander had officially presented him with a scroll of music bearing the Military Band's composition called 'The Kretschmer March'. Now he wanted to return the compliment, and it was decided that the lifebuoy from the 'ghost' tanker *Conch* should be painted up and handed over to the Army. It was an impressive ceremony, attended by staff officers, U-boat crews and a full military parade. Kretschmer handed over the lifebuoy formally, and a representative of the German Broadcasting Company asked to record the ceremony; but Kretschmer refused, as he also refused interviews to war correspondents, who were, however, allowed to be present and write about the ceremony. The broadcasting team won in the end. With Kassel's connivance, they had given a wristwatch-microphone to a sailor who stood behind Kretschmer holding up his right hand. The tiny microphone recorded everything the Commander said.

On February 17th Dönitz sent for Kretschmer and said: 'I want you to consider again taking a shore job just for a short spell. I want *U-99* to sail in three days. I have still time to put another officer in command.'

'No, sir.'

'Right. I understand Petersen will take over the duties of a Second Lieutenant. You will be receiving two midshipmen for a few weeks. They should arrive tomorrow.'

That morning four midshipmen had left Kiel bound for various assignments in Lorient. But while changing trains at Hamburg, the tall, fair-haired Volkmar König, aged eighteen and proud indeed of his acceptance in the U-boat Arm, missed his three friends and the train. He arrived in Lorient late, and found his absence had caused a few bad words to fly around Headquarters. He had been assigned with another midshipman to join *U-47*, commanded by Prien. But *U-47* had sailed on exercises that afternoon, and another midshipman had gone in his place. König was told to report to *U-99*. He met Kretschmer on the quayside beside the U-boat, saluted and reported for duty. Kretschmer looked him up and down for a moment, and said bitingly: 'What do you think you know about U-boats?'

König was nonplussed at this greeting. He had heard that, while a strict disciplinarian, Kretschmer was a reasonable man and one of the best to serve under. Doubts streamed into his mind.

'I know only what a midshipman's training course can teach me, sir.'

'Well, I suppose you will be telling us how we ought to run the war on your first trip. But I'll soon knock that out of you.'

Kretschmer walked off and left König to find his way on board, where he was greeted by the senior midshipman, Rubahn, who said: 'Well, did you meet the captain?'

'I did. Not what you might call the friendliest of introductions.'

'Forget it. He has by now.'

That same afternoon König was sent to the operations room at Headquarters to check the position of all other U-boats on the North Atlantic prior to their sailing. The Duty Officer showed him the large map with little pins on strings which represented U-boats. König gaped in astonishment. He had expected to see the map covered with pins; instead there were exactly four. König turned to the officer. 'If that is all there are in the North Atlantic, where are all the others?'

'Don't be silly,' came the reply. 'What others? We rarely have more in this field of operations than you see there.' It was König's first disillusionment.

At the completion of his exercise, Prien in *U-47* prepared to leave harbour early in the morning of the 19th. He arrived in his clean leather overalls and a dazzling white cap-cover; a band played and crowds of soldiers, dockyard workers and other U-boat crews crowded round to see him off; a young girl presented him with a bouquet of camellias, which flower early in Brittany. He plucked one and handed it to her gallantly, and put another in his buttonhole. Several fellow commanders came up to wish him luck, among them Kretschmer.

'Little Prien,' said Kretschmer, calling him by his nickname, 'I shall be following you in a couple of days. Have a convoy ready.'

'I shall do that thing,' replied Prien with a laugh. 'Just leave it to Papa's nose to smell something out.'

'Good luck and good hunting,' said Kretschmer, and shook his hand.

'Thank you, Otto. I have a feeling about this trip. I feel it is going to be a big one for us all. Good-bye.'

That night Kretschmer entertained the old and new officers, including the midshipmen, to a farewell party at Moulin de Rosmadec, at Pont Aven, near Lorient. Over coffee, brandy and the inevitable cigar for Kretschmer, he told Bargsten and Elfe, who were to take over their own commands, that, as he was no longer their commanding officer, they could use the occasion to make any complaints they liked about his methods of command. It would, he said, be instructive for the new officers.

Bargsten and Elfe chuckled to themselves. It was pleasant to talk over all they had been through together in the luxury of the restaurant. They could be detached now from the horror, the tension, the fear and the sickness that sweep in spasms over men who have seen too much of war. They were no longer part of the crew that gave *U-99* her soul, but some part of her would stay with them for ever – or until they died. They pretended to think deeply. Bargsten said at last: 'Well, all I can think of, sir, is the time we were running in to attack the *Invershannon* on the second trip and you gave me a really mighty blow on the back of the neck. It hurt for a couple of days afterwards.'

Kretschmer looked a little taken aback: 'Hit you? I don't believe it.'

'I don't suppose you even realised you had done it. You were concentrating on conning the ship into the attack, and I was standing in your way, looking at another target through my binoculars. Elfe told me later that you called out to me a couple of times to get back and put the setting on the director, but I didn't hear you. The next thing I knew you had struck me on the back of the neck and pushed me aside to the director. I think you were so wrapped up in the attack you didn't know what you were doing, sir. That's my complaint, and one I don't mind at all.'

Kretschmer turned to Knebel-Döberitz. 'That is what you can expect from me. You had better ask for a transfer before we sail tomorrow.'

Minor delays put their sailing date back to the 22nd, when they prepared to leave harbour at noon. It was the best send-off Kretschmer had received and was laid on by the Army, because the local regiment had adopted *U-99*, and partly because he now ranked as the highest scoring 'ace'. The military band played on the quayside while Kretschmer himself said good-bye to everyone present. The Army had commandeered a small river steamer and, with their band still playing, followed *U-99* to the harbour entrance. Before signalling farewell, the U-boat put her bows against the stern of the steamer and the mail was handed across in waterproof bags. The last sounds they heard as they headed out along the swept channel were the closing bars of 'The Kretschmer March'.

Notes

1 Lüth became a famous 'ace' in the days of the second 'Happy Time' which dawned when the Americans entered the war and the east coast of the United States, became a favourite U-boat hunting ground. He was killed just after the German surrender, in 1945, when, as Chief of the Midshipman's Training School, he returned to the base one night and was challenged by the sentry. There was a mix-up in the passwords, and the sentry shot him dead.

2 A few months before, Prien had agreed to write a propaganda book on his own career describing the sinking of the *Royal Oak*. Kretschmer had disapproved of this.

Eleven
The 'Aces' At Sea

On February 25th, 1941, *U-99* crossed St George's Channel and neared the North Atlantic patrol area lying slightly to the south of that allocated to *U-47*. Shortly after dawn next day Kassel intercepted a signal from Prien to U-boat Headquarters:

> *Enemy convoy in sight on westerly course at estimated speed seven knots. Am being driven off by airpatrols. Prien.*

Two days later Kretschmer was poking *U-99*'s nose through a thick fog searching for the convoy. It was an agonising day. He knew that Prien's navigator was second only to Petersen. If he relied on their combined position reports, the convoy should be on top of him – and to the conning-tower crew of *U-99*, who could barely see her foredeck in the thick, swirling fog, there might emerge at any moment a great steel hulk like some black monster to crush their frail little craft and send them to the bottom. The strain was too great to stand for long. Kretschmer dived to below periscope depth and told Kassel to sweep a full circle on the hydrophones. Their navigation had been good; almost too good. Hydrophone effect came from a wide arc to port. Kretschmer steered to intercept, and from the estimated range shouted by Kassel, decided to surface before getting too near. When they broke surface, the first thing they saw was a U-boat slowly following the convoy with her conning-tower watch gazing curiously at this new ally from below. It crossed their minds that it would have been unfortunate if, in all the vast lonely expanse of the Atlantic, a small 500-ton submarine had chosen to surface beneath a brother and topple her over. It was *U-47*, and following an exchange of signals, Kretschmer told Prien that Schepke had sailed just after him and might be around somewhere. As they chatted away by semaphore at close visibility distance, both boats followed in the wake of the still invisible convoy.

Suddenly the fog lifted and the two U-boats burst from behind the thick screen to find ships scattered ahead of them. Little more than three miles away were two destroyers, and one, with sharper lookouts than the other, began turning immediately in their direction. The two boats dived, Prien heading to the north and Kretschmer, deciding to get closer to the convoy, steered towards the approaching hunters. They heard the throbbing propellers pass overhead, then came the depth-charges, some distance away. More followed, and from their general direction they estimated that Prien was the target.

They stayed underwater the rest of the day because fog hampered surface operations. From Headquarters came a signal informing all U-boats in the area that coastal aircraft were being sent out to bomb the convoy. Nothing happened when they surfaced that night, but the fog became thicker and the convoy vanished. The next day they dived and stayed down to get hydrophone bearings. Catching the convoy again after surfacing at night, they saw a sight which caused some jealousy. Six Focke-Wulf bombers had attacked just before dusk, leaving three ships blazing and sinking behind the convoy. *U-99* passed the wrecks, but there was no sign of the main target.

Soon they sighted a single ship, ploughing westwards. Since evening the sea had become steadily rougher, and now great waves were tossing them about and reducing their speed to a maximum of ten knots. Kretschmer closed the steamer to within half a mile for his first shot, but the weather was too bad and the torpedo missed. It was no use firing again in such a sea, so he decided to steer a parallel course and wait until morning before making a second attempt. As he was altering course, another U-boat ahead of the ship fired tracer bullets, and the ship stopped. Kretschmer sheered off, as it was no longer his quarry, and later found his prize had been 'stolen' by Prien, who had successfully escaped the destroyer and had been following Kretschmer's propeller noises, thinking they came from the convoy.

In Lorient, Dönitz was growing impatient with his North Atlantic team, which, despite the presence of three 'aces', had failed so far to make a concerted attack. He ordered them to take up an interception 'stripe' across what his staff considered to be the probable course of the convoy. On this 'stripe' were *U-100* (Schepke), *U-47* (Prien), *U-99* (Kretschmer), *U-95* (Schreiber). They covered an area of twenty-five miles near to Iceland and began steaming eastwards in the hope of meeting the enemy. But while the three 'aces' went off, *U-95* misinterpreted orders and remained where she was, waiting for the convoy to arrive. As they moved off, Schepke, Prien and Kretschmer exchanged semaphore signals – somewhat frivolous ones – and Kretschmer remarked to Petersen that they could steam for weeks on other trips and never sight another U-boat, but on this one they kept tripping over Prien wherever they went.

On the conning-tower, Midshipman König gazed at the other U-boats, enthralled at a sight he had dreamed about but never imagined to be so frightening that it would be beautiful. The tiny, insignificant-looking submarines were being hurled high into the air by the mountainous swell, and then sent skidding down into the pits between waves, where they would be covered by raging seas before emerging high on the crest of another wave, where they hesitated for a brief second while the water drained off them before plunging downwards again. Often they just drove through the waves, which broke over them in foaming torrents.

Having obviously lost or mislaid the convoy, they broke off the 'stripe', Kretschmer heading towards the northern Hebrides. Prien headed eastwards a bit longer, and to his surprise nearly ran head-on into another convoy heading westwards from the North Minches. He signalled:

Enemy in sight on north-westerly course speed eight knots.

It was then that they all witnessed that strange phenomenon of the sea known as St Elmo's Light. As the sea pounded over the boat and the bridge, the hull and the crew on watch glowed as though covered in luminous paint. On the bridge Petersen flamed like a beacon. They were quiet after this, for mariners the world over say that the ship that glows in this electric effect is doomed to sink.

At 1 a.m. on March 7th, Kretschmer reached the reported convoy – a large formation with such a wide frontage that it took him more than an hour's steaming at full speed to cross the bows and fall back on the starboard side-the dark side. The slow merchant ships heaved and rolled ponderously in the heavy sea; and on the starboard beam Kretschmer sighted two destroyers quite close and another on the bow; an indication of a strong escort. Slowly, patiently, on an inward course, he dropped between the two beam destroyers and ran in alongside the convoy's starboard column, where a large tanker emerged from the shadows. They closed on a firing course, and soon saw it was not a tanker, as first thought, but an odd-shaped vessel that could be only a whale factory-ship. The torpedo hit amidships, and at once Kassel intercepted a signal saying that the *Terje Viken* had been torpedoed in the boiler-room and requested assistance. A quick check showed that this ship of more than 20,000 tons was the largest of its kind in the world. The next ship ahead was a tanker, and Kretschmer crept up alongside it to fire from a range of 500 yards. The torpedo hit in the stern, and she stopped.

With two ships stopped only a few hundred yards from each other and from him, Kretschmer decided to sink the second with his gun. It was an astonishing decision, and not perhaps a wise one. Every few seconds *U-99* rose on the crest of a wave, and the gun's crew could see the target clearly for just sufficient time to get off a couple of rounds. They sank back into the sea and visibility was blocked by the waves. Through his glasses Kretschmer could see the fall of shots and, to his anger, the shells seemed to be hitting nothing but the tops of waves. It was, to him, plain bad gunnery, and he was all the more furious because while he was hanging around these two ships the convoy was drawing ahead into the darkness. The target soon began replying with her stern gun and at the same time signalled for help, giving her name as the *Athelbeach*. Kretschmer closed and fired a second torpedo. It hit near the stern again and at once she toppled over and sank.

As dawn came up, Kretschmer returned to see what had happened to the *Terje Viken*. They intercepted a signal from Prien at 7.25 a.m. giving the convoy's position and new course before he went off the air. As *U-99* steamed back on her search, the presence of more U-boats was startlingly apparent. The stopped, burning and sinking wrecks of other ships wallowed despairingly every few hundred yards. They reached the position of the whaler but there was no sign of her. Two destroyers were cruising around slowly, picking up survivors, so Kretschmer withdrew discreetly. Just then Kassel intercepted another signal, this time from *U-70*, commanded by Lieutenant-Commander Matz, reporting that heavy seas had damaged his conning-tower, but that he intended expending his torpedoes before returning to base for repairs. They sighted him, racing across their bows and heading after the convoy. As they waved to each other, two corvettes came out of a rain-squall and bore down on the U-boats. Matz crash-dived on his course while Kretschmer turned and dived under the wreckage. It was a bright morning with a liberal sprinkling of rain-squalls, and it would have been hopeless to try to get away on the surface from such close range. In *U-99* they heard the first pattern of depth-charges reverberating through the water from a close distance and knew that Matz was under attack. Their own boat rocked and pitched under the impact of charges well-aimed and too close to be ignored. Ear-drums were split by the sharp crack of the explosions and the lights went out. Emergency lighting was switched on, and Kretschmer ordered every motor to be cut except the one electric engine needed for power.

They crept at 200 feet, still heading beneath the wreckage on the surface. It was still and quiet down there until the second pattern sent them flying in all directions as *U-99* heeled over from side to side like a living being and her rivets and joints grated ominously under the strain of sudden pressure caused by the blast. Knebel-Döberitz staggered along the length of the hull inspecting plates and, to their relief, reported no leaks. Unconsciously, Kretschmer was heading on a course that was to help him escape. Asdic sets were liable to become confused if there were any obstacles in the path of the beam and the corvette operator became confused by the turbulence caused by the depth-charges and the wreckage.

Throughout the attack, König slept soundly in his bunk. They counted more than a hundred charges before Kassel reported the propeller noises growing fainter, but they heard both corvettes attacking Matz.[1]

At noon, Kretschmer considered he had travelled far enough from the heaving battlefield and surfaced to take a look around. Shortly afterwards they intercepted a signal from Lieutenant-Commander Eckermann, commander of a new type of submarine, *U-A*, reporting to Lorient that he had been badly damaged and was returning to base. The 'pack' was being thinned out by a stubborn defence, but Kretschmer was still on his own operating independently. Throughout the night Prien, as shadower, had been sending out regular reports on the convoy's position, course and speed, and Kassel maintained a listening watch at his set, trying to pick it up now. They heard nothing and Kretschmer interpreted this to mean that *U-47* had been forced to dive and could no longer shadow their quarry. He wondered if he should perhaps replace Prien as shadower, but all afternoon avoided making a decision in the hope that some other U-boat would take over first. To Kretschmer, shadowing was a tedious task that ruled out his favourite method of attack. At intervals Dönitz, by now concerned about Prien's safety, kept transmitting: '*U-47* report position, conditions and successes…*U-47* report position.' The only reply was silence.

After dusk, Kretschmer tried to regain contact with the convoy and report its position. He succeeded at midnight and intercepted another signal from Lorient calling on Prien to report his position. U-boats could receive wireless signals while submerged at periscope depth on a special long-wave band, so Kretschmer thought it likely that Prien was either still submerged and too deep to receive, or his wireless had been damaged. Meanwhile, other 'wolves' in the pack, forced to retreat from this convoy by the powerful defence of the destroyer-corvette escort, made off to the northward and ran into another convoy, and the third battle of the patrol developed.

At dusk on the 14th, Kretschmer received a strange signal from Lorient telling him that a message had been intercepted from the *Terje Viken* to the Admiralty saying she had attempted to return to England but was sinking fast. She gave her position and asked for help urgently. He raced off on the surface to this position, determined to finish off the great ship, which by rights should already be at the bottom. He arrived there shortly after midnight: just too late. The last act of the *Terje Viken* was being played out to a gallery of two destroyers and a corvette which were picking up more survivors who had stayed aboard to the end. As the destroyer spotted Kretschmer and turned to head him off at full speed, *U-99* dived deep, and they heard the destroyer pass astern. After a decent interval, Kretschmer surfaced again and headed northwards on the surface, using the respite to reload his bow tubes. It was a lovely, quiet night after the storm of the last few days. The breeze was slight and cooling, and *U-99* pitched lightly in a merry swell that played down their sides with a quiet swish of water. Kretschmer smoked one cigar after another, and the word passed round that no targets were in sight.

Smoking below deck was forbidden, so the crew took turns to come on deck for a cigarette. Bergman vanished into the diesel engine-room and Kassel mischievously threw open the door in time to see his friend take a long pull at a cigarette by the air-vents. Bergman hastily stamped out the cigarette and turned to see who had disturbed him. When he saw Kassel he growled furiously, while the radio man smiled innocently and closed the door again.

For the next six days they patrolled their allotted area without sighting even a lone ship, but on March 15th detected smoke-trails at an estimated distance of thirty-five miles. As they reached the area, they saw an American destroyer[2] clearly silhouetted on the horizon heading for them. Kretschmer dived to periscope depth and they watched the destroyer come close to their earlier position, prowl around for a few minutes and then take off back to the convoy. But when Kretschmer surfaced, the smoke-trails had gone and the destroyer was travelling too fast to be followed.

That evening *U-99* received a signal from *U-110*, commanded by Lieutenant-Commander Lemp, sinker of the *Athenia*. He reported sighting a convoy between Iceland and the 61st parallel. Petersen worked out an interception course and they raced for the new sighting position at full speed. Further to the west, Schepke in *U-100* also received the report and followed suit. There was still no word from Prien and it was presumed he had been lost.

By early morning on the 16th, Kretschmer was in the convoy's estimated position, but with nothing in sight. He dived and heard faint propeller noises on the hydrophones bearing to southwards. They surfaced, but two hours later ran into fog and dived again to get more hydrophone bearings. Kassel nearly leapt from his seat in alarm as a loud jumbled noise crackled through his headphones. 'There are propeller noises all around us, sir,' he shouted. Despite the risk of collision, Kretschmer decided to surface. They came up into a thinning fog which had cleared enough for them to see they were inside the escort screen on the starboard side of the convoy with two destroyers to port and one coming towards them from ahead. Kretschmer dived, heading underneath the convoy itself and then slowed down to drop back gradually until he could surface well astern in safety. When they came up again the fog had lifted completely, and they sighted four trawlers ploughing their way northwards from the convoy, presumably to keep a rendezvous with another.

Although Lemp was the official shadower, Kretschmer stayed astern, reasoning that it was as good a position as any to spend the daylight hours. He would work up to the convoy at dusk. Throughout the afternoon he had to dive at intervals to avoid detection by a Sunderland aircraft flying round the convoy in wide sweeps. But he was by now a good five miles behind the stern escorts and hidden in a light mist. At one time he was mystified by the appearance behind him of a curious-looking ship that seemed to be an old-time lugger. Rightly, he diagnosed this as a rescue ship attached to the convoy to pick up survivors. They heard the sharp explosions of depth-charges on the convoy's starboard side, and a rapid check of U-boats in the vicinity showed it was Schepke who had been trying to work his way up to the bow for a dusk attack with a fan of torpedoes. By early evening, *U-99* was working up on the port side of the convoy, keeping in touch at masthead visibility. The weather looked as though it had cleared for the night, so Kretschmer left his officer-of-the-watch in charge while he went down to rest with his 'guest' for the trip, a Lieutenant-Commander Hesselbarth, who was to command his own ship when they returned.

Shortly after 3 p.m. he returned to the bridge and, to his anger and amazement, the watch had lost contact with the convoy. He altered course to bring it back in sight but they saw nothing. The convoy had altered course to starboard unnoticed by the officer-of-the-watch. Eventually, they had to dive to use the hydrophones and managed to pick up propeller noises very faint to the south. Kretschmer surfaced and made off on the bearing at full speed, making contact again shortly after dark. The convoy had altered course round Lousy Bank at the time his officer-of-the-watch had lost it. Kretschmer wasted no time. He had been on patrol for a month, taking part in three convoy battles and fuel was running low. He raced in between the two escorts on the port beam and attacked a large tanker in the middle of the outside port column. The range was just under a mile, and the torpedo hit just before the midships mast. There was a huge sheet of flame as high-octane petrol exploded and burned internally. Lying between the tanker and the outside destroyer escort, *U-99* was illuminated starkly in the white glare of the flames.

Surprised and not too happy at being exposed so unexpectedly and so nakedly, Kretschmer dived and made his way past the escort again into the protective blackness, well beyond the escort screen. He worked his way round to the stern on the surface and, passing the burning tanker wallowing and hissing in the water, crept between the stern escorts and entered the convoy inside the centre lane of ships. He was only a few yards from ships on either side of him as he slipped past them looking for a suitable target. He saw another large tanker two columns away and manoeuvred through gaps in the lines of merchant ships until he was running alongside his target. He fired one torpedo, and *U-99* rocked in the blast as the tanker erupted and he was revealed again in the glare of the blaze to every merchant ship around him.

He felt as if he was sun-bathing on a crowded beach without any clothes on. The flames gave way to a huge cloud of smoke which fell slowly like fog on the sea. Kretschmer steered into the middle of it and crossed into another lane.

Meanwhile, the escorts were firing starshell and snowflakes out to sea on either side, making it difficult for U-boats who wanted to fire fans outside the escort screen. For nearly fifteen minutes, Kretschmer travelled along with the convoy as though part of it before he spotted a third tanker. He conned *U-99* alongside it and scored another hit with one torpedo. This tanker stopped and black smoke poured from beneath its decks, while angry red flames licked its decks. He repeated his previous performance, seeking shelter in the smoke-clouds and then emerging in another lane to travel along as part of the convoy. By now depth-charges were being dropped several miles astern and on the starboard side. He saw two small escort vessels hovering round his three sinking tankers picking up survivors. Moving up to the front ships of the lanes, he saw two large freighters. He fired one torpedo at each and scored direct hits amidships on both almost simultaneously. The smaller one sank immediately, but the larger only settled slightly down into the water. He stopped alongside it and fired another torpedo while other ships were still passing by. At little more than 200 yards, this shot missed – another torpedo failure. The third torpedo at this target hit astern and she subsided below the surface on an even keel.

By this time the convoy had drawn ahead and Kretschmer put on speed to catch up again. Meanwhile, Kassel had been intercepting distress signals and noting the names of each ship. The first tanker had been the *Ferm*, the second *Bedouin* (both Norwegian) and the third a British tanker, *Franche Comte*. The small freighter was the *Venetia* and the larger one the *J B White*. *U-99* got into the convoy from astern again, and it seemed to Kretschmer as he smiled grimly to himself that he had thinned it out a little. The distances between the ships had grown larger. They sighted another tanker and, in confident mood, *U-99* went alongside the target and turned outwards for a shot from the stern tubes. The hit had extraordinary results. The ship broke in two, sagging inwards, but somehow she turned towards *U-99* and came at them in an attempt to ram. They had no torpedoes left and there was nothing to do but get away. Kassel reported this ship's wireless as giving her name as the *Korsham*. As they raced away, they saw the two clinging halves vanish into the sea with tremendous hissing and clouds of steam.

They left the convoy passing between two escorts firing starshell and vanished into the darkness, heading for home. Behind lay the wreckage-strewn battlefield of the fourth attack of the patrol, but they needed rest badly, having been at action stations on this last attack for nearly forty-eight hours.

It was quiet, the convoy had disappeared and Kretschmer decided to set course north of Lousy Bank. He went below to discuss the trip with the 'guest', Hesselbarth. It was exactly 3 a.m. when Petersen sent for coffee and sandwiches and wrote in the War Diary: 'Have taken over watch from Captain, who has gone below'. In the control-room, Kretschmer sat with Kassel and Hesselbarth totalling up tonnages, checking names and composing signals of success to Lorient. Above all, he was thinking that just about now at the Chez Elle in Paris…Suddenly, alarm-bells rang with a startling clang throughout the relaxed U-boat.

Notes
1 The corvettes were HMS *Camellia* and *Arbutus*, who continued the attack all day until one of their last patterns tore *U-70* in half. Matz was saved.
2 One of the fifty old US Navy destroyers given to Britain in exchange for a lease to harbour facilities in Bermuda.

Twelve
Trapped

For three days the convoy escort group under the command of Commander Donald Macintyre[1] in the destroyer *Walker* had been aware they were being shadowed. It was Macintyre's first trip as captain of *Walker* and senior officer of the escort. The days of escort group teams, efficiently worked up during weeks of exercises before taking over convoy duty, had yet to come. At present the urgent need of any sort of escort made these groups a loosely-knit bunch of ill-assorted ships relying more on the decisions of individual commanders than on any practised plan to defend their convoys. Commander Macintyre hardly knew his way round *Walker*'s bridge as the main attack developed, after dusk on the 16th, when a tanker burst into flame. The determined but ill-equipped escorts fought back desperately in an effort to tear the U-boats from the blackness of the Atlantic night – turning, twisting and firing starshell and snowflake rockets to illuminate the sea. But the hours dragged by with no trace of the enemy. It soon became apparent that the full weight of the attack was coming from the port side where, unknown to the escorts, were gathered Schepke, Kretschmer, Lemp and Schultz. On *Walker*'s bridge, Macintyre felt the despair of so many commanders in those days who could see convoys being ripped to pieces and had neither the ships nor the equipment to make the attackers reveal their whereabouts. Radar was still a primitive instrument, and the Asdic was of little use against a surfaced U-boat.

With the only other destroyer in the escort, *Vanoc*, in company, they turned to cover a large circle out to port, and on this sweep their luck broke. *Walker* sighted the fluorescent wash of a U-boat retreating on the surface. They gave chase at full speed and dropped a pattern of ten depth-charges over the whirlpool of water left by their quarry. It was Schepke. They lost contact and Macintyre decided to steam southwards to pick up the survivors of the tanker. When this had been done both destroyers set off to carry out another sweep to port of the convoy. Meanwhile Schepke had been damaged by the depth-charging and felt unable to stay below for a long period. He decided to risk inspecting the damage and probably escape on the surface. As *U-100* came up, the radar operator in *Vanoc* reported to the bridge that his screen showed a dark green blob that might be a U-boat. This radar sighting made naval history, for it was the first known time that those primitive and crude sets had led to a night attack on a U-boat. *Vanoc* reported by R/T to *Walker*, and on Macintyre's orders the two destroyers made a tight turn at high speed and raced along the bearing given by *Vanoc*'s radar operator.

After covering little more than a mile they sighted the tiny hull-down silhouette of *U-100* on the surface. A brief order from Macintyre sent Vanoc racing into the attack. The sleek destroyer headed straight for the conning-tower of *U-100*. Cries of alarm sounded thinly in the night air as the U-boat crew saw the knife-edge bows of the destroyer coming at them in a cloud of spray. Some of them jumped overboard and tried desperately to swim out of the way. On *Vanoc*'s bridge they heard the roar of Schepke's voice as he shouted in German: 'Don't panic. They are going to miss us. They will pass astern.' Then came the rending, grinding crash as *Vanoc* struck *U-100* amidships by the conning-tower, throwing the remainder of the crew into the water. Her bows cut both Schepke's legs off at the trunk and jammed him behind the periscope sheath. *Vanoc*, carried forward by her speed, ran right over the stricken U-boat before coming to a halt, straining to release herself with both engines pulling astern. Eventually they came clear with a sharp jolt and *U-100* rose high in the air. Schepke, still alive, was jerked free from the conning-tower and his body thrown into the air to fall helplessly into the sea. His white-covered cap was still worn with all its rakish dash as he thrashed wildly for a few seconds and then sank beneath the heavy swell, to be followed a few moments later by *U-100*. Despite his weaknesses, Schepke had died like an 'ace' – on his bridge.

Vanoc played her searchlight over the scene. Only five swimmers could be seen, and with *Walker* keeping an Asdic sweep around her, she picked up these survivors from a crew of nearly fifty and inspected the damage to her bows. On the bridge of *Walker*, Commander Macintyre waited impatiently for *Vanoc* to report her damage, when suddenly his Asdic operator shouted: 'Echo to starboard, sir.' He gave range and bearing and, to Macintyre's astonishment, it put the target almost directly under the stern of *Vanoc*; a most unlikely position. Macintyre and his officers felt inclined to believe that this echo was caused by the disturbance of the water after the collision or by *Vanoc*'s own wake. But the Asdic operator stubbornly resisted all suggestions that the echo was caused by something other than a U-boat. It was too firm too strong to be anything else. Still doubting, but not willing to risk missing a chance of attack, Macintyre increased speed and went into attack, while *Vanoc* drew out of the way. Could there be two U-boats where there had been only one a few seconds before?

As Petersen fell down through the conning-tower hatch, he reported a destroyer less than half a mile to starboard. 'Well, why the devil have you dived?' Kretschmer asked. 'Are you sure we could not have got away on the surface?'

Petersen looked worried. 'I don't think so, sir. They must have seen us.'

Kretschmer did not bother to reply. Kassel reported propeller noises approaching and they dived to 300 feet. As they waited for the attack to develop, Kretschmer extracted the story of what had happened from Petersen. The starboard forward lookout – a petty officer – had been dreaming and not properly alert. He had failed to spot the destroyer and report it to Petersen, who had sighted it by chance when they were so close he had to look up at camouflaged cream-and-green sides gleaming in the moonlight. Astonished at being so close, his first thought had been to dive. Despite the suddenness with which events had happened, Kretschmer still had doubts if Petersen had been wise, and told him so forcibly. All this time Kassel was reporting propeller noises, and now estimated there were two destroyers near them. He shouted that one was heading their way, and the first seven depth-charges came with unexpected suddenness.

There was a long series of cracks, and *U-99* nearly rolled right over in a circle. They were the closest depth-charges Kretschmer had experienced, and an unpleasant, ominous roaring filled his ears as blast-waves rocked against the boat, sending lights out and shattering every movable object. The glass dials of the instruments were smashed, the chronometers broken and many of the gauges had gone haywire, among them the depth-gauge. They had no way now of knowing how deep they were.

It was almost certain that the depth-charges were tossing them about wildly, and they might be deeper than they thought. The patterns continued to come down, all well aimed, and a pipe split, sending a jet of water into the crew's compartment forward of the control-room. The boat was listing badly, and oil began pouring into the control-room from a leak in the after fuel-tanks. Within a few minutes they were wading ankle deep in oil and sea-water and Kretschmer decided they would have to blow themselves to the surface. The second depth-gauge in the forward torpedo compartment seemed to be in order; unbelievably, they were at 600 feet, 100 feet below the depth of no return for a submarine. By rights the pressure outside would snap their hull into shreds at any moment. The engineer reported that they were getting no thrust from the propellers and were making no speed – a danger because, without speed, a U-boat must sink. Kretschmer ordered compressed air to be blown into the ballast tanks. 'Popp', the control-room Petty Officer, tugged at the air valve, but it would not budge. Petersen stood by the depth-gauge calling out depths as they plunged downwards...six fifty feet...seven hundred feet...There was a sharp crack from the stern and a slight leak appeared in the starboard side of the after-torpedo-room. This was the beginning of the end. Their only hope lay in the valve that 'Popp' could not move.

In U-boat Command Headquarters at Lorient, the radio-room was silent save for the monotonous hum of the electric generators and the regular chimes of a clock announcing each quarter of an hour. On a chart of the North Atlantic stood out the red flag of a missing U-boat, *U-47*. But, confidently, they waited for the success reports of the other 'aces' – Schepke and Kretschmer.

'Popp', helped by a sailor, tugged frantically at the air valve. It gave slightly and, cautiously, he pulled it open to avoid wasting the air. 'Seven hundred and twenty feet,' sang out Petersen, and Kretschmer jumped over to slap 'Popp' hard on the back and shout: 'Open it wide and fast.' The air rushed into the ballast tanks and for a moment the boat shuddered, then it rolled and Petersen sang out excitedly: 'Seven hundred...six seventy-five...six fifty... we are going up.' At 200 feet Kretschmer ordered the air to be turned off in an attempt to keep *U-99* at that depth, but the engines had not been repaired and there was a suspicion that the propellers were damaged. Without speed there was no way of controlling the boat, which continued its upward climb and rushed to the surface, where it arrived with such force that its nose hung out of the water before dropping back. Kretschmer rushed to the conning-tower, while the assistant radio operator, Stohrer, tapped out their first message to Lorient. It said 'Bombs...bombs'.

At Lorient, the wireless-room came to life. Alarm buzzers sounded and runners took the message to several staff officers, including the Commander-in-Chief. They came running to the wireless-room to listen. For days they had been worrying about the first of the 'aces' to get into trouble. Now here was a second. What was happening out there in the Atlantic?

The senior staff officer on duty ordered signals to be sent to the boats which had not reported during the night.

'All submarines accompanying *U-110* (convoy shadower) report position, conditions and success immediately.'

They waited, but there was no reply.

'*U-99* and *U-100* report position at once.'

Again neither ship replied. In the control-room of *U-99* the First Lieutenant grabbed the signal Kassel was dictating and read: 'Two destroyers – depth-charges – 53,000 tons – capture Kretschmer.'

It was the curt signal of a man who was going to fight his boat to the last. But Knebel-Döberitz inserted the word 'sunk', and when the full text was picked up by a nearby U-boat, *U-37*, and transmitted to Lorient, the staff there interpreted it as meaning that he had sunk two destroyers as well as 53,000 tons of shipping. Dönitz sensed the drama that was being played out on the high seas; that some of his top commanders were fighting for their lives. But he did not know how the fight was going or that his 'aces' were caught in a deadly trap.

When Kretschmer reached the conning-tower, *U-99* was lying on her side to starboard and a great patch of oil was spreading over the water around her. One destroyer was lying dead ahead beam-on and stopped. Kretschmer cursed at not having a torpedo. He was sure he could have hit, despite his own crippled position. Desperately, the engineer and his men strove to get the diesel motors working, in the hope they could get some steering way, but the propellers had been blown off or damaged by the explosions. They simply wallowed in the light swell.

The crew of the slow-moving, damaged *Vanoc* were startled to see a second U-boat shoot to the surface so close under their stern. A quick report to *Walker* brought the curt reply: 'Well, get out of the way.' *Vanoc* increased speed, turned and the three ships set at the corner of a triangle gazed at each other speculatively for a few seconds as their commanders adjusted themselves to this swift turn of events. While Kretschmer raged impotently at having no speed to get away and no torpedoes to attack, Commander Macintyre remembered that, with his only other destroyer damaged due to ramming one U-boat, he could not afford to damage himself. The convoy had to be protected for another four days at least. He was bound also by an Admiralty order that if it was possible, escort commanders should make every attempt to capture U-boats intact.

He decided to open fire with his main and small armament in an attempt to scare the U-boat crew into abandoning their ship. The two destroyers circled the target warily, keeping *U-99* under a vicious cross-fire from four-inch turrets, machine-guns and pom-poms. Showers of tracer bullets and shell splinters splattered on the side of *U-99*'s hull and conning-tower, but as she was listing away from the fire, the crew had plenty of protection on the other side of the boat. Kretschmer thought seriously for a moment of having his own gun manned and making a duel of it, in the hope of delaying the final attack until another U-boat came to his rescue. But he realised that any man who appeared above the deck level of the listing *U-99* would be killed before he could get to the gun. Miraculously, the shells of the large guns were missing widely, making big water-spouts all around them. He ordered all his crew out on to the deck on the starboard side in readiness to abandon ship and then, unable to do anything about their predicament, sat under the protection of the conning-tower and, to his men's amazement, proceeded to light a cigar.

It seemed that the two destroyers were being over-cautious. They drew off, obviously expecting to be torpedoed at any moment. With no teeth to bite back, Kretschmer thought it likely that a boarding party would be sent over to try to capture the U-boat. He ordered scuttling charges to be set, although the boat was quite noticeably sinking, if only slowly, but the scuttling men reported that the door to the compartment where the charges were kept was jammed.

There was nothing for it but to open all the hatches. When this had been done, Kretschmer made a short speech to his crew hanging on to the guard-rails. He told them how sorry he was he would not be able to take them home this trip, and warned them that they might have a short spell in the water before being taken prisoner. He then sent them below to put on the warmest clothes they could find and return to deck to wait for his order to abandon ship. He remembered his own experience in 1936, when he had been left in the Baltic by a mischievous commander. That had been his last experience of being alone in the sea. The crew returned wearing their lifebelts, and his own servant appeared carrying his peaked uniform cap, which he put on at the regulation angle. The First Lieutenant stayed below to see that all secret papers were destroyed, and the chief engineer checked if there was any more air left in the ballast tanks.

Suddenly, the stern of the boat sank with a jolt below the level of the water and the sea rushed in through the open galley hatch, and even through the conning-tower hatch itself. Kretschmer had just time to haul his First Lieutenant and engineer up to the conning-tower through the inrushing water. But the ballast tanks had been blown by the engineer and the stern rose again. Half the ship's company had been standing on the after-deck and had now been washed overboard. The tortured, straining *U-99* began drifting sideways away from the two waiting destroyers, leaving the men in the water behind. Kretschmer told Petersen to sling the portable battery flashlamp over his shoulder so that, if left alone in the water, they could flash their whereabouts to the destroyers. He also ordered him to call up the nearest destroyer with his lamp, and dictated a signal, letter by letter, very slowly in English: 'From Captain to Captain…Please pick up my men drifting towards you in the water stop I am sinking.'

The destroyer – it was *Walker* – read the message as 'I am sinking' and flashed an acknowledgement before approaching the men in the water with her searchlight playing on the swimmers. Kretschmer and the remainder of his crew watched while the men were hauled aboard with scramble nets. As *Walker* drew close to *U-99* on the starboard beam, Kretschmer realised at once that the destroyer could drift down on top of him and send a boarding party leaping across on to his decks. He decided then that no matter what chance there might be of avoiding capture, no British sailor would ever step aboard *U-99*. He discussed the position with Knebel-Döberitz and Schröder, the engineer, who immediately offered to go down and flood the ballast tanks.

The matter became urgent as they saw the *Walker* preparing to lower a boat. The engineer vanished below into the waterfilled control-room and was never seen again. He must have operated the ballast controls, letting the air out as water rushed in with a final hiss. Kretschmer shouted to the engineer to jump up to the conning-tower, but there was no reply. The stern went down, the nose came up and the U-boat that had menaced Allied shipping so successfully for nearly a year slid stern first to her grave in the waters she had prowled for so long. Kretschmer and his men were washed off the conning-tower and decks. There was no whirlpool or backwash to drag them down. They formed a line in the water and held hands like a human chain to make sure no one was lost. *Walker* came close and they swam the short distance to safety, where Kretschmer grabbed the corner of a scramble net hanging down the destroyer's side and counted his men going up.

Apart from the engineer who had gone down with *U-99*, two of the crew were missing. One had lost his lifebelt and could not swim, and another had received concussion during the depth-charging and, when they turned to help him up the nets, he went under and failed to reappear. When his officers and crew had gone up, Kretschmer tried to clamber up himself, but his sea-boots were so full of water they held him back. He could not lift his legs. Thinking all the survivors were on board, *Walker* was picking up speed and dragging him through the water at a rate that would force him to let go. Kretschmer thought this was to be his end, when his boatswain glanced over the side and shouted: 'There's the Captain', and came down to help him. When he was pulled on the destroyer's deck, weak after hours of action and tension, a large Colt .45 pistol was poked into his face by a cheerful, grinning British petty officer. He had imagined all sorts of receptions if he was ever captured, but hardly this. He began laughing, but soon stopped when the petty officer glanced covetously at his binoculars. Kretschmer thought suddenly that the glasses he valued so much should not fall into the hands of an enemy sailor and tried to sling them overboard. But he was too late. Another sailor grabbed them from him as he slipped the lanyard over his head.[2]

He was escorted aft to the Captain's day cabin, where he and his officers were stripped of their wet clothes and given large tots of rum. Lieutenant Osborne, *Walker*'s Engineer Officer, appeared with a reefer uniform, which he handed to Kretschmer. 'I think these should fit,' he said. Eventually, the *U-99* officers were taken away to the wardroom and Kretschmer was left alone in the day cabin with an armed sentry outside. He sank into an armchair and all the tension of a month of action drained away as waves of sleep poured over him.

This was the first successful night counter-attack made by convoy escorts against U-boats during the war. And it had bagged two 'aces'.

Some hours later he wakened to see a British officer wearing the three stripes of a commander sitting on a desk looking at him. It was Macintyre. As his brain cleared, Kretschmer said with a rueful grin: 'Thank you for picking up my men. That was good of you. I should like to say, however, how much I regret not having had any torpedoes with which to attack you. As it is, my sincere congratulations on your success.' Commander Macintyre took the proffered hand with a non-committal grunt and left the cabin. Alone, Kretschmer's thoughts raced back across the last hours of *U-99*.

Schepke was sunk; he suspected that Prien was dead. He alone of the three young volunteer trainees who had arrived with youthful enthusiasm at the Submarine School at Kiel in 1936, and who had won for themselves the adulation of their countrymen and the respect of their enemies, was alive. It seemed to him then – as it still does today – as though some powerful invisible force guided them to Kiel, schemed their rise to fame and then sent them to the same fatal rendezvous far out in the Atlantic. It was an uneasy thought that left him a little apprehensive of what special fate the same guiding hand had reserved for him. And while he paced up and down the confined space of the cabin, anxious staff officers at Lorient crowded the radio-room as the operator sent out the call across the quiet sea:

U-99 and U-100 report your positions, conditions and successes immediately...Report your positions...report your positions.

That morning, Kretschmer was allowed on deck for exercise. He walked thoughtfully up and down the quarter-deck. On the foredeck, his crew had been allowed to exercise while the mess decks were cleaned out. Macintyre decided to give his prisoners a lesson in how little they had really achieved despite what he rightly considered their bravery. With *Vanoc* still in company, they rejoined the convoy and put on speed to take up their positions ahead. From astern they raced proudly through the columns of the convoy, which, although subjected to the strain of attack for nearly forty-eight hours, was steaming along in perfect formation. Gaps in the columns had been closed and the long lines of ships sailed serenely, as though taking part in some fleet exercise. Macintyre was pleased with his charges as they passed each cheering ship – for the news of their success had gone ahead of them. On the foredeck, the crew of *U-99* looked around in vain for signs of destruction, but that had been left behind. This was another day – one of triumph – and it must have seemed to some of the German captives that it would take much more than the gallantry of a few to stop these ships reaching their destinations.

Once in position, Macintyre handed over the bridge to the officer-of-the-watch and went below to shave, clean up and talk again to Kretschmer. As yet, he was not sure which U-boat he had sunk. He had a suspicion that the five survivors in *Vanoc* and his own captives were deliberately trying to mislead him by giving faked numbers. Kretschmer had given his name and rank willingly enough, but nothing else. And in *Vanoc*, while they had been given Schepke's name by the survivors, the number of the U-boat had changed three times during the course of interrogation. Macintyre was determined to get the correct numbers – essential if the Admiralty were to determine the types. Now he saw Kretschmer gazing fixedly at *Walker*'s shield on the after-superstructure. The Captain who for so long had sailed under the insignia of the Golden Horseshoe had been captured by a destroyer carrying the crest of an Upturned Horseshoe. Macintyre guessed what was running through Kretschmer's mind and said gently: 'You had your horseshoe the wrong way up. The luck was bound to run out.'

In the evening the Merchant Navy officers who had been picked up were given mattresses on the cabin floor while Kretschmer was allowed to keep the captain's, bunk. Before turning in, Lieutenant Osborne came down to see if among them there were any bridge-players. He was lucky. Two survivors and Kretschmer joined him and they played long into the night.

In the wardroom, *U-99*'s officers talked with *Walker*'s off-watch officers and two young Merchant Navy officers, while forward in the Petty Officers' Mess a poignant drama was being played out to an unexpected end. Several of *Walker*'s petty officers and some Merchant Navy survivors sat on the wooden benches down one side facing *U-99* petty officers across the mess table. There was an ominous silence, neither side showing open friendliness or enmity. A steward came in and whispered to a chief petty officer that the U-boat officers were being given every consideration in the wardroom, and the German captain was playing bridge in the day cabin. Taking their cue from the officers, all except one, *Walker*'s crew relaxed and began to show signs of hospitality to their uninvited guests. Rum passed round and experiences were exchanged freely, but this one petty officer sat and glowered at Kassel, who shifted uncomfortably every time he met the hostile eyes. Suddenly the petty officer shouted: 'You bastards! My brother is dead.' There was another silence, and someone explained that his brother had been serving on a merchant ship that had been torpedoed. The rum was passed round again, and after further friendly gossip they settled down to sleep. The uncompromising petty officer relented enough to look hard at Kassel and say: 'Well, I suppose it might have been you. You were just lucky to be picked up.'

Lying on the hard bench with an old coat as a pillow, Kassel found he could not sleep. He turned from side to side and fidgeted until finally he fell into a light doze. Then he felt someone moving his head, and he opened his eyes to see the hostile sailor taking the coat from under his head and replacing it with a pillow.

Before sleep came to the wardroom there was a sticky moment when a Royal Naval Reserve officer turned to König and said: 'I was serving on the *Laurentic* when she was sunk. I wish I could find the bastards that did that.

The second salvo of torpedoes hit us as the boats were being lowered. It was an awful mess.' König who had not been with *U-99* on that trip, maintained a discreet silence. Mattresses were soon laid out and they turned in.

Next morning in the wardroom it was found that a souvenir hunter had ripped the submarine insignia from Knebel-Döberitz's jacket, which had been left in front of the electric fire to dry. A quick inquiry by *Walker*'s First Lieutenant disclosed that a Merchant Navy cadet was responsible. His senior officer made him spend the morning sewing the insignia back on to the jacket.

On the mess decks, members of *Walker*'s crew discovered they could swap Spanish war experiences with *U-99* sailors. They found that some of them had been patrolling off the Spanish coast in cruisers at the same time as several of the Germans had been patrolling in *U-35*, Kretschmer's old training submarine.

Kassel was snapped up by *Walker*'s radio operator, who invited him to look over the destroyer's wireless-room. On the way up a ladder they were stopped by an officer.

'Where are you taking this prisoner?'

'To the radio-room, sir. He is the U-boat's wireless operator.'

'Take him down below, you idiot. You ought to know better.'

They returned to the petty officers' mess with Kassel grinning at his opposite number's obvious discomfort.

On the third day they proceeded ahead of the destroyer *Vanoc* for Liverpool to hand over their prisoners. Steaming through the Minches, Macintyre received a signal from the Admiralty asking for positive identification of successes immediately, as the Prime Minister wished to make a statement in the House of Commons that night. He decided to accept the numbers given – *U-100* and *U-99* – and replied to that effect. The result was another signal to *Walker* conveying the congratulations of the Prime Minister and their Lordships. They were to implement this later by awarding Commander Macintyre his first Distinguished Service Order.

On the morning of the 21st *Walker* docked in Liverpool, and on the quayside to greet Macintyre was the Commander-in-Chief, Western Approaches, Sir Percy Noble, with high-ranking members of his staff. When the lines had been passed ashore, Kassel stood on a bench in the mess-decks and made a speech to *Walker*'s crew thanking them for saving their lives and for their hospitality during the past few days. In reply a chief petty officer said: 'We are damn glad we got you, but now we have to apologise for having to hand you over to the Army. They won't treat you so well. They haven't got any sense of humour, chums.'

U-99's crew were lined up on deck amidships while Commander Macintyre was piped ashore. He made his way across to Admiral Sir Percy

Noble and stood there chatting for a moment. An Army station wagon drove down the dock and two soldiers and an officer jumped out and stood by the gangway. At a signal, Kretschmer was escorted along the deck now wearing his own submarine clothes, leather jacket and peaked cap. He strode down the gangway, and there was a silence on the dockside as he stepped ashore. For a moment he looked at Macintyre and the group of officers standing round the Admiral and wondered if he should march across and formally thank the destroyer captain for his treatment. Instead, he gave a slight nod and stepped towards the waiting car with a soldier at each elbow. His watching crew on Walker's deck came smartly to attention and saluted as their commander was driven away.

Notes

1 Later Captain Macintyre, DSO and Bar, commanding officer of the cruiser *Diadem*. He ended the war as the Royal Navy's top-scoring U-boat 'killer' with seven U-boats confirmed to his three commands, *Hesperus*, *Walker* and *Bickerton*.

2 Captain Macintyre claimed these binoculars as his personal 'prize' and used them for the rest of the war. Though they had a few small globules of water in the lens, he said: 'They were far better than ours, and still one of my most treasured acquisitions of the war.'

Thirteen
The Secret Meeting

The march through the streets of Liverpool was an ordeal none of the survivors of *U-99*'s crew would forget. Liverpool was the operational centre of the Battle of the Atlantic. There the convoys gathered, and there the sailors kept wives, sweethearts and girlfriends. News of the *Walker* and *Vanoc* successes had spread round the city, and as the Germans were marched out through the dockyard gates bound for Lime Street station, they were greeted with angry demonstrations by hundreds of women, many of whom might have lost relatives at sea. To them the crew of *U-99* were murderers – the first they had been able to see alive. It was only natural that they should seize the occasion to vent the sorrow, and in some cases the inevitable hate, they had nursed for U-boat crews in general.

The forty-two German sailors sensed the simmering tension, and for a while thought it likely they would end their lives dangling from the lamp-posts of Liverpool. But the crowds were held back behind police cordons lining the route to Lime Street station. The demonstration caused the prisoners to miss the London train, and now they had to be marched back into the streets to Walton Gaol. Here the petty officers were separated from the men and each group was locked in a large communal cell. The officers shared an ordinary cell designed to hold one criminal, while Kretschmer, who had been taken, straight to the prison by car, was already locked in a cell by himself. He had no idea of what Britain did with prisoners-of-war, but as he paced the tiny confines of the cell, he felt that this was to be his home for the rest of the war.

His suspicions were confirmed when night came, and they were given a straw mattress and a single blanket each. Only the imperturbable Midshipman König and his commander slept that night. The rest of the crew lay awake wondering what would become of them.

The Army escort called for them again in the morning. Kretschmer was taken away alone by car and the crew were marched direct to Lime Street station. There were no crowds, and the early risers paid them scant attention as they threaded their way to the station. They caught the train this time and were taken to London and sent to the Number One Cage in Kensington for interrogation. Meanwhile, Kretschmer was locked in the dressing-room hut of the local football ground at Preston, on which an army unit was encamped. Here he was searched again and given his first bath. With clean sheets and a proper bunk at his disposal, he slept for nearly twelve hours. Next day he was shaken awake, given some hot cocoa and driven to the station with two army officers. A special compartment had been reserved for them on the London train. The trip passed quickly. Both the escorting officers had brought flasks of tea and sandwiches, which they shared with their prisoner. They talked of British and European history, and Kretschmer was amused to find he knew more ancient English history than his escorts.

In London he was driven to Kensington for classification, and there met his interrogator – a naval intelligence officer he at once nicknamed 'Bernhardt', because of his uncanny likeness to the Dutch Prince. During the next week every day was spent in interrogation before he was moved to the central transit camp at Cockfosters to await his travel orders to a permanent prison camp.

On April 3rd 'Bernhardt' called for him, and said he was to be ready within half an hour for a drive into London.

Since the capture of Kretschmer and the sinking of *U-99* had been confirmed, Captain Creasy had been playing with the idea that if he saw the 'ace' himself, something might emerge from the talk that would give him a clue as to how Dönitz was planning his offensive campaign. He felt, however, that some embarrassment might be caused politically if he had Kretschmer brought to the Admiralty. The alternative was to see him secretly at his private flat across the park in Buckingham Gate. He waited for the formal political and morale interrogations to end and gave instructions for Kretschmer to be brought into London.

At lunchtime on April 3rd, Creasy drove to his flat and explained to his wife that he had sent for a U-boat commander, now a prisoner, to be brought to the flat that afternoon. He said he intended to interview the commander alone in the hope that he might talk more freely. His wife pleaded with him to let at least one escort remain in the room during the visit, and made it clear she thought it very possible that the young U-boat captain would take advantage of the opportunity to knock her husband over the head and escape through the window. Captain Creasy calmed her fears, and she agreed to stay in the bedroom out of sight during the interview. An hour later they had finished lunch, and Creasy prepared for his visitor.

At that time a brown-and-green camouflaged car was threading its way across Trafalgar Square, through Admiralty Arch and down the Mall. In the back seat, Kretschmer sat silent listening to 'Bernhardt's' rueful description of how a recent alcoholic forty-eight-hour leave had led to strained relations between himself and his fiancée.

The car pulled to a stop outside a block of flats and he was escorted to the first floor, where a servant answered the door and ushered them into the lounge. Captain Creasy stepped forward with outstretched hand to welcome the enemy who had done more to wreck his peace of mind than any other. It was a strangely dignified meeting, with Kretschmer snapping to attention and saluting, as Creasy introduced himself. Then the Captain turned to 'Bernhardt' and said: 'Please join my wife in the next room and wait with her until I call you. I want to talk to Commander Kretschmer alone.'

With a look of surprise 'Bernhardt' left the room and Creasy nodded to Kretschmer to sit down while he poured out two glasses of port. They raised their glasses to drink and Kretschmer was offered a cigar.

'I understand you smoke cigars only. I hope these will do,' said Creasy with a grin. Kretschmer took one suspiciously. He was certain that this was some sort of trap to extract information from him and made up his mind he would say nothing other than give the information required under international law. But under the friendly questioning and sailor-to-sailor approach, he began to feel more at case.

At first Creasy volunteered information. He told the prisoner that the severe depth-charging he had undergone on his first trip into the Atlantic had been delivered by one of the first corvettes ever built and put into service by the Royal Navy. He explained the purpose of the corvette and discussed tactics.

Kretschmer relaxed and argued freely. Creasy explained that, as a destroyer officer, he had always been amazed at the way in which U-boats stayed on the surface in the worst possible weather and even managed to attack. 'How do you people do it?' he asked.

Kretschmer told him of the leather strap and chains for the bridge personnel and of the special hatch gratings that allowed water to drain off the decks without entering the boat itself, Creasy nodded.

'Well, destroyers are bad enough, but I should hate to have to stay on top in some of the weather in which you have had to operate. Our chaps like to stay down in that sort of weather. Incidentally, how did you manage to keep dry?'

For some reason, Kretschmer suspected a trap, and did not tell his host of the 'Mickey Mouse' all-in-one overall suit that kept U-boat crews dry in the worst of storms. Then came another question.

'About Prien; can you tell me if any of his crew were rescued?'

'I'm sorry, sir. I know nothing of what happened to Prien.'

'Well, you must know that we sank him about five days before you were captured. He was depth-charged successfully by the destroyer *Wolverine*. Incidentally, during the last attack the explosion of the charges was followed by a brilliant orange flash which spread across the surface of the water. Can you give me any idea of what might have caused that – something inside the submarine?

'I'm sorry, sir. But I have never heard of such a flash before, and what you tell me of Prien is news to me.'

Kretschmer was on his guard now. He had known of Prien's death but was admitting nothing. Creasy acknowledged his guest's suspicions with a smile.

'Commander, I can assure you of one thing. I know more about your operations than you think. Do you realise I could give you almost as accurate an account of your trips as your War Diary shows.'

Kretschmer gave him a quick look of disbelief. 'I find that hard to credit, sir.'

'All right, let's start with your arrival at Lorient and your decision to use captured British uniforms until your own could be brought down from Kiel.'

Creasy then proceeded to give the prisoner a remarkably accurate trip-by-trip description of his operations. Kretschmer sat back amazed as the full impact of the account struck him, and he thought with a shock of how many Frenchmen in Lorient could be responsible for passing information of such an intimate nature to London. The implications of this intelligence appalled him. How much more did the Admiralty know of the U-boat Arm's operational plans? He was further astonished at Creasy's free use of the personal names of his German opponents. He referred to Prien, Dönitz, Raeder and Schepke as though he had known them all his life. To the best of Kretschmer's knowledge, no one in the U-boat Command knew the names of any of their opponents in the Royal Navy. He decided at once that this was a regrettable omission, for it brought to the war a curious personal note totally lacking on the German side. He was shaken again when Creasy referred to Schepke's end.

'Poor Schepke!' he said. 'We are very sorry about that. It was a horrible death for a bold commander. Please believe me when I say that while we are glad he was sunk, we would have preferred him to have died differently.'

His growing astonishment at this intimate discussion of men with whom he had trained and fought warmed Kretschmer to this aloof, yet friendly Royal Naval officer who, contrary to everything he had been led to expect by German propaganda, was treating him as an honourable enemy worthy of courtesy, even in defeat. Yet the ruthless operational commander was still alive to the dangers of over-friendliness.

Creasy switched the conversation to Dönitz, discussing the personality of the German Admiral and sympathising with his difficulties in having to rely on such tenuous influences to get the production schedule he demanded.

This was the trap. Above all things, Creasy wanted to know more and more about the character of the U-boat chief. Unwittingly, Kretschmer fell into it – if not completely. As the talk around deepened, he suspected that there was something about Dönitz that Creasy wanted to know, and he lapsed into non-committal replies. But Creasy was content. He had not learned all he would have liked, but he felt he knew his opponent better now. In addition, Kretschmer's own character and personality had given Creasy a clue to the type of men that commanded the U-boats; the strength of character and training that the escort groups were having to fight. To Creasy this was of far greater value than any particular detail of a purely technical nature about a U-boat which Kretschmer might let slip.

He changed the subject and produced some photographs of the Norwegian campaign in which he had served as a destroyer officer. They talked around the war at sea for a few minutes and then Creasy heard signs of movement in the next room. He did not know until later that his wife was growing more and more anxious as she waited for the sound of a scuffle that would herald Kretschmer's break for freedom. He smiled to himself and poured out two more drinks. He tried a few more random questions to see if the German could be drawn.

'You were depth-charged on nearly every trip, I think. How was it? Were our attacks good? Did the charges explode anywhere near you?'

Kretschmer, almost wincing at the recollection of some attacks that had nearly blown him to bits, replied diffidently: 'Not really, sir. The noise of the explosions was so terrific we used to think they were close. But as we became more experienced we found that most attacks were well wide of the mark.' And he looked innocently back at Creasy's hard stare.

At four o'clock Creasy ended the interview. He called 'Bernhardt' from the bedroom where he had been given tea by Mrs Creasy and said he would drive with them as far as the Admiralty. He reassured his wife, whose fear for her husband's safety had now been replaced by an intense curiosity to see for herself this 'dastardly villain' from the wilds of the Atlantic, and they left for the return drive to Cockfosters.

As they approached Buckingham Palace, Creasy pointed out the damage nearby caused by recent air raids. Kretschmer was genuinely shocked at the fact that these bombs had so narrowly missed the Palace, and was clearly unhappy that a non-military target should have been so nearly hit. He noticed that people walking along the Mall carried gasmasks, which struck him as curious, for no one in Germany carried such equipment, and only a few had ever seen a gas-mask. Creasy showed him St James's Park through the windows, and explained that he liked to walk to the Admiralty each morning at this time of the year because the flowers and the trees gave the first sign of approaching spring. The car stopped outside the Admiralty and Creasy got out.

Kretschmer thanked him for his hospitality and they shook hands before the car drove off.

As they threaded their way through the traffic towards North London, 'Bernhardt' said: 'You are the only prisoner I have ever known or heard about that has been given this sort of treatment. Captain Creasy must have thought you pretty important. Perhaps there is still some luck left in that horseshoe of yours.'

Kretschmer smiled faintly. 'Perhaps. We shall know soon enough when the invasion begins…'

Fourteen
War Behind Bars

At Cockfosters, a converted mansion set in its own grounds, officer-prisoners lived in the main building separated from other ranks housed in the outbuildings. Kretschmer was allotted a small bedroom on the first floor equipped with a single bed, a cupboard and table. His clothes were taken away, and in their place he was given a collarless khaki shirt and a pair of shorts, a toothbrush, a razor and a gas-mask. He soon made himself a collar from the shirt tails.

During the first week the Army officers assigned to guard duties decided to play football with some of their men on a nearby field. The officers' team was three players short, so Kretschmer and two other German officers were invited to take part. It was his first real exercise since landing, at Liverpool, and he entered into the spirit of the game a little too enthusiastically. One British sergeant he barged a bit too hard fell over and glared at him angrily. For the rest of the game he played more cautiously, remembering he was a prisoner and the opposing eleven were his guards.

Some days later he found that his crew, living in the converted stables, were going through a rough time. Their bedclothes were dirty and their food poor. When they complained they were told it did not matter, as they were all going to be shot any day. He guessed that if these allegations were true they were part of a campaign aimed at forcing from the men information concerning Lorient and U-boat tactics in general. He sent a message across telling them that the British were bluffing and on no account were they to reveal more than their name, rank and unit.

One morning, after two weeks in captivity, the naval interrogation officer, 'Bernhardt', invited him to tea in the guards' mess, and when they had taken their seats in a corner handed him a slip of paper sent to Cockfosters by the Admiralty. It informed Kretschmer that he had been promoted to *Korvettenkapitän* as from March 1st. The announcement of Kretschmer's promotion – which also promoted Prien posthumously to the same rank –

had been made by the German radio. It was monitored by the Admiralty, who had taken the trouble to inform Kretschmer officially. During the tea, he met several other British officers, and as a result received several invitations to take wine with them before dinner on more or less alternate days.

During the third week, he and his crew were taken back to the No. 1 Cage in Kensington Gardens for further questioning. This was mainly of a political nature, designed to extract what each one of them thought of the war. Kretschmer replied to the effect that he was a U-boat officer not conversant with high strategy, but in his opinion Germany should have marched eastwards. However, as the West had become the front, it was just as inevitable that Germany would win. The war in Greece had already begun, and his interrogators were interested in his estimate of how the German-Italian forces could hope to win. They implied that the involvement of German troops marked the end of Germany.

'We will win in six weeks,' he said bluntly. In fact, the Greek war ended seven weeks after German troops marched in.

He was asked if he or any of his crew were members of the Nazi Party, to which he said no. He did not expect to be believed, but, to his surprise, the interrogators said they knew that already. They astonished him further by reciting to him a list of his activities since he had left school at the age of sixteen. He was never able to find out how this detailed intelligence had been obtained, and again doubted if Germany knew much about any British commanders. After three days at the cage he was told to pack up his belongings in readiness for transfer to a permanent PoW camp. The following day the crew, with Warrant Officer Petersen in charge, were sent to a camp for 'other ranks' at Bury, near Manchester. Forty-eight hours later Kretschmer and his officers, including their 'guest' – Hesselbarth – were taken to Euston station to be escorted to the north of England. While waiting for their train, Kretschmer's cardboard box in which his gas-mask and laundry were packed, dropped and burst open, scattering his meagre possessions over the platform. The Army Transport Officer escorting him stooped down, picked everything up and re-tied the string round the box. Kretschmer was both astonished and pleased at a courtesy which a prisoner could hardly expect from a guard. The train took them to Lake Windermere, where they were herded into a truck and taken to a large country mansion on a mountain slope overlooking the lake. They had arrived at Grizedale Hall, officially known as PoW Camp No.1. Here Kretschmer became the Senior German Officer commanding 100 naval and Luftwaffe prisoners for the next year.

Meanwhile, Kretschmer had been keeping Admiral Dönitz in touch with developments. At the outbreak of war, Dönitz had issued a private code to be used by U-boat officers in the event of capture. He had assumed they would be allowed to write to their next-of-kin, and had arranged that all relatives should forward letters from captured officers to his headquarters. Kretschmer wrote several times to his mother, and each letter was sent on to Dönitz for scrutiny. The code worked in this way. His first letter said that while staying at Lorient he had attended a party given by Lemp. He mentioned that Schepke had been present and listed the names of a dozen other officers. These names were fictitious, and a numbers code spelled the names of the destroyers *Walker* and *Vanoc*. Further information concerning his own health hid the name Cockfosters and a brief account of his interview with Captain Creasy. Further letters gave news of his crew and the loss of his engineer. Although screened by War Office censors, all these letters got through. When broken, the code showed he had been lost while attacking a convoy shadowed by Lemp.

After his arrival, Kretschmer was sent for by Major, now Lt Colonel, James Reynolds Veitch, of the Grenadier Guards, who commanded the camp, and told that, as Senior German Officer, he would be responsible for the organisation of the prisoners' activities within the limits laid down by International Law. Veitch made it clear that he considered it his main task to prevent escapes and to administer the camp correctly with no favours and no brutality. He expected the prisoners to behave decently, and in return they would receive proper treatment from the camp authorities. The 100 officers were housed in dormitories on the upper floors, while the ground floor had been turned into a common room, mess hall and kitchen. Barbed wire cut off the larger part of the grounds, leaving them a strip about fifty yards wide round the entire building for exercise.

Veitch had only recently taken over as commandant, and had spent days inspecting the security arrangements to prevent escapes. Extra wire fences were ordered, and as the foundations consisted of granite blocks set into the rocky mountain-side, tunnelling seemed a remote and futile pastime. But he was amazed one day to find that mountain sheep were getting through the barbed wire into the camp compound.

If animals could get in, prisoners could get out, and a search organised by Veitch revealed a break in the barbed wire which the prisoners had not yet found. Several more tons of wire were ordered and a new barrier put up outside the first. Veitch firmly believed the prisoners were now secure inside. This, in fact, was true until early October, when Kretschmer organised the first escape.

In August 1940, *U-570*, commanded by Lieutenant-Commander Rahmlow, surrendered in the North Atlantic to a Hudson aircraft of Coastal Command piloted by Squadron Leader J.H. Thompson. The U-boat had been bombed while diving, and had been brought back to the surface with a white-backed naval chart flying from its periscope as a sign of surrender. As the Hudson was running short of fuel, Squadron Leader Thompson radioed for a relief plane and surface ships to take over and receive the surrender of the first U-boat in history to give itself up to an aircraft. Another aircraft soon took over from Thompson, and twelve hours later two destroyers arrived to take the U-boat in tow. One of them tried to send a boarding party across, but the sea was too rough to lower a boat. In spite of this, they ordered Rahmlow to attempt to reach them in a rubber dinghy. He completed this difficult operation successfully, and in doing so left his ship with the First Lieutenant in command. At Grizedale Hall, Kretschmer and other naval officers read of this astonishing incident in British newspapers, which confirmed that *U-570* was the first U-boat of the war to be captured intact. The report caused consternation through the camp, and to bring the affair out into the open, Luftwaffe officers invited Kretschmer to lecture the prisoners on what he would have done under similar circumstances. He said: 'There are no doubts in my mind. I would have gone on diving despite the air attack, and should have considered my escape certain if there were no surface vessels with Asdic less than twelve hours' steaming away. If the bombs had damaged me severely I would have come to the surface and fought it out with the aircraft. My anti-aircraft gun's crew were excellent and as the aircraft had to come in low to bomb with any accuracy, I think our chances of shooting it down would have been good. In any event I must see Rahmlow before saying anything more definite.'

In September the First Lieutenant, Second Lieutenant and Engineer Officer of *U-570* arrived at Grizedale Hall, where the angry prisoners refused to welcome them until the question of their behaviour at sea had been settled. Kretschmer called a meeting of other senior officers to discuss what action should be taken. Under the Geneva Convention, prisoners were not allowed to sit as a court-martial board on other prisoners; nor were courts of inquiry allowed. Kretschmer avoided this issue by setting up a secret Council of Honour which was to establish whether the captain and officers of *U-570* were guilty of cowardice in face of the enemy. On this Council were Lieutenant-Commander Hesselbarth and two other U-boat officers. The sittings were held in secret, and all prisoners were warned not to talk about it in the presence of guards. Questions to be decided were:

1 *Had Rahmlow and his officers shown cowardice?*
2 *Had Rahmlow been at fault in abandoning his command by paddling over to the destroyer?*
3 *Why had* U-570 *not been scuttled to avoid capture?*

First to appear before the Council were the Second Lieutenant and Engineer Officer. It was soon established that, as subordinates, they had obeyed orders, and the Council decided that while these two officers could have acted more vigorously by objecting strongly to the surrender, they had not been guilty of cowardice. That evening Kretschmer called the camp together in the common room and formally announced the Council's findings. He instructed that the two officers were no longer to be ignored and should be allowed to become part of the camp community and treated according to their rank. He shook hands with each of them and formally welcomed them to Grizedale Hall.

The following morning the Council sat to consider the case of the First Lieutenant. His was divorced from the others on the assumption that, as the senior executive officer, he had been in a position to protest against the surrender, and if necessary place Rahmlow under arrest and assume command himself – a natural act if he considered he could have saved the U-boat. Secondly, when Rahmlow left the boat to board the British destroyer, the command automatically passed into the hands of the First Lieutenant, who should have taken scuttling action. In any event, it was his duty to have made sure that the U-boat did not fall decisively into enemy hands.

The Council opened the questioning by asking for details of the attack, such as the period between the original sighting and the dropping of the first bomb, the height of the aircraft and the accuracy of the bombing. The witness was told that opportunities would be given him to put forward every possible explanation in his own defence. He was assured that the questions were not designed to trap him but to help him to extricate himself from an awkward situation. The interrogation followed these lines:

'Did you realise that Naval Battle Instructions lay down that no U-boat should be allowed to fall into enemy hands?'

'Yes.'

'Why did you not take some action to carry out this order by countermanding your commander's surrender?'

'My first thought was for the lives of the crew. In the heat of the moment it seemed to me that their safety was of primary importance to the capture of the boat.'

'Did you not realise that the capture of your boat would reveal to the enemy secrets which might lead to the deaths of hundreds of other sailors in future?'

'I do now, but at that time my own crew occupied my mind.'

'Surely you must have realised that with complete knowledge of our equipment and weapons, the enemy has been presented with an opportunity to stifle the whole U-boat offensive.'

'Yes.'

'Do you think it right, then, that you valued your own life and those of your crew above the lives of many crews yet to sail. Do you think that fair?'

'Yes.'

Members of the Council could not contain gasps of astonishment. The questions had been so phrased that a normal man would have known exactly what reply he was expected to give. Instead this officer was insisting that his commander and himself had been right in saving themselves while not bothering to think of the consequences of their actions. Further questioning by the Council failed to persuade the First Lieutenant to change his replies, and at another camp meeting that night Kretschmer announced the Council of Honour's opinion and his own decision. The First Lieutenant had been found guilty of cowardice in the face of the enemy, and when the Germans occupied England[1] he was to be handed over to the occupation authorities for formal court-martial. Meanwhile he was not to be allowed to take part in any of the camp activities. This sentence, in effect, isolated him from the rest of the PoW community. Two other naval officers of his term were ordered by Kretschmer to be responsible for looking after him.

The strain of not only being a prisoner but of being excommunicated by his countrymen was too much for the First Lieutenant. A few days later one of the guardians reported that he realised now that he had behaved like a coward and wished to be allowed to atone by committing suicide. Kretschmer replied by saying that such a stupid suggestion made him even more of a coward. The affair might have rested there but for reports in various newspapers saying that *U-570* had been taken to Barrow-in-Furness, where she was moored to a buoy in a narrow channel.

After this information had been confirmed by a talkative guard it was passed to Kretschmer, who immediately called a meeting of senior officers in his room to tell them of a plan which might serve the two-fold purpose of destroying the U-boat and giving the First Lieutenant a chance to regain his honour. He was to be told to escape with the mission of getting to Barrow, boarding the U-boat and scuttling it. If he agreed to this plan the Council of Honour would see to it that this mission was taken into account at his eventual court-martial.

The officer agreed at once and the plan was put into action. In an amazingly short time sufficient information had been extracted from newspapers, magazines, books and prisoners' memories, for Kretschmer to draw a chart of the harbour and fix the most likely place for *U-570* to be moored. Another committee of officers drew up a map giving three roughly estimated routes from Grizedale Hall to the Barrow area by cross-country, road and rail.

A tailoring department turned out civilian clothes, and papers were forged describing the bearer as a Dutch seaman on leave. This unit also turned out emergency ration cards and an identity card obtained for them by a guard in exchange for money. The 'cover' story, to be used if questioned, was that he had been in London on leave, spent all his money and was now hitch-hiking back to the Clyde to join his ship.

When all preparations were ready, they waited for the right moment. Late one October afternoon, the whole camp held a sing-song near the outer fence between two sentry posts. Both guards leaned over the rails of their covered huts to watch, while out of sight, directly underneath one tower, two prisoners cut a hole in the barbed wire and twisted the loose ends round the fence-poles. At nightfall the sing-song ended and the prisoners came back to their huts. At 10 p.m. the First Lieutenant was lowered out of a first-floor window of the main building and in a brief spurt crossed the yard to the fence to slip through the hole into the surrounding woods, and freedom. Two hours later the guards made a routine count of the prisoners in bed. For some reason they seemed to suspect trouble, and turned down the bedclothes covering every prisoner. They soon found one bed with an overcoat buttoned up over two pillows.

The alarm was up. The whole camp stayed awake that night waiting tensely for the First Lieutenant to be recaptured. But nothing happened, and in the morning the prisoners estimated with some excitement that if he travelled fast, he, even on foot, should be well clear of the camp. But in the afternoon they heard the faint burst of firing in the distance and with sinking hearts realised he must have been found. About an hour later Kretschmer was sent for by Major Veitch and told brusquely that the First Lieutenant was dead. He had been found on the slopes of the nearby fell hiding in a stone sheep shelter. He had told his cover story to the Home Guards who had found him, and they had been inclined to believe it. But, to make sure, they decided to bring him back to the camp for identification with the promise that if his story were true they would see he got to the Clyde in plenty of time to catch his ship.

As they were marching back to the camp, the First Lieutenant, knowing he would be identified at Grizedale Hall immediately, leapt from the track and ran for it. The Home Guard patrol called out to him three times to stop or they would shoot. He ignored their warnings and was about to disappear into a densely-wooded copse when they opened fire and a bullet hit his back. He was still alive when they reached his writhing body and carried him to a nearby farmhouse, where the farmer's wife bathed the wound while a Home Guard private was sent for a doctor. The First Lieutenant was dead before the doctor arrived.

Veitch told the expressionless Kretschmer how much he regretted that such a gallant escape attempt had ended so fatally. Captain C.H. Sleigh, camp Intelligence officer, asked if Kretschmer could throw any light on the meaning of certain documents found hidden in the dead man's clothes – a map of the north of England and what appeared to be a chart. He also wanted to know how they had been supplied. Kretschmer shook his head in pretended puzzlement. Sleigh looked grim and demanded angrily how these documents had been acquired, implying he knew that other brains than the dead man's had planned this escape. How, he asked, could one man have provided himself with such excellent identity papers without collaboration? Kretschmer nodded his agreement but denied any knowledge of the escape. Sleigh indicated he knew something was wrong between the dead man and the rest of the camp and intimated that he intended to get to the bottom of it. Kretschmer ignored this and asked that the dead man be buried with full military honours. Veitch agreed, and three days later twelve Senior German Officers in full uniform and wearing decorations were taken to the nearby village of Ambleside, where the coffin, draped with the Royal Navy's battle ensign, was laid out beside a newly dug grave. A British guard of honour fired three volleys and the coffin was lowered slowly into the earth – the whole ceremony being in strict accordance with the Geneva Convention.

Kretschmer had asked for and been given permission to make a speech at the graveside. Now, as Veitch called on him, he looked terribly strained and shook his head. On return to camp, however, he announced that his indictment of the First Lieutenant's cowardice should be wiped out and replaced with the regained honour he now deserved. Three hours later Lieutenant-Commander Rahmlow arrived at the camp.

Notes

1 At that time the prisoners at Grizedale Hall were convinced that the invasion of England was imminent and would succeed. Kretschmer had no illusions about the First Lieutenant's fate. He would be shot.

Fifteen
Bowmanville

The arrival of Rahmlow so soon after the burial of his First Lieutenant was a shock to the whole camp. Kretschmer had known Rahmlow only vaguely at Lorient where he had not been liked, and it was improbable that he was going to find much affection at Grizedale Hall. As soon as he had been assigned a bunk he was brought to Kretschmer, proffered his hand enthusiastically and said how nice it was that two 'aces' like themselves should be reunited. Kretschmer ignored Rahmlow's hand, told him coldly that they had just returned from burying his First Lieutenant and described the developments that had led up to the shooting. Rahmlow tried to explain but Kretschmer cut him short with a brief instruction that he would be given a chance to explain his actions before the same Council of Honour that had heard his officers. Rumours reached the authorities about the dissension. Veitch, on the advice of Sleigh who by now had a pretty good idea of what was going on, was alarmed at the prospect of a second death and repercussions from the War Office. He placed Rahmlow in the punishment block for his own safety, and the following day sent him to another PoW camp near Carlisle, which housed mainly Luftwaffe officers, and where it was unlikely that the full story of *U-570* would be known.

On the same day another U-boat commander also arrived at Grizedale Hall. His U-boat had been caught on the surface in the North Atlantic by two Canadian corvettes, one of which, HMCS *Moosejaw*, attempted to ram her. In the high swell and heavy seas the corvette was thrown off course and the two ships hit beam to beam and ran along beside each other. Before the U-boat rebounded off *Moosejaw*'s side the German commander jumped from his conning-tower on to the corvette's fo'c'sle, and in doing so abandoned his command. Luckily, his First Lieutenant managed to scuttle the U-boat before she could be captured. Kretschmer told him he would have to face the Council of Honour that had dealt with the case of *U-570*. This officer agreed that it would be the proper course and placed himself at the Council's disposal. The authorities got wind of what was happening and he, also, was transferred. In the afternoon he was gone.

The Admiralty, to whom Veitch had sent the map and chart, sent an Intelligence investigator to the camp. This officer, an RNVR Lieutenant, discovered nothing, but Admiralty Intelligence in London, on further study of the case, connected the fact that at the time of the escape of an officer of *U-570* that submarine was lying in Barrow. Checks on both documents showed that the map revealed several routes to districts near Barrow, and that the chart was a fairly accurate survey of the harbour. When this information was sent to Veitch, who had heard by then of the Council of Honour proceedings from Sleigh, he was not long in guessing that the escape was part of some plan aimed at destroying *U-570*. He took the view that the Council of Honour, no matter what it was called, was in practice a court-martial and therefore illegal under the Geneva Convention. He sent a full report to the War Office, who would be responsible for disciplinary action against Kretschmer and the Council board, but for some reason the authorities in London decided to let the matter rest. Veitch, however, called Kretschmer to his office and told him bluntly that, as the dead officer had escaped on a mission tantamount to an act of war, in that it could be classed as intended sabotage, he as senior German officer was responsible and could be dealt with by British Military Law. No punitive action was to be taken on this occasion, but most certainly would if there was any repetition.

Shortly after the *U-570* incident, Major Veitch also sent for Kretschmer to issue orders that all PoW's were to be confined to their quarters immediately for an emergency search of the camp buildings and grounds, and a special count. This took more than two hours, and when it was over Kretschmer asked Sleigh what had been the reason. It was then he learned that two airmen claiming to be prisoners-of-war were being held by an RAF unit near Hull. The RAF had telephoned to say that both men spoke impeccable English and German and had made a forced landing in a Hurricane fighter nearby. It was suspected that they were RAF deserters, but they insisted they had come from a prison camp near Carlisle. This camp had reported no escapes and no prisoners missing, so a routine check was being made on all camps in the vicinity.

Nearly a week later Sleigh met Kretschmer in the exercise yard and told him the RAF were putting the two men on court-martial as deserters. On the eve of the trial the commandant of the Carlisle camp reported that an unexpected count had revealed two prisoners missing, and it was then that the real story emerged. The two Luftwaffe pilots had dressed in workmen's overalls and with ladders balanced on their shoulders walked out of the camp's main gates whistling cheerfully. They had reached a fighter aerodrome, climbed into a Hurricane and taken off, heading for Germany.

But as they passed over the English coast the engine coughed. They were running out of fuel. There had been just enough petrol left to make a wide sweep and land in a field north of Hull. A farmer had given them tea, telephoned the nearest RAF field, and a car had been sent to pick them up. Their absence had been so successfully hidden in the camp that despite their continued assertions that they were PoW's the RAF had launched an almost national investigation aimed at proving they were deserters. The court-martial was cancelled and both prisoners were returned to their camp loaded with presents from an amused RAF mess.

On Boxing Day, Major Veitch held a formal parade of both guards and prisoners. He read out a letter from the Admiralty informing him that Kretschmer had been awarded the Swords to the Oak Leaves of the Knight's Cross – the highest award Germany could offer a naval officer at that time.

Towards the end of May 1942, Kretschmer received official notification from Major Veitch that all the prisoners in the camp were to be transferred to Canada at short notice. For several days they packed up personal belongings and camp equipment which was the communal property of all prisoners. And on the day they entrained for the Clyde, where they were to board a liner, a long column of Army lorries took their luggage to Ambleside station. Certain that some attempt to escape would be made during this period of moving, Veitch doubled the guards, and each lorry-load of equipment was inspected by his chief security officer.

On one lorry the load was topped by a comfortable looking armchair. A private travelling in charge of the load sat in it for the fifteen-minute ride and helped to unload it at the station. Then he sat in it again to rest and smoke a cigarette, at the same time unconsciously stroking one of the arms with his hand. He was astonished to feel the whole chair wriggle beneath him. Leaping to his feet, he gazed at this phenomenon in further amazement as from beneath the cover came a series of sneezes and giggles. Now thoroughly alarmed, he called the sergeant. and together they ripped the chair to pieces. Strapped inside the framework, with his legs pulled under the seat, was a German officer who had been sewn into the upholstery by his comrades. Unwittingly the caressing motion of the private's hand along the would-be escaper's thigh had been more than he could bear, and despite all efforts to control himself, he had lapsed into convulsive giggles and allowed his head to move into a wad of horsehair, which jammed around his nose, causing him to sneeze fitfully. When this was reported to Veitch, he found that his chief security officer had actually sat in the chair a few minutes before it was loaded.

Four days later they were bound for Canada and eating the best food they had received since becoming prisoners. Steaks were on the menu every day, and as many of the prisoners – mostly Army and Luftwaffe – were sick, the naval men had double helpings of everything. Their main worry was that some determined U-boat would torpedo them.

On arrival in Canada they were put on a special train, and it was more steaks all the way to Bowmanville Camp, near Lake Ontario. When they marched in through the gates they found about 170 Army and Luftwaffe prisoners already in occupation, but it was still a bleak-looking camp, little more than a long series of huts surrounded by barbed wire. Two Army Generals, captured in North Africa, were, in theory, the senior officers. Neither had any interest in the camp and refused to deal with the Canadian Commandant, Colonel Bull, preferring to retreat inside themselves and live their lives remote from the rest of the camp community.

Kretschmer found that a Colonel Hefele of the Luftwaffe had assumed the duties of senior German officer, and after a few days they agreed to share this role between them. But it was the energy of the new arrivals that transformed the camp. Under Kretschmer's direction, and with the complete co-operation of Hefele, the desolate waste inside the barbed wire became an active settlement. Sports fields were built, flowers and vegetables planted, a large swimming-pool was set up in one corner, tennis-courts were laid out and the huts converted to provide more spacious accommodation. A furniture factory was established and various committees set up to organise daily routines, including physical-training exercises, sports leagues, camp concerts and university standard educational courses. Kretschmer was determined that from the Naval point of view younger officers should not suffer by imprisonment. The midshipmen were given courses in navigation and seamanship, as they would have done in Germany. They kept to a timetable of terms, taking their 'holidays' at the customary periods.

Beneath this surface activity an undercover organisation grew up to handle all escape plans. Inside this organisation was a tailoring unit to provide civilian clothes; a forgery department which provided false papers and passports for getting across the border into the United States, not yet in the war; a map-making cell which could provide escapees with detailed maps of any given part of Canada. Presiding over it all were Kretschmer and Hefele, who, with a small committee, co-ordinated a long-term escape programme, and by the end of the year were ready for the first successful escape of a German officer from a Canadian camp.

Throughout 1942, Americans of German origin maintained a flow of food-parcels and clothing to the prisoners in Canada. Inside each parcel was the name and address of the sender. In the New Year a young Luftwaffe pilot, Lieutenant Krug, noticed that a consistent stream of parcels came from one address in Detroit, just across the border from Montreal. His plan was to cross the St. Lawrence River into America and visit this address in the hope of getting help for the next stage of his journey, which he thought would be

Mexico. One morning Krug and another officer, dressed in workmen's overalls and carrying a measuring tape and a pot of yellow paint, were escorted to the fence by a third officer wearing a stolen Canadian sergeant's uniform. The two 'workmen' proceeded to paint yellow rings round one fence-pole after another, while the 'escort' looked on with an air of boredom. The guards in the towers watched the activities diffidently and paid no attention when the 'workmen' placed a ladder against the wire, climbed over and proceeded to measure distances between the poles. They paid no more attention when Krug and his 'mate' shouldered the ladder, waved good-bye to the 'escort' and the guards, and walked off down the road as though they had finished their job and were going home.

About a mile down the road the two men stripped off their overalls, under which they were wearing dark-blue suits, and separated. The other officer was recaptured in a few hours, but Krug walked five miles to the nearest station and bought a railway ticket to Toronto. He thumbed a lift from there to Montreal, and after crossing the St Lawrence by night in a 'borrowed' rowing-boat, reached Detroit. From there he made his way via Chicago to San Antonio in Texas, where he was eventually arrested by the FBI and taken to Washington for questioning. As the United States was not at war, the German Embassy secured his release and flew him to Lisbon, where he changed planes for Berlin. The German radio proclaimed him a hero, and he was awarded the Knight's Cross for what was rightly described as a brave and daring escape. Six months later Krug was killed flying a Stuka divebomber on the Russian front.

Then came another chapter in the case of *U-570*. Rahmlow arrived at Bowmanville, and at once Kretschmer reported to a committee of senior officers what had transpired at Grizedale Hall, including the death of the First Lieutenant and Rahmlow's transfer to another camp. After listening to this report, the committee decided to set up another Council to hear Rahmlow's version of the case and to decide if he had acted in accordance with his duty. The Board was dominated by Luftwaffe and Army officers and consisted of six members and a chairman. Like his First Lieutenant before him, Rahmlow made no attempt at apology for a course of action which he honestly regarded as amply justified to avoid the useless loss of the life of men for whom he was responsible. Such an attempt would hardly weigh with young U-boat officers in the first flush of victory. It was to be some years before considerations like these became intelligible.

Meanwhile, across the Atlantic a bitter row was blowing up between the British and German Governments over the handcuffs used by British Commandos who took German prisoners during their raid on the Channel Islands. Hitler announced that he would place an equal number of British prisoners-of-war in chains unless the Germans were unmanacled. Then came

165

the Dieppe raid, and 100 British and Canadian prisoners taken by the Germans were placed in chains and sent back to Germany. The German radio announced they were to be kept chained as a reprisal against the British action. Churchill's reply was to inform the House of Commons that 100 German Army officers imprisoned in Canada were to be manacled until the British prisoners were released. And one summer morning, Kretschmer, by now more active as Camp Leader than Hefele, was summoned to Colonel Bull's office to be informed that 100 of Bowmanville's inmates were to be shackled and sent for a prolonged stay to an empty farmhouse nearby. The commandant expressed his regret at having to take such action, but pointed out that he had to obey orders. To Kretschmer's vigorous protests, Colonel Bull replied that if necessary he would use force to carry out his orders. Kretschmer then stated bluntly that force would be necessary, as he could not agree that prisoners-of-war should be shackled in contravention of international law. Colonel Bull looked grim as he said:

'Your people started this, and it's up to them to finish it. I have my orders, and I shall carry them out. That's all.'

'I understand, but we shall resist force with force,' replied Kretschmer, equally grimly.

Cordial relations between prisoners and guards had been built up over a year of facing each other 'across the wire'. Now Colonel Bull felt sorry that this friendliness, which had made possible the smooth running of the camp, was about to be destroyed. He called in his senior officers and prepared to march guards into the camp to take out 100 officers by force. Meanwhile, Kretschmer set up a resistance headquarters in the large kitchen, one of the few brick buildings in the camp. About 150 officers, petty officers and ratings barricaded themselves inside, armed with sticks and iron bars. In another brick hut a further 100 officers of all three Services prepared to fight off the guards and submit to a long siege. At 2 p.m. on a Saturday the first wave of guards marched in, armed with police truncheons and rifles with fixed bayonets. They rushed the kitchen first, and a pitched battle was fought on the doorstep and beneath the windows.

They withdrew, and the prisoners claimed the first round. Another rush followed, this time on the second building, but the guards were beaten off again. Isolated groups of prisoners had set up strong-points in wooden huts between the two main headquarters, and the third attack was directed against these. For more than an hour the battle raged as axes were used to break down doors and fighting took place inside the huts themselves. To relieve the pressure, the two main bodies of prisoners unbarricaded themselves and charged both flanks of the guards, who then withdrew in disorder. There was a brief respite while the wounded of both sides, suffering mainly from broken bones, bloody noses and cracked heads, were removed to safety. The guards advanced in the fourth attack behind a screen of fire-hoses. The powerful jets, aimed through the windows of the huts, threw the barricades to one side and sent the defenders tumbling in all directions. The prisoners still fought back stubbornly, but by six in the evening they were overwhelmed.

Kretschmer refused to hand over 100 prisoners for the shackling, and at nightfall the opposing forces were deadlocked. By agreement, however, the prisoners marched from their huts to begin repairing the damage. At a brief parade, Colonel Bull announced that he had sent for a battalion of regular troops at a nearby camp to reinforce the guards and extract the hostages he required. As the prisoners left their huts, an engineer captain standing by the kitchen door slapped each one over the head and face with his cane. The prisoners said nothing, but made it clear that, in the near future, they would avenge what they regarded as an insult.

The following day was Sunday, and the regular troops were not expected to arrive before Monday morning. But Kretschmer sent a message to the guards that the engineer officer would be advised not to enter the camp again until feeling had died down. Instead, he appeared at the camp gates an hour later and rashly, if bravely, began walking around. Kretschmer was talking to two other officers near one of the huts when the captain appeared round the corner with an elderly guard generally liked by all the prisoners. He leapt on the captain and knocked him to the ground, and one of his companions gave the guard a light tap on the chin to keep him out of action, while Kretschmer set about beating up the captain to pay him off in full for his use of the cane. The three Germans then dragged the Canadian into a hut.

As the battle had begun on the question of shackling prisoners, Kretschmer decided to tie the captain's hands behind his back with strips of cloth, which could have been broken easily had the captain tried. But the elderly guard they had left outside recovered and rushed out giving the alarm. Inside the hut the prisoners prepared to march out with their captive between them and proceed to the gate with mock solemnity. But as they appeared, a guard on one of the towers opened fire with a rifle. Kretschmer pulled the captain flat on his face and dropped down beside him. The Germans crawled back to the hut with bullets kicking up the dust around them, leaving the Canadian where he was.

Once inside the protection of the hut, Kretschmer called out to see if anyone was hurt, and his own midshipman, König, reported proudly that a bullet had hit his leg, tearing the flesh. They gathered round a window to see what their late captive was up to, and were just in time to see him clamber to his feet and rush to the gate.

No further action developed until the following morning, when the regular Army battalion arrived and advanced through the gates wearing tin hats and carrying fixed bayonets, clubs and hoses. Drawn across the main entrance with Kretschmer in the middle was a thin line of prisoners armed with fire-axes, hockey-sticks and stones. They wore cushions and pillows lashed round their heads. A pitched battle took place, and gradually this first line of defence dropped back to prepared positions in their huts. Too late, the troops realised they had walked into a trap; for as they moved between the huts, shouting prisoners appeared on the roof-tops hurling bricks into their closely-massed enemy, forcing the soldiers to withdraw. A few minutes later about 400 troops charged each hut, forcing the doors and climbing through the windows.

All afternoon the struggle went on, with both sides whooping with joy as they slugged it out – the Canadian soldiers having good-naturedly thrown aside their bayonets to use the same weapons as the defenders. By early evening the battle was over and a mixed, sorry-looking procession of Canadian infantrymen and German officers paraded before an emergency first-aid station set up by doctors of both sides. At nightfall the whole camp lined up to watch silently as 100 German Army officers were handcuffed and marched off to the farmhouse. After a few days the handcuffs were worn for roll calls only – about twice a day – a procedure started by the guards and winked at by the camp authorities. In less than a week, the whole affair died. In effect, little had been achieved by either side, but the battle had provided both guards and prisoners with a weekend of relief from monotony and boredom.

Kretschmer's agile mind, always looking for new methods to force the pace of war even from behind wire, found another outlet for his energies. The repatriation of wounded prisoners, which up till then had been a trickle, was becoming more organised, and almost monthly German officers were being sent to the east coast to be returned to the Fatherland. To Kretschmer they presented an unequalled opportunity of getting information back to Germany. He organised a naval espionage group whose main task was to locate the major war industries and military bases in Canada and the United States. They applied for nearly every newspaper and magazine printed in the New World, a request that was granted.

Within a short time this espionage group found, to their own surprise, that by careful reading of both articles and advertisements they could accumulate an astonishing amount of vital information. For instance, one magazine carried a full-page advertisement by an American firm manufacturing marine engines, claiming that their products were being used to power a new aircraft-carrier under construction in Brooklyn Navy Yard. A week later an obscure technical magazine contained an article on the American shipbuilding programme which gave the name of the new carrier and the performance of her engines as claimed by the manufacturers. A month afterwards a repatriated German officer took with him the name of the carrier, its tonnage, the number of aircraft it carried, its speed and expected date of completion – all the information needed for Admiral Dönitz to send U-boats to lie in ambush for the carrier on its maiden voyage. From then on every prisoner leaving Bowmanville for Germany took with him important intelligence covering such items as the location of Army training bases, fighter and bomber airfields, torpedo and other armament factories and principal convoy bases.

This group, which became known in Bowmanville as the 'Lorient Espionage Unit', managed to build a powerful radio transmitter and receiver, which they hid in the large centre leg of the common-room table. It was taken out nightly, and brief transmissions were made in an effort to contact Dönitz's headquarters or U-boats at sea. The unit also maintained a flow of information coded into their ordinary letters home. After the German surrender and the occupation of Berlin, American Intelligence officers found among the Luftwaffe records a complete plan for a bombing offensive against the United States and Canada. This included a list of priority targets, among them military bases and industrial centres compiled from information supplied by the 'Lorient Espionage Unit'.

Kretschmer decided it was time to organise his own escape. His First Lieutenant, Knebel-Döberitz, had for some time been urging that they persuade Dönitz to send a U-boat to the entrance of the St Lawrence River to take off as many captured commanders as possible. Now Kretschmer prepared to put this plan into action. The senior U-boat commanders in Bowmanville were himself, Knebel-Döberitz, Lieutenant Elfe, one-time Second Lieutenant of *U-99*, whose own command *U-93* had been sunk by HMS *Hesperus* in the South Atlantic, and Lieutenant Commander Ey, whose command, *U-433*, had been sunk by HMS *Marigold*. It was decided that these four should make the escape. They planned to dig a 100-yard-long tunnel from one hut and come up inside the forest about twenty yards from the wire. Two more tunnels were to be started from the same hut in different directions to act as 'dummies' should the guards discover the digging before it was completed. More than 150 prisoners were to assist in the building of these tunnels, and efforts were made by both radio transmission and letter to contact Dönitz.

In the selected hut an extra wardrobe was built which stretched from floor to ceiling, large enough for two prisoners to work behind its closed doors on the entrance of the tunnel. A hole was cut through the top of the wardrobe and the ceiling so that the dirt could be passed up into the attic. The shaft went down ten feet below the wardrobe and then opened up into a cave-like room large enough to take two crouching prisoners. In the attic German engineers built a system of wooden railway lines leading to each corner. Boxes, which had once held tinned fruit, were fitted with wooden wheels, and as the dirt came up in home-made sacks, it was poured into the boxes, and the prisoners in the corners pulled them by rope and packed the dirt deep against the sides of the roof.

It took more than a month to complete the shaft and begin digging horizontally in the direction of the fence. Work went on night and day, with the prisoners taking over in shifts; two at the tunnel face, one in the cave pulling the dirt back, and hitching the sacks to the 'lift', one in the wardrobe to guide the 'lift' and four in the attic to stow the dirt and lower the empty bags. More prisoners worked in the same way on the two 'dummy' tunnels, but at the end of the fourth month these were abandoned and work was concentrated on the main escape tunnel.

Meanwhile, they established contact with Dönitz by letter in code, and it had been agreed that when an escape deadline could be reached a large ocean-going submarine would lie off an agreed rendezvous on the Canadian cast coast. Everything depended now on the success of the tunnel. After six months, towards the end of 1943, the tunnel resembled a modern coal-mine. It was large enough for diggers at the face to kneel, the dirt was hauled back through the shaft – a distance of some seventy-five yards – on a wooden railway line, and the engineers had tapped the camp electricity system to run an electric cable with bulbs at intervals down the tunnel to provide light. Further, more than 500 fruit tins had been welded together to provide an air pipe to the tunnel-face. Curiously, throughout all this period the camp authorities gave no sign that they suspected an escape was being planned. Kretschmer's main worry was the attic, where so much dirt had been stored that the ceiling was beginning to sag under the weight. Three German artists had made four life-size dummies 'which on the night of the escape were to be dressed in uniform and used to disguise the absence of the escapers.[1] But during rehearsals, despite all the efforts of the creators, they refused obstinately to walk. For some reason it was impossible to make their legs properly manoeuvrable.

By this time progress had reached a steady daily average, and, Kretschmer decided on a date for the break-out, which was sent to Dönitz, whose reply – coded into a letter from Knebel-Döberitz's mother – said that *U-577*, a 740-tonner commanded by Lieutenant-Commander Schauenburg, would surface for two hours each night for two weeks in a tiny bay north of the St Lawrence estuary. This meant that Kretschmer and his three companions would have a maximum of fourteen days to reach the rendezvous point after escaping from the camp. In the ninth month the tunnel was 106 yards long and branched up to within about two feet from the surface. The four officers were equipped with civilian suits, shoes, shirts, trilby hats, identity cards and papers describing them as merchant seamen. In addition, a national newspaper had reproduced a military order carrying the signature of the Canadian commander of the Eastern Seaboard. In case their rendezvous area with *U-577* lay in an area prohibited to civilians, the forging unit copied this signature on official permits giving them the right to move freely in restricted coastal regions. About a week before the escape deadline, Kretschmer sent another coded letter to Germany giving the news that all was well and the rendezvous would be kept.

One night the attic fell in, smothering the sleeping prisoners with tons of dirt. Frantically they tried to clear away all signs of the disaster, but the loud splintering crack as the whole ceiling sagged and split brought the guards running to the hut, and the search was on for the tunnel. Throughout the next day the anxious prisoners diverted the guards from the wardrobe and allowed the first 'dummy' tunnel to be found. Close inspection of this showed it was full of water and must have been abandoned some time ago. The second tunnel was uncovered, but the new commandant, a Major Taylor, reasoned that it was too small to have yielded the amount of dirt that had fallen from the attic. The prisoners, who had worked for the better part of a year below the earth, waited resignedly for the main tunnel to be discovered. The search went on for more than twenty-four hours, and to their elation it was called off without the third tunnel being found.

Kretschmer decided to wait no longer, but to break out that night. The day dragged on. In the afternoon a prisoner fond of gardening went in search of some decent top soil for his flower-bed. He found some near the wire fence, and while the guards in the towers joked with him he commenced shovelling the dirt into a sack. Suddenly, to the amazement of the guards, he dug a bit deeper than normal and the shovel vanished up to the handle in the ground, the prisoner falling flat on his face. The roof of the tunnel had collapsed, and even while the alarm was being given a whole stretch of the camp ground fell inwards.

The secret was out. The guards placed small charges of dynamite along the route of the tunnel and removed the wardrobe covering the shaft. Kretschmer held an emergency meeting in another hut at which it was decided to try and contact *U-577* by radio and tell her of the disaster. He was frightened that if she hung around too long she might well be sunk. Lieutenant-Commander Heyda[2] thereupon suggested that he should try to make a lone escape the following evening, and find his way to the rendezvous and tell *U-577* what had happened. His plan was daring. Wooden pylons carrying electric current into the camp crossed one corner with one pylon actually inside the wire. He wanted to build a boatswain's chair with two wooden trolleys which would fit over the electric wires and swing him to the next pylon outside the camp. After considerable argument, and with the unlikelihood of reaching *U-577* by radio, Kretschmer agreed.

They tore nails from the floorboards of a hut and fitted them into the soles of his boots to act as spikes for climbing the pylon, and by noon the following day the boatswain's chair, complete with trolleys, was ready. After exercise that afternoon, Heyda, in his civilian clothes, and with the boatswain's chair under his coat, hid in the sports hut while one of the 'dummies' took his place during the parade count. That night he climbed the pylon, sat precariously on the wooden seat, held on to the ropes and with a murmured prayer swung down the wires. To cover him the prisoners organised a mass fight inside one of the huts. Guards came running from all directions to quell what they thought was a threatened riot.

By the time the camp had quietened down, Heyda, whose first attempt had been a complete success, was well clear. He travelled by train half-way across Canada to the east coast and, four nights later, reached the appointed rendezvous. From a sheltered vantage point, he looked out across the bay, and to his amazement saw three corvettes and a destroyer at anchor. He suspected immediately that, somehow, the Canadian authorities had broken the code by which the rendezvous had been made, and had sent this small force to trap Schauenburg. All he could do was reach a point nearest the beach where he could wait for developments. As he was making his way down a cliff-side he was startled by a loud challenge. He stopped, and was immediately surrounded by a Canadian Army patrol. He showed the officer in charge his papers, including his false permit to be in a prohibited area, and, with no further fuss, the officer saluted and advised him not to take his walks late at night. He went with them to the nearest main road, and with a cheerful wave left the patrol and walked away from the area.

All next day he slept in a wood, and the following night made another attempt to reach the beach. But once again he was stopped by a patrol, and this time taken to their headquarters for examination. An officer inspected his papers under an electric light, and again they were passed and accepted. With an almost audible sigh of relief, Heyda replaced them in his pocket, said good night to the officer and turned to leave the hut. As he reached the door the officer called out: 'Stop! I believe you are a German prisoner-of-war.'

Heyda turned slowly. 'What makes you think that?'

The officer grinned and said: 'That hat you are wearing was never bought in a shop. It has a seam running right down the middle at the back – the sort of thing that would happen if it was home-made in a prison camp.'

Three days later Heyda was back in Bowmanville, and after hearing his story the prisoners waited to hear that *U-577* had been ambushed and sunk by the naval force. Later Kretschmer learned that Schauenburg had seen the ships through his periscope on the first night and withdrawn. This had been repeated every night for a week, and finally Dönitz had been informed that, as it was impracticable to keep the rendezvous, *U-577* had resumed her normal patrol in the North Atlantic.[3]

This was Kretschmer's only attempt to escape. After this he received instructions from Dönitz to make no further plans, as the flow of information from the 'Lorient Espionage Unit' under his direction had become a vital section of German Naval Intelligence. These orders were underlined later by a German radio announcement that Kretschmer had been promoted to Captain.

Notes

1 An identical ruse was used by British prisoners in Germany, the story of which is known today as 'Albert RN'

2 Former commander of *U-434* which had been sunk by the destroyer, HMS *Stanley*.

3 *U-577* survived the war.

Sixteen
With The Crew

The crew of *U-99* had left England for Canada at the same time as their officers, but had been taken to Monteith Camp for 'other ranks', also near Lake Ontario. Nearly 4,000 men were housed there, and Petersen, as the senior warrant officer took over as Camp Leader. Within a few days of their arrival in May 1942 they met their first skunk. It had hidden itself beneath the floorboards of the kitchen and settled down to sleep. Providing a skunk is not disturbed there is no defensive bad odour to offend sensitive nostrils. But one afternoon Clasen saw it run from the kitchen and, thinking it was a rabbit, gave chase enthusiastically. When he managed to corner it and approached close for the fatal pounce, the creature lifted its tail and gave the astonished prisoner the full effect of its defences. His jacket stank, and laughing guards explained what had happened. He spent days trying to remove the smell but resisted all the pleadings of his fellow-prisoners to throw away the jacket. One night, while he was sleeping, a deputation of *U-99* men stole it from his bedside and burned it.

Monteith artists contrived to make a non-walking 'dummy' prisoner to cover escapes. It was put to bed, and guards who shone torches on the sleeping prisoners never discovered that the tousled head that moved from hut to hut was in reality a fake. This 'dummy' was used mostly by a paratrooper called Brosik, who had been one of the first prisoners to arrive in Canada, and who had escaped more times than any other PoW He earned the title 'Escape King' by such adventures as leaving the camp once in an empty bread carton, then through the wire fence, and on another occasion through a tunnel. His planned break-outs came every autumn, but he never missed an opportunity during the other three seasons.

He was fond of music and his will to escape suffered after D-Day, when Montgomery's forces captured a whole military band intact. The musicians were sent with their instruments to Monteith, where they gave weekly concerts. The camp commandant was so impressed, he invited a Mr

MacMillan, director of Canada's leading symphony orchestra, to visit the camp to hear a performance. Afterwards, MacMillan told the audience: 'You have the second best orchestra in Canada. Mine is always the best.'

Early in 1945 several hundred prisoners were transferred to Medicine Hat, in Alberta, where the local farmers had applied for Germans to work on their farms. Labour was desperately short, and those prisoners willing to work on parole were asked to volunteer for transfer. Among these was Kassel, who was put in charge of the prisoner-labour units working on a large-scale irrigation project covering several farms. He was taken to the camp at Medicine Hat first and then told to get ready to move to the tiny country town of Brooks, the base for the project's labour force. It was a long train journey and the compartment used by Kassel and his escort – a corporal and a private – became stuffy and warm, particularly to Kassel, who was wearing a naval greatcoat to cover his German uniform. The restaurant car was full of troops going home on leave, and the two soldiers guarding the PoW kept gazing longingly down the corridor at the sound of laughter and clinking glasses. One of them could stand it no longer. He leaned across confidentially to Kassel and said: 'Look, we are going up to the dining-car to have a drink. You stay here and look after our rifles and we will bring you back some beer.' Kassel nodded agreement – he was on parole, anyway – and tucked the two rifles beside him in the corner while the escorts disappeared along the corridor.

An hour passed before the train stopped for a few minutes at a country station and an Army officer climbed into the compartment to sit opposite Kassel. As the train moved out he looked hard at Kassel's coat and remarked that the Navy were wearing curious greatcoats these days. He talked for a while about the war and his own part in it and then dropped off to sleep while Kassel, finding it unbearably hot, discarded the coat. Some time later the officer wakened and his eyes bulged at the sight of a German naval uniform complete with Iron Cross sitting opposite him.

'Why, you are a Nazi,' he burst out in astonishment. Then he saw the two rifles and started visibly. Kassel was used by this time to being called a Nazi. 'No,' he replied courteously, ' I am not a Nazi, I am a German.'

He explained what had happened and asked the officer not to say anything that might get the two guards into trouble. The Canadian had been edging towards the door as Kassel spoke, and now he jumped up and ran towards the dining-car shouting something to the effect that a Nazi was loose on the train, armed with two rifles. A crowd of celebrating soldiers jostled their way to the compartment to look for themselves and burst into laughter when Kassel waved cheerfully at them. Beer, cigarettes and food were passed into the compartment, and a few minutes later the two guards appeared, both drunk; so drunk, in fact, that they decided to leave the train at the station before

Brooks and send for a lorry to pick up Kassel while they continued drinking on the train.

On the platform, Kassel had to hold their rifles while they went to the stationmaster's office and rang for transport. They returned and tried to work out how they could leave him without someone signing the delivery note, it being customary for prisoners to be signed for during escort change-overs as 'One body delivered'. The corporal told Kassel that he would have to sign the delivery note himself. Kassel replied that he could not do that very well, as he was the body to be delivered. But the corporal muttered angrily and insisted, until eventually the private supported Kassel's view, and a civilian standing nearby also took sides against the corporal. Whereupon a general discussion, carried on loudly and drunkenly by the two soldiers, was held on the platform, with Kassel grinning hugely and carrying the rifles under his arm. In the end the corporal announced sternly that they had been arguing long enough. He would ring Brooks again and get a decision from his sergeant.

He vanished with the private, and neither was seen again. Kassel talked with the civilian for a while before an old Model T Ford drew up and a farmer stuck his head from the window and shouted: 'Where is the prisoner for Brooks?' Kassel shook hands with the civilian, boarded the ancient car and drove off. The next morning a Calgary newspaper printed a report of the whole incident under the headlines:

KIND-HEARTED NAZI TAKES CARE OF STIFF GUARDS

The civilian had been the newspaper's local representative. Kassel remained in the farming areas of Alberta until the end of the war. One day his men received an inspection visit from an officer of the Medicine Hat Camp. While the officer talked to the farm owner, Kassel gossiped with the jeep driver and commiserated with him on the tedious task of driving officers from one farm to another. The driver said he had been a merchant seaman earlier in the war, but his ship had been torpedoed and sunk. He himself had been injured, and when he came out of hospital had been drafted into the Army for service at home. Kassel asked the name of his ship, and was startled to be told, *Magog*. The former sailor was about to launch into a description of the sinking when Kassel interrupted. 'Don't bother to tell me. I know all about it. While you were in the boats, the U-boat came alongside and your captain was given a bottle of brandy and some food. Then, if I remember rightly, the U-boat drifted away and your captain stood up in the lifeboat and thanked our captain.'

It was the soldier's turn to be shaken. He looked at Kassel disbelievingly: 'How do you know all that?'

Kassel smiled blandly. 'I should know it. The U-boat was mine, *U-99*, and your ship was the first or second we sank in the Atlantic. I remember it well.'

For a moment Kassel thought the soldier would leap at his throat, but instead, he recovered his composure, grinned and explored under the driver's seat to produce two bottles of beer, which they finished before the inspecting officer returned and Kassel's new-found friend vanished in a cloud of dust.

Towards the end of 1946 a general movement of prisoners from Canada to England began, and the crew of *U-99* were reunited with their officers on board the SS *Aquitania*, bound for Liverpool. On arrival, the men were sent to a prison camp at Oldham, while Kretschmer and his officers were escorted to Lodge Moor Camp, near Sheffield. This was the time of the great sort-out, when the British Government was trying to ensure that the first prisoners to be sent home were those untainted by the heritage of Nazism, and not in support of the military caste system. In general, U-boat commanders were considered by the authorities to fall automatically into the class of dangerous prisoners and were to be among the last to leave England.

Early in the New Year, 1947, forty U-boat captains, all classified as unrelenting militarists, were sent to Scotland, to Watton Camp, near Caithness, where they were lumped together with Luftwaffe fighter pilots and SS officers accused of Nazi sympathies.

After nearly two months at Watton, Kretschmer became ill and was sent to a PoW hospital at Carmarthen, in Wales, to be treated for a stomach complaint, and there he learned that the spectre of his Council of Honour had risen again to haunt his dreams of a quick release.

Seventeen
Home Port

In the early weeks of 1947 thousands of German prisoners thought they could secure their release more quickly by denouncing many of their comrades as Nazis, while at the same time admitting that they themselves had learned their lesson. For prisoners said to be known Nazis, the practice led to the setting up of special camps where they were left to be dealt with last of all. This applied particularly to the Army and Luftwaffe, which provided the vast majority of prisoners; but, on the naval side, an Allied order classed U-boat captains as militarists, and therefore equally unsuitable for rapid discharge.

One Admiralty interrogator had been assigned the questioning of the forty U-boat captains at Watton. Rahmlow maintained his previous defence and again urged his point that further resistance by his U-boat would have been futile.

After weeks of questioning, the forty 'dangerous' U-boat captains were reduced to twenty-five, and the Admiralty interrogator began a systematic search of naval camps for further evidence which might prove Kretschmer to be directly responsible for the death of *U-570*'s First Lieutenant.

At this stage it seems likely that the *U-570* affair had developed into a personal feud between the two captains. There is little doubt that Kretschmer was a militarist inasmuch that once Germany went to war he became a brilliant, daring and even reckless captain. Rahmlow was patently a man with whom humanitarian considerations weighed heavily; and he was not perhaps fully alive to the effect his views might have on his brother-officers. In any event, there could never be anything else but friction between a commander of Kretschmer's temperament and Rahmlow, who had obeyed instinctively the bidding of his conscience.

News of the interrogator's inquiries reached Kretschmer in Carmarthen Hospital through the senior British medical officer, who said bluntly: 'Someone is after your blood. I have been asked if you are fit for interrogation on a serious charge.' Kretschmer's illness had already passed, but knowing he would receive no pension in Germany or have any money to pay for medical attention, he had stayed at the hospital at the British Government's expense to make himself fit for whatever living he could earn in Germany. The interrogator was told that Kretschmer was ready to undergo severe questioning. A week later the two men met in a private room set aside by the hospital authorities. The interrogator wasted no time in formalities.

'Did you send a prisoner-of-war from Grizedale Hall to Barrow for the purpose of scuttling a U-boat?'

'No, I did not send him. He was asked if he would like to volunteer for the mission.'

'Why did you hold a court-martial you knew to be illegal?'

'I did not hold a court-martial. The Council of Honour was set up only for us to decide if the officers of *U-570* had carried out their duty. After all, no submarine had ever surrendered to an aircraft before and we wanted to know how it had happened.'

'You realise that if I find you responsible for the death of Rahmlow's officer you will be tried by a military court and might receive the death sentence?'

'There is nothing I can do about that. You should realise that the officer was willing to undertake the mission and had he not run away from the Home Guards, or at least had he stopped when they warned they would shoot, he would be alive today, living not in disgrace, but respected by all of us for a gallant attempt. In any event, the War Office investigated the matter and decided to take no action.'

'What about Rahmlow? Why did you have him persecuted at Bowmanville?'

'I was not responsible for his isolation. He was heard by an independent Board, who refused to allow me to appear.'

From then on the questioning became milder and he was asked to give the names of German officers who could support his testimony. He mentioned several officers who knew the details intimately. The interrogator left, and a few days later Kretschmer was amazed to hear that one of these officers, who was also a close friend,[1] had been interviewed and had 'confessed' that the Honour Councils and the death of the prisoner had been the result of Kretschmer's own scheming, and that other officers taking part had done so only to fill in vacant chairs and act in 'token' capacities.

The interrogator returned to Carmarthen to inform Kretschmer that he would probably have to face a British court-martial and, even if he escaped the gallows, would certainly be among the last returned to Germany. Kretschmer received this warning with stoical indifference.

Shortly after this, in February 1947, Kretschmer rejoined the other twenty-four 'dangerous' U-boat commanders at Featherstone Camp, near

Haltwhistle, and among the first he met was the friend who, in his view, had betrayed him. This officer admitted signing the statement, but said he had done so for personal reasons. It seemed that, while outside camp on parole, he had become friendly with an English girl who accompanied him on long country walks. He had decided there would be no future for him in a wrecked Germany, and hoped to be able to marry the girl and settle down in England. When questioned by the interrogator he had thought it probable that to admit tacit approval of the Honour Councils would have jeopardised his chances of being allowed to stay. For that reason he had placed the blame on Kretschmer alone, knowing that, if anyone could shoulder the entire responsibility and get away with it, Kretschmer could. It was a backhanded compliment, but Kretschmer accepted the explanation, more in sorrow than in anger, and asked the officer to sign another statement retracting the first and giving his reasons fully for doing so. When this had been done, Kretschmer hid the document inside his tunic. His friend's embarrassment was all the more acute, for in the meantime he had asked the girl to marry him if he were allowed to stay, but she had turned him down, apparently finding an occasional stroll across the fields more entertaining than a final walk to the altar.

Kretschmer was expecting an escort to call any day to march him away for court-martial, but as weeks passed he felt the Admiralty had followed the example of the War Office and let the matter drop. In March, the U-boat captains, excluding Rahmlow, who had been released earlier, were taken to Sudbury to prepare for transfer to Germany. With personal luggage not exceeding 100lb each, they were loaded on to a train for Harwich, where they embarked for the Hook of Holland. There they entrained for Munsterlager, in the Rhineland, for a further period of imprisonment. They stayed at this prison camp for a few days before being transferred to Neuengamme, near Hamburg, in readiness to appear before the British Naval Review Board for demilitarisation and eventual release.

After three weeks at this camp, Kretschmer was taken to Royal Navy Headquarters in Hamburg and shown into the office of a Lieutenant-Commander responsible for the preparation of documents to be handed in to the Board. On his desk lay the full report of the Admiralty interrogator's inquiries throughout the PoW camps in England. The purpose of this interview was threefold. Could Kretschmer offer a satisfactory explanation of the report? Did he repent his many acts of war carried on behind barbed wire? And would he abandon his stubborn refusal to accept that Germany had been wrong and the Allies right?

Kretschmer had been waiting for such a moment to produce the hidden document in which his 'friend' had withdrawn the original betrayal. He handed it over. The Lieutenant-Commander called in a senior officer, and they studied this second statement closely. Kretschmer was then taken back to Neuengamme and left alone for another six weeks. He was beginning to wonder if he would have to face trial in Germany, not so much for the *U-570* affair, but for his success at sea when he was summoned to Hamburg again. This time he was to appear in the final act of his war career – the Naval Review Board were to hear his case.

The 'court' sat in a small, bare room at Naval Headquarters, two commanders sitting on either side of the President of the Review Board – a Colonel of the Royal Marines – behind a long table. Each had a copy of Kretschmer's record before him. The prisoner sat with the Lieutenant-Commander at another table. To his considerable surprise, he saw Rahmlow sitting in the corridor outside waiting to be called as a witness. Kretschmer felt the atmosphere of the room menacing; the questions were put coldly, and he thought his chances of release slender indeed. In his answers he re-told the story of his career and, at the end, the Lieutenant-Commander rose and, more in the manner of a defence counsel, said that further inquiries in England and Germany concerning the *U-570* affair substantiated the prisoner's version.

The Board told Kretschmer to wait outside, and Rahmlow was called in. Kretschmer learned later that the one-time captain of *U-570* was examined closely on the reasons why he had surrendered his command and what had happened to him in successive prison camps. Nearly two hours passed before Kretschmer was recalled and to his surprise found that the grim reserve of the Board had given way to friendly informality. He was offered a cigarette, which he refused, and the President turned to him again: 'The war is over, Captain Kretschmer, and there is no political objection to your release. If there were, you would be appearing before another court. But you have proved yourself an unusually active and stubborn enemy, and we must warn you that if you break any law of occupation you will be liable to severe punishment. We find nothing in your service record to which we can seriously object, and therefore you are now formally released from captivity to return to your home. You will have to wait here for your discharge papers to be completed, and will then be free to go. You should know that civil life in Germany is at the best difficult and, after six years of imprisonment, you may find it hard to fit into it. But we wish you good luck in anything you choose to do.'

To the dazed Kretschmer the next few days of packing up, collecting papers and saying good-bye to guards and fellow-prisoners passed with incredible rapidity. In the brilliant sunshine of a clear summer's morning, he walked out of the station at Kiel and made his way to the docks. It was here that he had boarded his first submarine eleven years before; it was here that he had first seen the dark, laughing eyes of Schepke and the faintly bored, cynical smile of the precise Prien; it was here that he had heard Dönitz tell the young volunteers: 'The future of each of you depends on your individual efforts to meet the standards I require of you…'

The docks had hummed with activity as sleek new ships slid from beneath vast webs of scaffolding, and the bright-eyed youngster from the clean, crisp air of the Silesian mountains had gazed with nervous excitement at the outward signs of the new Navy pulsating with the vigour of his generation. Now rusting wrecks littered the harbour; the haughty cranes and bright steel scaffolding lay in sad confusion and, in the east, his mountain home was occupied by the Russians. Schepke and Prien had gone down with their ships in the fury of the battle, and Dönitz languished in a prison cell.

In sombre mood, one of the most decorated and celebrated sea captains of a defeated nation walked away towards the house in which he would stay with a friend[2] as a demilitarised civilian. But he had reached his home port and here he would build a place of his own.

Notes

1 Captain Kretschmer has asked that this officer's name be withheld because of a promise he made never to reveal his betrayer's identity publicly.

2 He was the commander of the first U-boat to be numbered *U-99* in the First World War.

Epilogue, 1955

Kretschmer has married a doctor with a large practice and made his home in Kiel. Old enmities have faded and there is no longer any bitterness between himself and Rahmlow, who is also still alive. Things are said and done under the strain of war that have no meaning in peacetime, when old comrades have time to reflect and respect their individual convictions. He studied maritime law at Kiel University, and would have qualified but for the 'Cold War' and West Germany's consequent swift return to nationhood and rearmament. He was soon called to Bonn to take an appointment with a public relations department, and today can expect with some certainty to be offered high rank in the new German Navy, which is to include a submarine force. Of the crew, König is still unmarried and running his own business in Hamburg, manufacturing plastic goods; Kassel is married and has become the export sales manager of a Hamburg firm manufacturing machinery for the world's cigarette industry; Clasen, also in Hamburg, is building merchant ships after helping to send so many others to the bottom.

In May last year I accompanied Captain and Mrs Kretschmer to a ceremony at Laboe, near Kiel, during which the German Navy's wa memorial, built like the prow of a Viking galley, was formally returned to the keeping of the Navy League, of which Kretschmer is President. It was a moving, solemn affair, with the only uniforms in sight those of the British, American and Italian Naval representatives. In the crypt below the memorial lay the stained battle ensigns of warships that had fought in such famous encounters as Jutland and the Falkland Isles, while above a naval band in civilian clothes played nostalgic marches not heard in Germany for eight years.

Kretschmer received the memorial formally from the President of Schleswig-Holstein in words that show plainly that the eager spirit of the 'Atlantic wolf' is still dominant.

The battle at sea was fought with chivalry and without hatred. The element of the sea will always be a bond between seafarers of all nations. Thus the shared life at sea in war and peace, where each shares the life of everyone else and masks soon fall away, has brought us together after the collapse of the Reich, in this German Navy League. But we are not a League of tradition, living only in the past. On the contrary, sailors don't look backwards for long, they always look ahead and into the future, and seek the world and their fate beyond the horizon. We have recognised the task set to our generation, and we will help in its completion. In this the things we have learnt at sea will be useful to us: team work, open-mindedness and global thinking, comradeship and tolerance. We want our whole nation – men and women, workers and farmers, politicians and soldiers – to understand and appreciate the economic, political and cultural importance of the sea. They must learn to think in a world-wide sense, so that our fate should be free from continental limitations and in peaceful collaboration with other nations. Our will for peace is joined with a will for peace with freedom. We wish to make this quite clear, so that there should be no doubts as to our positive stand as regards the question of a European get-together for common defence…

Appendix A

Confidential Report on Kretschmer sent by Admiral Dönitz to Naval Headquarters in Berlin at the end of 1939.

CURRENT REPORT ON KAPITÄNLEUTNANT OTTO KRETSCHMER ON RELINQUISHING HIS COMMAND AS FLOTILLA CHIEF.

Kapitänleutnant Kretschmer has been commander of *U-23* attached to U-Flotilla Weddigen since the autumn change of commands in 1937.

For his age he is of unusually quiet but inwardly strong and definite character. Very sympathetic, modest and well-bred in manners and appearance. Never tries to make much of himself. Outwardly well-groomed and of good appearance, socially reserved but well-versed. Mentally alert, varied interests, well read, interesting to talk to, once he has got over a certain shyness and reserve. Inclined to be a lone wolf and make up his mind on all things for himself, but in spite of this popular with his colleagues, through his basically cheerful and comradely manner, as well as his dry humour.

He faultlessly carried out his duties as a U-boat commander during two years of peace, training and leading his crew well, and sailing his boat well in every way, when his special aptitude for good seamanship was particularly noted. A careful and safe navigator. During exercises he shows tactical aptitude and understanding.

On several enemy actions Kretschmer proved himself outstandingly, and after he had already been decorated with the EK 2 *Klasse*, in December, he was additionally awarded the EK 1 *Klasse* after a specially difficult and daringly and safely executed special assignment. His outstanding characteristics in action were his unconcern, calm, decisiveness and great ability with which things were carried out. He is a U-boat commander specially suited for the carrying out of difficult tasks, and who is mentally and physically fresh, so that a further successful career may be expected for him.

K is now specially suited to be commander of a large U-boat. Later use as flotilla chief and as 'Referent' or 'Asto' seems suitable, when he has reached the necessary seniority. He will satisfactorily fill any post given to him and is worth watching for the future.

Kiel, 31.12.39.

Appendix B

Confidential Report on Kretschmer's character and ability from his Flotilla Leader for sending on to Berlin.

CURRENT REPORT ON *KAPITÄNLEUTNANT* KRETSCHMER ON RELINQUISHING THE COMMAND OF *U-23* FOR THE PERIOD 1.1.1940-1.4.1940.

Kapitänleutnant Kretschmer is a very quiet and reserved, but able and energetic officer. Talented, clear in his judgement, safe and sure in his aim, he shows favourable characteristics for his post.

Kretschmer is very popular among his subordinates and colleagues, who are quick to recognise his true merit in spite of his reserve.

I can fully confirm the very favourable report which my predecessor made on Kretschmer's work and duties.

During three further successful actions against the enemy, Kretschmer attacked unceasingly and brought out the best efforts from himself and his crew.

He was always full of ideas on how to shorten time in harbour and how to increase the number of torpedoes that could be carried.

His great ability, calm and decisiveness made it possible for him to go on specially difficult assignments several times without pause.

Kapitänleutnant Kretschmer is eminently suited to be commander of a large U-boat.

On Board, 14th March, 1940.
Signed: ECKERMANN Agreed: DÖNITZ

Appendix C

Confidential Report on Kretschmer's suitability for higher command from Dönitz to Admiral Raeder.

REPORT ON U-BOAT COMMANDERS

1.12.1940 – at the change-over of the Flotilla Chief, on *Kapitänleutnant* Otto Kretschmer, Commander *U-99*.

(1) Suited for what position? U-boat commander, later Flotilla Chief.
(2) Suitable for promotion? *Kapitänleutnant*, Year 1930.
(3) Is position being filled? Yes.
(4) General report: *Kapitänleutnant* Kretschmer was commander of *U-99* from 18.4.40-2.9.40 in the 7th U-boat flotilla. The special success which lie achieved in the shortest time with his new boat was due to his outstanding ability, his unshakeable calm and his joy in attack. He managed, in a short time, to transmit these qualities to his crew.
A character of integrity and reserve, with a clear and independent judgement in all things.

Very quiet and reserved, yet a faultless and popular comrade.

Appendix D

Congratulations on award of Knight's Cross to Kretschmer after the 'Night of the Long Knives'.

WIRELESS MESSAGE. 5th November, 1940.

To *Kapitänleutnant* Kretschmer
In grateful acknowledgement of your heroic achievement in the battle for the future of our people I bestow on you, on the occasion of the sinking of 200,000 BRT[1] (tons) of enemy merchant shipping as the 6th officer of the German Wehrmacht the Oakleaf to the Knight's Cross of the Iron Cross.
Adolf Hitler

To *U-99* for the Commander
My best congratulations, with proud acknowledgement of your achievement, on your being awarded the Oakleaf to the Knight's Cross.
Commander-in-Chief[2]

To *U-99*
Congratulations. Carry on the same way.
Your BDU[3]

Appendix E

The file card used at Lorient U-boat Headquarters to denote that U-99 was overdue and presumed missing.

Postcard from
    Naval Document Centre
    British Naval Headquarters
    24a Hamburg-Alsterdorf.

U-99 *Fregattenkapitän* Kretschmer ★★4 17.3.41.
Ship left Lorient 22.2.41
Last message on 17.3.41 6 a.m. to convoy lost.
Commander and part of crew prisoners. North Atlantic.
One star: 17.3.41 Two stars: 17.3.41
Ship sunk by HMS *Walker*, 17.3.41, 16°-00' N., 12°-00' W.

Appendix F

Extracts from German Wehrmacht communiqués on the U-boat war.

19th July 1940. The German U-boat force has further successes to report. A U-boat has sunk 31,300 BRT[5] of enemy merchant shipping, another U-boat[6] managed to shoot up a large armed merchant steamer out of a strongly guarded convoy.

3rd August 1940. A U-boat under the command of *Kapitänleutnant* Kretschmer sank, on one journey, seven armed enemy merchant ships with a tonnage of 56,118 BRT, among them three tankers which were part of convoys. This brings the total sinkings of this U-boat to 117,367 BRT of enemy merchant shipping and the British destroyer *Daring*.

8th August 1940. The Knight's Cross of the Iron Cross has been awarded to: *Fregattenkapitän* Fritz Berger, Chief of a Destroyer Flotilla, *Korvettenkapitän* Max-Eckart Wolff, commander of a destroyer, *Korvettenkapitän* Rudolf Peterson, Chief of a flotilla of fast boats, *Kapitänleutnant* Otto Kretschmer, commander of a U-boat.

19th October 1940. German U-boats have sunk, in the last few days, thirty-one enemy merchant ships with a total tonnage of 173,650 BRT. Of these, twenty-six steam-ships were sunk out of strongly guarded convoys. These successes belong to: U-boat commanded by *Kapitänleutnant* Frauenheim (ten steamers and 51,000 BRT), U-boat commanded by *Kapitänleutnant* Kretschmer (seven steamers with 45,000 BRT), U-boat commanded by *Kapitänleutnant* Möhle (seven steamers with 44,050 BRT). Two further U-boats sank four steamers with 21,000 BRT and three steamers with 12,600 BRT.

4th November 1940. The U-boat under the command of *Kapitänleutnant* Kretschmer has sunk the two British Auxiliary Cruisers *Laurentic* (18,724 BRT) and *Patroclus* (11,314 BRT) as well as the armed merchant ship *Casanare* of 5,376 BRT. This success brings *Kapitänleutnant* Kretschmer's total tonnage sunk to 217,198 BRT, and he is thus the second U-boat commander to sink more than 200,000 BRT.

4th November 1940. The Oakleaf to the Knight's Cross to the Iron Cross. The Führer and Commander-in-Chief of the Wehrmacht has awarded the Oakleaf to *Kapitänleutnant* Kretschmer for sinking 200,000 BRT of enemy shipping.

17th December 1940. Special report: *Kapitänleutnant* Kretschmer, returned from a trip on active service, reports the sinking of 34,935 BRT. Thus this officer, with a total sinking of 252,100 BRT, is the first U-boat commander to pass the 250,000-ton mark. This total includes three auxiliary cruisers and the British destroyer *Daring*.

20th March 1941. The U-boats commanded by *Korvettenkapitän* Kretschmer and *Kapitänleutnant* Schepke have not returned from action against the enemy. Both boats took part, under the most difficult conditions, in the destruction of enemy convoys. *Korvettenkapitän* Kretschmer has now sunk a total of 313,611 BRT[7] apart from the sinking of three enemy destroyers,[8] two of them on his last trip, among them the auxiliary cruisers *Laurentic*, *Patroclus* and *Forfar*, and *Kapitänleutnant* Schepke has sunk 233,871 tons of enemy shipping. These two commanders, who had been awarded the Oakleaf the Knight's Cross of the Iron Cross in recognition of their exceptional services in the battle of the German people, have, together with their brave crews, won eternal glory.

Notes

1 BRT = British Registered Tonnage.

2 Admiral Raeder.

3 BDU = Commander-in-Chief, U-boats.

4 One star denoted a U-boat overdue. Two stars indicated overdue and presumed lost.

5 BRT = British Registered Tonnage.

6 *U-99*.

7 This figure omits the *Terje Viken* (20,000 tons) and the destroyer *Daring*.

8 This was a misrepresentation of Kretschmer's last signal to Lorient.